EXPERIMENTS ON DECISIONS UNDER RISK

EXPERIMENTS ON DECISIONS UNDER RISK: THE EXPECTED UTILITY HYPOTHESIS

Paul J. H. Schoemaker
Graduate School of Business
University of Chicago
Center for Decision Research

Springer-Science+Business Media, B.V.

Library of Congress Cataloging in Publication Data

Schoemaker, Paul J. H.
Experiments on decisions under risk.

Bibliography: p.
Includes index.
1. Risk. 2. Utility theory. I. Title.
HB615.S36 658.4'03 79-27948

ISBN 978-94-017-5042-4 ISBN 978-94-017-5040-0 (eBook)
DOI 10.1007/978-94-017-5040-0

Originally published by Martinus Nijhoff Publishing in 1980
Softcover reprint of the hardcover 1st edition 1980

To my wife Joyce
and
my parents

CONTENTS

FOREWORD xv

PREFACE xvii

ACKNOWLEDGMENTS xxi

1 INTRODUCTION 1

1.1 Background 1
1.2 Decision under Risk 3
1.3 The Experimental Approach 4
1.3.1 Challenges 5
1.3.2 Misconceptions 6
1.3.3 Some Specific Issues 8
1.4 Plan of This Book 9

2 EXPECTED UTILITY THEORY 11

2.1 Background 11
2.2 Von Neumann-Morgenstern Utility 13
2.3 Empirical Evidence 16
2.3.1 Experimental Studies 17
2.3.2 Field Studies 22
2.4 Conclusions 26

3 ALTERNATIVE DESCRIPTIVE MODELS 28

3.1 Schematic Overview 28
3.2 Holistic Judgment Models 31
3.3 The Information-Processing Perspective 36
3.4 Non-holistic Judgment Models 41
3.5 Conclusions 44

4 A POSITIVISTIC TEST OF EU THEORY: PREFERENCES FOR INFORMATION 45

4.1 The Positivistic View 45
4.2 The Basic Problem 46
4.2.1 Mathematical Structuring 47
4.2.2 The Preference for Information 50
4.2.3 Generalization to *n* Urns 52
4.3 The Experiment 56
4.4 Results 57
4.5 Conclusions 64

5 AN EXPERIMENTAL STUDY OF INSURANCE DECISIONS 66

5.1 Issues to Be Examined 67
5.2 The Experiment 69
5.3 Results 71
5.3.1 Pure Risk Alternatives 71
5.3.2 Other Factors Affecting Risk Preferences 73
5.3.3 Insurance Preferences 78

5.3.4 Context and Format Effects **81**
5.3.5 An Illegitimate Portfolio Effect **83**
5.3.6 Comprehensive Insurance **85**
5.3.7 Scale Effects **86**
5.4 Conclusions **87**

6 STATISTICAL KNOWLEDGE AND GAMBLING DECISIONS: MOMENTS VS. RISK DIMENSIONS **91**

6.1 Literature **92**
6.2 Hypotheses **94**
6.3 The Experiment **94**
6.4 Results **98**
6.4.1 Cognitive Strain **98**
6.4.2 Decision Quality **101**
6.4.3 Decision Strategy **102**
6.5 Regression Findings **104**
6.6 Conclusions **107**

7 RISK TAKING AND PROBLEM CONTEXT IN THE DOMAIN OF LOSSES **109**

7.1 Background **110**
7.2 Hypotheses **111**
7.2.1 A Markowitz Type of Utility Function **112**
7.2.2 The Influence of Problem Context **115**
7.3 The Experiment **116**
7.4 Results **117**
7.4.1 Insurance Preferences **118**
7.4.2 The Effect of Context **122**
7.5 Conclusions **124**

8 EPILOGUE **126**

8.1 General Findings **127**
8.2 An Integrative Framework **129**
8.2.1 The Dependent Variable **129**
8.2.2 The Independent Variables **130**

8.2.3 The Mapping Function **131**
8.2.4 The Present Research **134**
8.3 Toward a General Theory **135**

APPENDIXES

I A Generalization of the Formulas for EU with Information **141**
II Questionnaire of the Preferences for Information Study **143**
III Questionnaire of the Insurance Study **148**
IV Analysis of a Duplex Gamble **157**
V Questionnaire of the Statistical Knowledge Study **158**
VI EU Analysis of Dimension Preferences **166**
VII Questionnaire of the Risk Taking and Context Effect Study **169**
VIII Insurance and EU Theory **177**

NOTES **181**

REFERENCES **189**

NAME INDEX **205**

SUBJECT INDEX **209**

FIGURES

3.1	Classification Scheme for Descriptive Models	29
4.1	Graphic Illustration of the Proof of Preference for Information	53
6.1	Example of a Duplex Gamble	95
7.1	EU Analysis: Keeping the Premium Constant	112
7.2	EU Analysis: Keeping the Loss Constant	114
7.3	EU Analysis: Keeping the Probability Constant	115
7.4	Preferences for Insurance	119
7.5	Partial Replication of the Study of Slovic et al. (1977)	119
7.6	The Effect of Context	123
8.1	Graphic Illustration of the Conceptual Framework	133
8.2	Minor and Major Critical Values	133
VIII.1	A Graphic Analysis of the Insurance Decision	179
VIII.2	Two General Shapes of the Utility Function	179

TABLES

2.1 The Allais Paradox Stated in Lottery Form **19**
2.2 Kunreuther's Study on Flood and Earthquake Insurance **25**
3.1 Choices among Two-Dimensional Alternatives **43**
4.1 Optimal EU Preferences for Information **50**
4.2 Risk Attitude and Information Preference: The Case of Small Amounts ($10–$20) **59**
4.3 Risk Attitude and Information Preference: The Case of Large Amounts ($500–$1,000) **60**
4.4 Narrowing the Probability Range **62**
5.1 Socioeconomic Profiles of Student and Client Respondents **70**
5.2 Preferences for Safe and Risky Alternatives with Equal Expected Losses **72**
5.3 Differences between Risk Seekers and Risk Averters **75**
5.4 Strength of Preference and Use of Intuition **76**
5.5 Effect of Statistical Knowledge on the Use of Intuition **77**
5.6 Summary of the First Insurance Question **78**
5.7 Frequencies of Absolute Rankings **79**

5.8 Frequencies of Relative Rankings 80
5.9 Question 5: Frequencies of Absolute Rankings 81
5.10 Effect of a Reduction in the Probability of Loss 81
5.11 The Deductible Effect 82
5.12 Question 11: Absolute Preferences for Insurance Portfolios 84
5.13 Rank Orderings of Joint Insurance Alternatives 84
5.14 Preferences for Comprehensive Insurance 86
5.15 Responses to the Scale-Effect Question 88
6.1 Listing of the 31 Duplex Gambles 96
6.2 Perceived Task Difficulty 98
6.3 Perceived Boredom of Task 99
6.4 Time Needed to Develop a Decision Rule 99
6.5 Parts of Bet on Which Subjects Focused 100
6.6 Mean Absolute Differences in Bids of Repeat Gambles 101
6.7 Frequencies of Irrational Bids 102
6.8 Use of Expected Value 103
6.9 Degrees of Fit of Three Regression Models 105
7.1 Questions Used in the Experiment 110

FOREWORD

In this valuable book, Paul Schoemaker summarizes recent experimental and field research that he and others have undertaken regarding the descriptive validity of expected utility theory as a model of choice under uncertainty. His principal message is that this paradigm is too narrow in its conception and misses some of the important elements of a descriptive model of individual choice. In particular, Schoemaker calls attention to the importance of individual differences, task effects, and context effects as they influence behavior.

The expected utility hypothesis has come under scrutiny in recent years from a number of different quarters. This book brings together these many studies and relates them to the large body of literature on individual decision making under risk. Although this paradigm may be appropriate for describing behavior under many conditions of uncertainty, Schoemaker presents convincing evidence that it does not do well with respect to protection against low-probability events. For example, he shows that the insurance purchase decision is influenced by the way information is presented to the client, as well as by the statistical knowledge of the respondents.

The book provides an impetus for looking in detail at the interaction between descriptive and prescriptive behavior. If one finds that presenting the same quantitative information in different forms will affect behavior, then this has definite implications for policy. Insurance companies and their agents have understood the importance of this phenomenon for years. They recognize that humans are limited in their ability to process information; hence, they place their emphasis on the dimensions of the problem that insurance is designed to protect against—namely, the potential loss. It is rare that insurance agents emphasize the small chances of a disastrous event; instead, they stress the protection that a policy will provide should such a catastrophe occur. In essence, the agent's task is to translate an individual's perception that an event has such a low probability that it is not worth his concern into a full appreciation of the financial loss that might occur without protection against that particular contingency—for example, loss of life, severe injury, or property damage. This book provides firms with more formal justification for concern about the way in which they present information to clients.

On a broader level, the findings from the experiments and the conceptual framework that Schoemaker proposes in the final chapter raise a host of questions that need to be explored. What role does past experience play in individuals' processing of information and in their final decisions? How can we incorporate our understanding of the diffusion of information among people, the adoption of innovations, and learning over time into a model of choice under uncertainty? At the level of the firm, we need to increase our understanding of the importance of organizational design for prescriptive behavior and the role that the different cognitive styles of managers play in their decisions. Finally, because consumers cannot accurately process information on risks affecting themselves and society, there now exists at a public policy level an emerging set of questions about the importance of informational incentives and the appropriate role of regulations. These questions and others require integration across the disciplines in the social sciences. I look forward to joining Schoemaker and others in this important task.

HOWARD KUNREUTHER
Professor of Decision Sciences
The Wharton School
University of Pennsylvania

PREFACE

This book examines individual decision making under risk. It represents research conducted during the second half of the 1970s, at which time I became concerned with the behavioral aspects of risk. My initial interest in risk started while completing an undergraduate major in physics. The debate between deterministic and probabilistic views of the universe brought into focus the essentially subjective nature of risk. No model of the physical reality can be independent of man's own role; in particular, uncertainty cannot be ascribed to physical phenomena without addressing the subtle relationships between our intellectual makeup and the nature of the world as we experience it through our senses. During subsequent graduate studies in finance and economics, my focus shifted to the role of risk and uncertainty in social, rather than physical, realities. In the process of examining the pricing and transfer of risk in financial markets, I became dissatisfied with the economic conceptualizations of risk. I felt a need to examine attitudes toward risk, and perceptions thereof, at the more basic level of individual decision making. In the context of the then newly emerging Department of Decision Sciences at the Wharton School, I wrote a Ph.D. thesis on economic and psychological questions of decision under risk, employing the methodology of laboratory experimentation. The present book is an outgrowth of these and subsequent activities.

Of central concern to the present book is the expected utility hypothesis, both as a prescriptive and a predictive model. Two aspects are examined. First, to what extent can behavior be modeled from the assumption that people act as if they maximize expected utility? Second, how operational is the theory as a prescriptive model, given that it rests in part on behavioral axioms? These aspects are, of course, of major interest to economics, psychology, and decision analysis.

The book consists of four theoretical and four empirical chapters, the latter involving experimental research. All the decision tasks examined concern single decision makers, objective risk (i.e., stated probabilities), one-dimensional outcomes (money), and a single time period.

The first chapter discusses the notions of risk and probability. The experimental method is analyzed in the context of prevailing misconceptions and various threats to its validity. Chapter 2 reviews expected utility theory: its roots, axiomatic development, operationalization, as well as important empirical evidence (both field and laboratory). Chapter 3 discusses and classifies alternative descriptive models, including a review of the tenets of bounded rationality theory.

Chapters 4 through 7 discuss four separate, but related, empirical studies. Chapter 4 consists of a positivistic test of expected utility theory, involving preferences for information. Chapter 5 focuses on the domain of losses, examining such issues as risk aversion, insurance preferences, statistical knowledge, decision style, and biases due to problem presentation and context. The respondents in this study were about two hundred students and one hundred clients of an insurance agency. Chapter 6 examines further the effect of statistical knowledge on decision rules. It offers a reconciliation of moment and risk-dimension approaches. Chapter 7 focuses on risk aversion for losses and the influence of problem context, particularly its implications for normative decision theory. The final chapter summarizes the implications of the research findings for both aspects of the expected utility hypothesis; a framework is developed for studying decisions under risk, and several issues are discussed as central to the development of a more general descriptive theory.

As suggested above, the book is directed at decision consultants, policy analysts, psychologists, economists, and finance and insurance experts. Although the book does not presuppose prior study in these areas, a bachelor's degree in one of the above fields would be helpful. In certain sections, a basic knowledge of calculus is assumed. In addition, core concepts of probability theory and statistics are utilized in discussing and interpreting the empirical results. However, no serious loss of comprehension is implied for those not initiated in these disciplines. The book is suitable for graduate courses on decisions under risk, in which capacity it is used, for example, at the University of Chicago. Although useful in the classroom, its main orientation is not that of a textbook; rather, the book provides a review, report, and synthesis of past and recent findings regarding the expected utility hypothesis.

ACKNOWLEDGMENTS

As evidenced by the extensive list of references included in this book, my intellectual indebtedness is quite intractable. In addition, my family, teachers, friends, and colleagues, as well as various institutions, contributed greatly to the intellectual basis from which the book was written. I would like to acknowledge explicitly those friends and colleagues whose comments on earlier drafts offered helpful insights. In alphabetical order, they are Professors Martin Bariff (Case Western), Hillel Einhorn (Chicago), Baruch Fischhoff (Decision Research), Jay Galbraith (Wharton), Rob Gerritsen (Wharton), John Hershey (Wharton), David Hildebrand (Wharton), Dorit Hochbaum (Carnegie-Mellon), Robin Hogarth (Chicago), Reverend Homan (St. Joseph's), Giorgio Inzerilli (Wharton), Daniel Kahneman (British Columbia), Paul Kleindorfer (Wharton), Howard Kunreuther (Wharton), Joop van Nunen (Delft), John Payne (Duke), John Pratt (Harvard), Howard Raiffa (Harvard), Jay Russo (Chicago), Alan Shapiro (Southern California), Paul Slovic (Decision Research), Amos Tversky (Stanford), and Robert Verrecchia (Chicago).

Mr. John Cantrill of the Fred W. Leonard Agency is gratefully acknowledged for encouraging his clients to participate in the experiment described in Chapter 5.

Special mention should be made of my colleague, friend, and former Ph.D. advisor, Dr. Howard Kunreuther, whose initial guidance and subsequent encouragement are in large part responsible for the present research. Drs. John Hershey and Howard Kunreuther are both acknowledged for their kind permission to reprint parts of work that we published jointly elsewhere. Journal reprint permissions are noted on the opening pages of Chapters 5, 6, and 7. Institutional support from the Wharton School and the Graduate School of Business at the University of Chicago is also gratefully acknowledged. Helpful research assistance was provided by my former students, Messrs. Garret Davies, Blair Haas, Michael Peck, and Fred van der Werff. Within the Martinus Nijhoff organization, in Boston, special mention goes to the director, Mr. Philip Jones, for valuable assistance at the drafting stage of the book, and to Ms. Sarah Evans for her fine editing of the completed manuscript. Finally, my wife Joyce is acknowledged for graciously enduring our joint sacrifices. The book's dedication measures in only small part her importance in completing this work.

EXPERIMENTS ON DECISIONS UNDER RISK

1 INTRODUCTION

The objective of this introductory chapter is to provide an overview of the domain, the methodology, and the organization of this book. The research reported here represents an exploration along the boundaries between economics and psychology, focusing on questions of value, risk, and preference.

Choice in the face of risk involves an important class of individual and societal decisions. People are constantly engaged in risk assessments, and society at large faces some difficult choices involving risk-benefit tradeoffs. Nuclear power plants, strategic arms limitations, genetic engineering, and pollution are just a few examples of situations in which certain or expected benefits must be weighted against uncertain, unlikely, but possibly severe, losses involving human lives. Hence, judgment under risk constitutes an important area of study.

1.1 BACKGROUND

In this book, two important approaches to understanding decision making under risk are compared. The first of these approaches focuses on a well-established economic decision model called "expected utility theory"; the second involves an information-processing view of decision making that is generally incompatible with traditional utility theory. Since these two approaches may lead to quite different suggestions on how to predict or influence behavior (e.g., for policy purposes), each was researched as to its merits.

The examination of alternative models generally proceeds slowly. Within an academic discipline, there often exists a dominant paradigm that defines for several generations of scientists the legitimate problems and methods of a research field. Examples of such paradigms are Aristotle's *Physica*, Newton's *Principia* and *Opticks*, Darwin's *Origin of Species*, and, in a more limited sense, the rational man conception of economics.[1] In essence, this conception holds (1) that people have preference structures that obey certain axioms of well-behavedness so that (2) a mathematical representation can be rendered of these preference structures and (3) choice can be modeled as maximizing an imputed objective function (e.g., expected utility) subject to certain economic constraints. Hence, choice in complex situations is assumed to follow from basic taste and preferences in a logical and predictable way, without explicit concern for cognitive limitations and problem representation. As Pareto (1909) put it, once we have obtained "a photograph of his tastes . . . the individual may disappear" (p. 61).

This idealized conception of rational man has its roots in Greek philosophy, in which an ideal person was viewed as someone leading "a placid life amid external turmoil by the application of reason to conduct" (Lee, 1971, p. 5) — that is, someone acting in accordance with his or her basic needs and ideals. In early economic theory, this conception referred to a person who knows his or her best interests and acts accordingly (Smith, 1776) — that is, a person who chooses on the basis of deliberation and informed reasoning, rather than emotion or habit (Marshall, 1890).

The rational-economic man conception is being increasingly challenged, primarily from outside of economics.[2] For example, Slovic (1972b), a psychologist, wrote that one of his favorite posters showed an individual in a gas mask surrounded by a cloud of polluted air juxtaposed with the following quote from Shakespeare:

> What a piece of work is man! How noble in reason! How infinite in faculty! In form and moving how express and admirable! In action how like an angel! In apprehension how like a god! The beauty of the world! The paragon of animals! [*Hamlet*, act 2, scene 2]

Similarly, Simon (1957), currently a professor of psychology and computer science, has been emphasizing the boundedness of rationality. His well-known view can briefly be described as follows: "The capacity of the human mind for formulating and solving complex problems is very small compared with the size of the problems whose solution is required for objectively rational behavior in the real world — or even for a reasonable approximation to such objective rationality." Even though Simon was recently (1978) awarded the Nobel Prize in economics, neither his view nor his career has been in the mainstream of this discipline. Simon's bounded rationality theory will be discussed further in Chapter 3.

Having thus drawn the main lines, this book hopes to shift research and thought on economic questions of value, preference, and risk in the direction of psychology, in particular toward information-processing views. The research will show that current economic theory is inadequate in accounting for observed laboratory behaviors. Although the decisions studied here by necessity cover only a small domain of economic choice, they constitute a cornerstone of economic theory.

1.2 DECISION UNDER RISK

Decision situations are often conceptually distinguished on the basis of the types of information available about the consequences associated with different courses of action. If for each alternative it is known a priori what outcome will result, the situation is one of decision under certainty. If the outcomes that may occur and their relative likelihoods are known, the situation is one of objective risk. Finally, if only possible outcomes are known, but no objective likelihoods, the case is one of uncertainty. We shall return later to the problematic distinction between risk and uncertainty.

Additionally, there is the case of conflict in which the outcomes depend in a known manner on the actions of others whose welfare, for that choice situation, is opposite to that of the decision maker. Other distinctions can be made on the basis of the number of attributes considered (one vs. multiple), the number of decision entities (individual vs. group), the role of time (e.g., static vs. dynamic decision making), or the nature of the solution space (e.g., implicitly vs. explicitly defined or discrete vs. continuous).

The concern of this book is with individual decision making under risk, usually involving a small number of alternatives of rather low complexity. The possible outcomes are all monetary. They will materialize in the current period, and their relative likelihoods are assumed to be known objectively, which brings us to the notion of objective risk or objective probability.

Going back in history, De La Place (1951) defined probability as a ratio of favorable to possible cases when these cases would be "mutually symmetric" (meaning equally likely). Bernoulli (1713) had earlier evaded this circular definition by distinguishing the concept from its measurement; probability was viewed as a degree of belief, to be measured in a frequency or ratio sense. The frequency approach was placed on a solid axiomatic footing by Venn (1866), Von Mises (1957, 1964), and Reichenbach (1949). They defined probabilities as the limiting values of ratios of outcomes associated with an infinite sequence of independent trials. Whether this abstraction has its image in reality, in principle, or as approximation depends on one's "religion"; a determinist may rule out true randomness (its only source being imperfect knowledge), whereas others may take the position of fundamentally irreducible uncertainty, as, for example, in Heisenberg's uncertainty principle (see Lindsay, 1968; Burks, 1977). The limited-knowledge view was favored by Keynes (1921), who founded the so-called logical school of probability.

An alternative approach to probability is the subjectivist's view of Ramsey (1931), DeFinetti (1937, 1974), Savage (1954), and Pratt, Raiffa, and Schlaifer (1965). In this view, probabilities are degrees of beliefs that can be assessed from revealed preferences among bets. Under certain behavioral axioms, which deal with internal consistency, the subjectively derived probabilities can be shown to behave as mathematical probabilities. An attempt to merge subjective and objective approaches into a rational learning system along Bayesian lines can be found in Carnap (1971). A brief introduction to the various probability conceptions is offered in Lee (1971) and Winkler (1972). A classic in the field is Kyburg and Smokler (1964). For a formal treatment of the subject, see Kyburg (1974).

Given the philosophical difficulty surrounding the notion of probability, we shall proceed as if objective risk exists and is meaningful psychologically. To quote Churchman (1961, p. 139), "Almost everyone knows what it means to say that an event is only probable — except those who have devoted their lives to thinking about the matter." In the present research, the view is taken that a .7 chance of event E occurring is interpreted by a subject in analogy to a thought experiment of infinitely many trials yielding, in the limit, 70 percent occurrences of the event E. This frequency-view assumption is complemented with a subjectivist's assumption that for each subject, assuming a known value or utility function, the degree of belief concerning the occurrence of E will be measured as exactly .7, using traditional betting procedures (i.e., there are no probability distortions).

1.3 THE EXPERIMENTAL APPROACH

Scientific inquiry can be separated into situations in which the investigator observes naturally occurring phenomena versus those in which the phenomena are wholly or partly the result of the investigator's instigation or intervention. The latter cases are referred to as experimentation. They are characterized by the existence of explicit prior hypotheses and criteria for assessing the extent to which experimental outcomes support or disconfirm particular theories.

True experimental design involves intervening in a system for the purpose of comparing the ensuing results with those of a control system that did not receive the intervention, but that is similar in all other essential regards. Such a pure design often cannot be attained, and researchers must settle for quasi-experimental designs (Campbell and Stanley, 1963). This latter type of design involves an intelligent scheduling of observations in order to approximate the ideal of a full control in assigning stimuli or treatments to persons or groups.

A second useful distinction within the class of experimental designs is that between field and laboratory experiments. The purpose of field experiments is to observe systems whose primary reason for functioning is unrelated to any given experimental design, even though certain manipulations or interventions are introduced for the sake of experimentation. An example would be experimental manipulation of the price structure of insurance policies to test different models of consumer decision making. In contrast, in the laboratory there exist social systems whose raison d'être rests entirely with the purposes of the experiment. Such laboratory experiments often involve abstractions from natural settings in order to examine relationships among variables in a reduced and more fundamental form (McGrath, 1964).

Within the social sciences, laboratory experiments are found predominantly within the field of psychology. The laboratory method is usually aimed at (1) making clear the temporal antecedent of cause before effect, (2) demonstrating that a hypothesized cause and effect indeed co-vary, (3) ruling out other variables that might explain the results, or (4) eliminating alternative hypotheses about the constructs involved in the relationship examined (Cook and Campbell, 1976). The laboratory method represents a systematic way of obtaining knowledge about some social reality (i.e., planned experience), acting from explicit prior beliefs and models about that reality.

1.3.1 Challenges

The challenges of good experimentation revolve around four types of validity, which are referred to as internal, external, statistical-conclusion, and construct validity (Cook and Campbell, 1976).

Internal validity concerns the reasoning process that relates effects to hypothesized causes. If several explanations can account for the same results, but only one is recognized and promoted by a researcher, the experiment will have questionable internal validity. To assure high internal validity, one must ascertain before conducting the experiment that each conceivable set of results can be argued either to favor or to disconfirm the hypothesis, without there being indeterminacy. Of course, the argumentation or reasoning involved in mapping outcomes into explanations must be acceptable to other experts in the field, making the final test one of consensus.

External validity concerns the extent to which experimental results generalize to larger populations (persons, organizations, or markets), to other time periods, and to other settings (e.g., in our case, to other decision situations). To judge external validity, one must identify the essential features of the experimental setting and relate these features to other contexts. After one has identified the relevant dimensions conceptually, one might use statistical theory to assess the sample's representativeness along some, or all, of these dimensions.

The third type of validity, called statistical-conclusion validity, deals with the validity of quantitative judgments about the extent to which cause and effect co-vary. It asks whether statistical theory is properly utilized to support a presumed causal relationship, given the assumptions underlying the statistical measures and the data to which statistical theory is applied.

Finally, there is the important area of construct validity, which refers to the correctness of connecting experimental treatments and outcomes, on the one hand, with theoretical constructs and abstractions, on the other. For example, construct validity is concerned with the question of how to obtain workable and acceptable constructs or measures for such abstract concepts as rationality, cognitive strain, or decision quality. To operationalize these concepts, one needs a clear delineation of the domains to which they apply, an identification of the multiple facets inherent in each concept, overlapping measures of these multiple facets, and, finally, a rule for combining the various measures into more basic factors, or possibly a scalar index.

1.3.2 Misconceptions

The use of experimentation, particularly in social science, has given rise to several misconceptions about this method. As Weick (1967) has pointed out, common, but not necessarily valid, criticisms of experimentation are that (1) experiments demonstrate the obvious, (2) experiments are artificial,

(3) laboratory contexts are oversimplified, and (4) hypotheses testing leads to myopia.

As for the first criticism, there may be a confusion between explicitness and obviousness (Weick, 1967). Once an experiment has been designed (i.e., variables have been identified and operationalized) and predictions are refined, the situation may become so explicit that the experiment's outcomes can be predicted with great confidence (i.e., they become obvious). However, at that point, much of the research has been completed, and it need not have been obvious initially that the chosen design would afford a good test of the theory under investigation. Furthermore, the illusion of obviousness may exist because alternative theories are not recognized. In that case, many implicit disconfirmations remain unnoticed, giving the impression of obviousness.

A different response to the criticism of "obviousness" is that events that have already occurred generally appear more likely when judged in retrospect (i.e., with hindsight). This well-documented "knew-it-all-along" effect (which is briefly reviewed in Wood, 1978) appears to operate in widely different contexts and has been shown to apply to retrospective assessments of experimental outcomes as well (Fischhoff, 1975, 1976, 1977; Fischhoff and Beyth, 1975; Schoemaker, 1978). Finally, much "obvious" knowledge that does not appear to need empirical verification may in fact be wrong. In his study of prevalent beliefs about American soldiers, Lazarsfeld (1949, pp. 177–78) provided dramatic examples of this phenomenon.

The second criticism, that of artificiality, really concerns unrepresentativeness rather than "unrealness." Human behavior in the laboratory is as real as behavior anywhere. The main difference is that laboratory settings are unrepresentative of daily life, which, in itself, need not be bad. The question of representativeness is related to the third criticism, that of oversimplification. Often the objective of experimentation is not so much to simulate or approximate natural settings as it is to create settings whose contexts allow for convincing arguments that certain findings support or disconfirm a given theory. For example, the experimental studies of Isaac and Plott (1979) and Smith (1976) tested economic theory by arguing that if economic price theory holds in the natural setting (as economists suggest), it must also hold in the experimental one. The reason for studying the experimental setting instead of the natural one is, of course, that the latter may not allow for a conclusive disconfirmation in case the theory is wrong, whereas the laboratory setting, owing to its controls and design, would.

Finally, the criticism that hypotheses induce myopia is really a question of structured observation versus unstructured observation. A given hypothesis may be narrowly focused in order to direct subsequent analyses in more profitable directions. When experimentation is viewed as a sequence of hypotheses and designs in which earlier conjectures shape subsequent ones, the single-hypothesis myopia will be recognized as a necessary condition for a systematic search path through potential tests and data analyses.

Of course, there are legitimate limitations and criticisms of the experimental approach; however, these do not include the ones described above. The legitimate concerns about experimentation all deal with one or several of the four types of validity that we discussed earlier. In general, experimentalists are well aware of the pitfalls of experimentation, as witnessed by the extensive list and categorization of threats to validity constructed by Campbell and Stanley (1963). Misconceptions about experimentation, however, often exist among those who are trained in other traditions of scientific inquiry and theory testing.

1.3.3 Some Specific Issues

The relevance of the experimental research described in this book to the field of economics rests on three key assumptions:

1. The decision situations analyzed in this research are of similar or lower complexity than the decision situations underlying behavior typically studied in economics (i.e., behavior of individuals, households, firms, and other aggregates).
2. The types of decision behavior and preferences examined here are similar to those studied in economics (i.e., general directions of preferences among finite alternatives, aggregated across individuals).
3. The different motivational (and other) conditions between the laboratory and the real world do not impact in essential ways on the cognitive processes underlying people's decision making.

The above premises imply that if economic theory, particularly the expected utility hypothesis, is to hold (approximately) in the real world, it should also hold in the controlled settings of the research presented in this book. If it does not, the decision about what kinds of alternative (typically more complex) descriptive models to adopt will critically depend on the trade-offs one wishes to make between parsimony and prediction error.

Regarding the second assumption, one might object that in contrast to the experiments presented here, economic theory focuses mainly on decision behavior under conditions of competition and conflict. This concern, however, enters the theory primarily at the level of models of (dis)equilibria, which form the bridge between microeconomics and macroeconomics (Quirk and Saposnik, 1968). The research described here addresses economic behavior and models that are antecedent to general equilibria theories, models that lie at the foundation of microeconomics, particularly the theory of consumer behavior. To quote Henderson and Quandt (1971), "The basic postulate of the theory of consumer behavior is that the consumer maximizes utility" (p. 48).

With respect to the third premise, it should be noted that all choices examined here concerned hypothetical decision situations. As many of the choices involved losses only, it was ethically objectionable to have subjects actually exposed to negative risks. The alternative of providing subjects with an initial endowment with which they could then have played some of the gambles was deemed undesirable because very large losses were involved and because a "protect-your-nest-egg" tendency could well have led to different responses.

Nevertheless, the issue of real versus hypothetical payoffs is an important one that may limit the external validity of the present research findings. However, a study by Slovic (1969a) on the differential effects of real versus hypothetical payoffs on choices among gambles showed the effects to be more motivational than cognitive.[3] When the gambles were real, subjects tended to be less wishful and more cautious. A similar conservatism effect under the real payoff condition was found in other studies reviewed by Kogan and Wallach (1974). Since many of the present research issues are concerned with the presence or absence of risk aversion or risk taking rather than with their exact degree, the hypothetical versus real payoff differences may not be too troublesome.

1.4 PLAN OF THIS BOOK

As its title suggests, this book is concerned with the expected utility hypothesis. The objective is not so much to ascertain the general validity or falsehood of the expected utility hypothesis (as it is probably neither), but rather to identify the conditions under which it may or may not offer an approximate description of decision making under risk. The importance of the expected utility model derives from its status as a normative benchmark against which to judge behavior, as well as from its widespread usage (descriptively) in economics and psychology.

Chapter 2 offers a discussion of expected utility theory in both its normative and descriptive forms. Evidence from laboratory and field studies is briefly reviewed to assess the status of expected utility theory as a descriptive model. Chapter 3 gives an overview of various alternative descriptive models. It provides a background for some of the concepts and interpretations offered later in discussing the experimental results and completes the review of previous literature.[4]

Chapter 4 is the first of the research chapters. It is the most mathematical and aims at a positivistic test of the expected utility hypothesis. A major portion of the chapter is devoted to the development of an urn paradigm that is resistant to ex-post-facto utility rationalizations. Chapter 5 focuses on the domain of losses, particularly insurance decisions. It examines various issues, including risk aversion, decision style, comprehensive insurance, context biases, illegitimate portfolio influences, and scale effects.

Chapter 6 examines in more detail an issue that arose in Chapter 5 in regard to the effect of statistical knowledge on gambling decisions. The task studied involves a type of gamble (called a duplex bet) that has been utilized in previous studies. The chapter also addresses the conflicting nature of previous research findings concerning this type of gamble. Finally, Chapter 7, which is the last of the research chapters, focuses again on the domain of losses. This chapter also pursues further an issue raised in Chapter 4 — namely, the influence of problem context on revealed risk-taking attitudes. In general, the research chapters offer little discussion of previous literature since much of this material is covered in Chapters 2 and 3.

Chapter 8, which is the final chapter, offers an epilogue on the general nature and implications of the research findings and reassesses the status of the expected utility hypothesis. It sketches a framework for classifying existing research studies on decisions under risk and offers conjectures as to profitable directions for future research.

2 EXPECTED UTILITY THEORY

The case of decision making under risk is one in which considerable consensus exists among decision experts as to how one ought to choose. The theory advises which alternative to select in complex decision situations on the basis of one's *basic* taste and preferences about risk and the intrinsic value of the attribute(s) under consideration. Both of these elements are captured through a utility function so that maximizing expected utility becomes the guide to rational behavior in more complex situations.

2.1 BACKGROUND

The mathematical form of the expected utility model can be traced back to Cramer (1728) and Bernoulli (1738), who sought to explain the so-called St. Petersburg paradox. The question was why people would pay only a small sum for a game of infinite mathematical expectation. The game consists of flipping a coin as many times as is necessary to obtain "heads" for the first time. Say this number of tosses equals n; the payoff would then be $\$2^n$. Of course, the expected value of this game is infinite (i.e., $\Sigma_{n=1}^{\infty}(\frac{1}{2})^n 2^n = \infty$). However, few people would pay more than $100, or even $10, to play the game once.

To account for this paradox, Bernoulli suggested that people maximize "moral expectation" rather than expected monetary value and that moral expectation (or the utility of wealth) exhibits diminishing marginal utility (i.e., equal increments of wealth add to utility at a decreasing rate). In particular, Bernoulli suggested that "the utility resulting from any small increase in wealth will be inversely proportionate to the quantity of goods previously possessed" (1738, p. 25). The utility function he suggested was

$$U(x) = b\left[\log \frac{\alpha + x}{\alpha}\right]$$

in which b is a constant, α the initial wealth level, and x the increase in wealth.[1] Note that $U'(x) = b/(\alpha + x)$, which is inversely proportionate to the total wealth possessed (i.e., $\alpha + x$).

Applying this formula to the St. Petersburg game will yield a final value, V_{max}, which can be determined as follows:

$$\begin{aligned}
U(V_{max}) &= \sum_{n=1}^{\infty} \left(\frac{1}{2}\right)^n b \log \frac{\alpha + 2^n}{\alpha} \\
&= b\Sigma \left(\frac{1}{2}\right)^n \{\log(\alpha + 2^n) - \log\alpha\} \\
&= b\Sigma \left(\frac{1}{2}\right)^n \log(\alpha + 2^n) - b \log\alpha \left\{\Sigma \left(\frac{1}{2}\right)^n\right\} \\
&= b\Sigma \log (\alpha + 2^n)^{(1/2)^n} - b \log\alpha \\
&= b \log \prod_{n=1}^{\infty} (\alpha + 2^n)^{(1/2)^n} - b \log\alpha \\
&= b \log \left[\frac{\Pi(\alpha + 2^n)^{(1/2)^n}}{\alpha}\right].
\end{aligned}$$

Hence,

$$U(V_{max}) = b \log \left[\frac{\alpha + V_{max}}{\alpha}\right] = b \log \left[\frac{\Pi(\alpha + 2^n)^{(1/2)^n}}{\alpha}\right]$$

or

$$V_{max} = \left[\prod_{n=1}^{\infty} (\alpha + 2^n)^{(1/2)^n}\right] - \alpha < (\alpha + 2)^2 - \alpha \text{ (for } \alpha \geq 0).$$

The value of V_{max} is finite in this case, as it will be for many other concave utility functions.[2] Bernoulli was thus one of the first to suggest that people maximize expected utility rather than mathematical expectation.

For a long time, the economic community debated how exactly to measure utility and whether it could be measured in an absolute sense. For example, Edgeworth (1881), an exponent of neoclassical utility theory, firmly believed in the ultimate possibility of a science of pleasure and pain. It was not until the work of Hicks (1939) that utilitarianism was abandoned by translating economic theory into an ordinal-preference language that does not require any absolute measurements of the utilities of commodities. (For a review of the historical developments of economic choice theory, see Walsh, 1970.) However, more recently the cardinalist view was revived by Von Neumann and Morgenstern (1947), who developed an important new utility theory as an underpinning in their economic theory of games. This utility theory expanded economic theory into the realm of risky commodities and is the predominant economic choice model of today. As a normative model, the theory embodies the essence of rational decision making under risk and assumes that no one would *knowingly* want to violate its axioms. As a descriptive model, it states that people behave *as if* they obey the axioms (i.e., as if they maximize expected utility).

2.2 VON NEUMANN-MORGENSTERN UTILITY

Von Neumann-Morgenstern (NM) utility theory (hereafter also referred to as expected utility theory) makes a set of assumptions about preference orderings and proves that to obey the axioms, one must always prefer the alternative with the highest expected utility. It differs in this sense from the Bernoulli postulate, which directly states that people should maximize expected utility. The axioms, described informally, are as follows:

1. *The complete ordering axiom*: For any two lotteries, L_1 and L_2, the decision maker prefers either L_1 to L_2 or L_2 to L_1, or else is indifferent. Furthermore, if L_1 is preferred to L_2 and L_2 to a lottery, L_3, then L_1 must also be preferred to L_3 (called transitivity).
2. *The continuity axiom*: If \$$x$ is preferred to \$$y$ and \$$y$ to \$$z$, then there must exist some probability p (between 0 and 1) so that the decision maker is indifferent between a sure amount \$$y$ and a lottery offering \$$x$ or \$$z$ with probabilities p and $(1 - p)$, respectively.
3. *The independence axiom*: If the decision maker is indifferent between alternatives x and y, then he should also be indifferent between two lotteries offering x and z in the first lottery and y and z in the second, with probabilities p and $(1 - p)$ in each lottery for any z and p value.

4. *The unequal probability axiom:* If x is preferred to y, then lottery L_1 should be preferred to L_2 when both lotteries contain only the outcomes x and y and when the probability of winning x is greater in L_1 than in L_2.
5. *The axiom of complexity*: If two lotteries, L_1 and L_2, offer outcomes x and y for L_1 and produce two new lotteries, L_3 and L_4, as the outcomes for lottery L_2, with L_3 and L_4 offering only x and y, then the decision maker should be indifferent between L_1 and L_2 if, and only if, the expected values of L_1 and L_2 are identical. (This axiom guarantees that probabilities are calculated in accordance with traditional probability calculus.)

The above axioms are sufficient to prove that there exists a utility index, unique up to positive linear transformations, so that computing expected utilities will yield a preference ordering among lotteries in accordance with the axioms. A very readable proof of this important theorem is contained in Baumol (1972, pp. 548–51). Alternative sets of axioms, which result in the same general theorem, are presented in Savage (1954); Luce and Raiffa (1977); Pratt, Raiffa, and Schlaifer (1965); and Fishburn (1970). It should be noted that the above axioms, particularly those of continuity and complexity, rule out any fondness or dislike for gambling for its own sake.

Although not directly related to the axiomatic theory of Von Neumann and Morgenstern, the next few paragraphs will be devoted to the practical issues of constructing a Von Neumann-Morgenstern utility function.

In constructing the utility index, $U(x)$, one is free to choose the origin and the unit of measurement. By way of illustration, let us set $U(-\$1,000)$ equal to 0 and $U(\$10,000)$ equal to 100 utiles. Given these two reference points, the NM utility index is constructed from such simple questions as, "What amount for certain is as attractive as a 50-50 lottery offering –\$1,000 or \$10,000?" Let us say the answer is $\$x^*$; we then compute $U(x^*)$ as $\frac{1}{2}U(-\$1,000) + \frac{1}{2}U(\$10,000)$, or 50 utiles. As long as the so-called reference lottery contains amounts for which the utilities are known, new utility points can be obtained. Thus, the next lottery would contain as outcomes either x^* and –\$1,000 or x^* and \$10,000. Indifference amounts for these lotteries will provide new outcomes for subsequent lotteries, and so many well-distributed points can be plotted. On the basis of the points thus obtained, a utility function can be interpolated. It should be noted that probabilities other than 50-50 can be used in the reference lotteries. Practical experience, however, suggests that 50-50 probabilities are least subject to probability distortions and therefore offer a more faithful representation of the decision maker's preferences.[3] For the same reason, it may be advisable to ask for indifference amounts (also called certainty equivalents), as outlined above, rather than indifference probabilities (as the second axiom proposes).

Suppose now that many points have been found; how should one interpolate a function? According to Keeney and Raiffa (1976), a good procedure is to ascertain general properties of the utility function in order to limit the class of functions from which to fit a curve. Useful characteristics to look for are ranges of monotonicity, as well as ranges of constant, increasing, or decreasing risk aversion. For example, if constant risk aversion holds, meaning that the certainty equivalents of lotteries are unaffected by changes in financial position, the utility function must be exponential (Pratt, 1964). The choice of the class of functions, however, remains subjective (see Meyer and Pratt, 1968). The same holds true for the choice of goodness-of-fit criteria, such as least squares, maximum likelihood, or others, which may lead to different estimations depending on one's assumptions regarding the error terms.

In fitting a curve, it is worthwhile to assess how easily one can work with various functional forms mathematically. In the case of exponential functions or powers of x, it has been tabulated what the value would be of $E[e^{-s\tilde{x}}]$ or $E(\tilde{x}^s)$ when $\tilde{x}$ assumes a beta, binomial, Cauchy, exponential, gamma, geometric, normal, Poission, or uniform density function (e.g., see table 4.6 in Keeney and Raiffa, 1976, p. 202). Of course, such tabulations greatly facilitate expected utility calculations. For example, if $\tilde{x}$ is normally distributed with mean μ and variance σ^2, the expected utility of $\tilde{x}$, assuming $U(x) = e^{-sx}$, will be $e^{-s\mu + s^2\sigma^2/2}$.

It is interesting to note that for quadratic utility functions (i.e., $U(x) = ax^2 + bx + c$), the expected utility of a lottery depends only on its mean (μ) and variance (σ^2). For example, consider a lottery ($\tilde{x}$) that offers outcomes O_1 through O_n with probabilities p_1 through p_n. The expected utility of this lottery will be:

$$
\begin{aligned}
E[U(\tilde{x})] &= \sum_{i=1}^{n} p_i U(O_i) \\
&= \Sigma p_i [aO_i^2 + bO_i + c] \\
&= aE(\tilde{x}^2) + bE(\tilde{x}) + c \\
&= a(\sigma^2 + \mu^2) + b\mu + c \\
&= f(\mu, \sigma^2).
\end{aligned}
$$

More detailed discussions of expected utility theory, particularly from an applied perspective, can be found in Chapter 4 of Keeney and Raiffa (1976).[4] In subsequent chapters, these authors extend the one-dimensional treatment to n dimensions, in which case the representation problem becomes more complex. In this book, however, we will not consider the multidimensional case.

As remarked earlier, the NM utility theory and Bernoulli's model, despite their mathematical similarity, differ in important ways. The NM utility index is a confounded measure of risk-taking attitude and the intrinsic worth of the attribute. In the classical economist's view, cardinal utility refers only to the intrinsic pleasure of the attribute under conditions of certainty. It is the author's interpretation that Bernoulli proposed to maximize the expectation of this latter type of utility rather than that of the NM type.

The cardinal nature of NM utility theory must therefore be interpreted carefully. Even though NM utility functions are unique up to positive linear transformations, it does not follow that if for certain outcomes $A \succ B \succ C \succ D$ and $U(A) - U(B) > U(C) - U(D)$, the change from B to A would be more preferable than the change from D to C. As an interval scale, the NM utility index provides only ordinal rankings among lotteries (Baumol, 1958). Differences in expected utility are difficult to interpret psychologically because of the confounded nature of the NM utility measure. Similarly, the notion of marginal utility has quite a different meaning in the NM sense than it has in classical economics. Whereas in classical economics it refers to changes in introspective pleasure sensation, in NM theory marginal utility refers only to "the marginal rate of substitution between X and the probability of winning the prespecified prize (E) of the standard lottery ticket" (Baumol, 1972, p. 548).

Having specified what is meant by rational decision behavior, we will now examine whether people in fact maximize expected utility in the Von Neumann-Morgenstern sense.

2.3 EMPIRICAL EVIDENCE

Expected utility (EU) theory has been, and continues to be, widely used in economics and psychology as a descriptive model. In this section, we will briefly assess its empirical status on the basis of some important experimental and field research. The review is not intended to be complete; its aim instead is to highlight the more important studies. (More specialized evidence will be cited in the research chapters.) The section is divided into experimental studies and field studies. The former tend to offer more direct evidence demonstrably related to specific axioms, while the latter are more indirect, testing whether people behave *as if* they maximize expected utility. The EU hypothesis is considered in both its general form, where no restrictions are imposed on $U(x)$ other than monotonicity (in the case of money), and in its traditional economic form, where $U(x)$ is assumed to be concave ($U'' < 0$), implying risk aversion.

2.3.1 Experimental Studies

One of the first experimental tests of EU was conducted by Mosteller and Nogee (1951), who used Harvard students and National Guardsmen as subjects. Their aims were (1) to observe betting behavior with real money (using small amounts) in a controlled laboratory situation, (2) to construct NM utility functions for each of the subjects, and (3) to determine if predictions could be made from these curves. Following the psychological tradition of establishing indifference or preference stochastically (i.e., from repeated trials), Mosteller and Nogee constructed probabilistic utility functions. Their data suggested that subjects' choices were indeed probabilistic. Despite this lack of perfect consistency (as assumed in the NM axioms), they concluded that the utility curves had considerable predictive power. The higher the expected utility of a bet, the greater the probability it would be chosen. The EU model was more accurate in this regard than the expected monetary value (EV) model.

Another important and well-designed experiment was conducted by Davidson, Suppes, and Siegel (1957). Using nineteen Stanford business students, six utility points were assessed per subject via indifference judgments. A major difference between their study and the Mosteller-Nogee experiment was that the utility measurement involved a single chance event whose subjective probability was determined experimentally. The general conclusions were: (1) their procedure offered a practical approach to measuring utility for small amounts, (2) people chose as if they attempted to maximize EU, (3) the utility functions were generally not linear, and • upon remeasurement, subjects appeared quite consistent.

In 1948, Friedman and Savage had proposed a utility curve, defined on final income levels, which could reconcile people's seemingly contradictory preferences for both actuarially unfair insurance and unfair lotteries. Essentially, the curve suggested increasing marginal utility in the middle range of income levels. (Such risk-taking tendencies were later empirically demonstrated in Mosteller and Nogee's 1951 experiments.) As an alternative to this risk-taking hypothesis, Yaari (1965) proposed a general psychological law according to which low probabilities are exaggerated and high ones are underestimated. From several experiments, he concluded that the acceptance of unfair gambles is better explained by optimism regarding low-probability events than by the notion of increasing marginal utility of wealth.

As a follow-up to Yaari's hypothesis, Rosett (1971) conducted five related experiments on probability perceptions and the presumed convexity of acceptance sets for two outcome gambles defined on a given event, E. His general conclusions were that experimental results greatly depend on the exact conditions of the experiment, particularly the decisions made by the experimenter about unstated assumptions of the theory under study. Furthermore, Rosett concluded that most of the unfair gambles that were accepted could be explained by very small nonconvexities of the acceptance set, although some probability exaggeration was observed as well. Finally, Rosett found that conformity with the EU hypothesis depends to a considerable extent on the complexity of the experiment. In favorable cases, 73 percent of the alleged biases were consistent with EU; in more complex, unfavorable designs, as few as 16 percent.

An important challenge to EU was proposed by Allais (1953), who asked people to choose one alternative in each of the following two situations:

Situation 1
- 1*a*: $1 million for certain.
- 1*b*: $5 million with a probability of .1; $1 million with a probability of .89; and $0 with a probability of .01.

Situation 2
- 2*a*: $1 million with a probability of .11 and $0 with a probability of .89.
- 2*b*: $5 million with a probability of .1 and $0 with a probability of .9.

A prevalent response pattern, even among experts, is to prefer 1*a* to 1*b* in the first case, and 2*b* to 2*a* in the second. The first preference implies, of course, that $U(1) > .1U(5) + .89U(1) + .01U(0)$ where the amounts are in millions. Combining terms, this simplifies to $.11U(1) > .1U(5) + .01U(0)$. The second preference, however, implies exactly the opposite: $.1U(5) + .9U(0) > .11U(1) + .89U(0)$ or $.1U(5) + .01U(0) > .11U(1)$.

The inconsistency can be made very clear by restating the choice as a lottery with 100 numbered tickets and prizes as shown in Table 2.1. The problem in both situations is now simply a choice between an outright gift of $1 million and a 10-to-1 chance of getting $5 million. Hence, the situations are identical within the EU framework.

Table 2.1. The Allais Paradox Stated in Lottery Form

		Number Drawn		
		1	*2–11*	*12–100*
Situation 1	1*a*:	1	1	1
	1*b*:	0	5	1
Situation 2	2*a*:	1	1	0
	2*b*:	0	5	0

Note: Prizes are in millions of dollars.

Tversky (1975) discussed a generalization of the Allais paradox in terms of a certainty effect and a reference effect that are sources of error in judgments. The certainty effect states that consequences obtained with certainty loom larger than those that are uncertain. An example of this effect is the incompatible preferences that subjects stated regarding the following choices:

Situation 1
- 1*a*: A certain loss of \$45.
- 1*b*: A 50–50 chance of losing \$100 or \$0.

Situation 2
- 2*a*: A .1 chance of losing \$45 and a .9 chance of losing \$0.
- 2*b*: A .05 chance of losing \$100 and a .95 chance of losing \$0.

Most subjects preferred situation 1*b* to 1*a* and 2*a* to 2*b*, which violates EU theory. The former preference implies that $U(-45) < .5U(-100) + .5U(0)$, whereas the latter preference implies the reverse inequality.

The reference effect states that people evaluate options in relation to their status quo, adaption level, or expectations rather than in relation to final asset positions, as EU theory assumes. This effect may lead to changes in preferences because of differences in the formulation of a decision problem.

Further experimental evidence against EU was provided by Ellsberg (1961), who showed that subjects prefer a small variance in the probability of winning over a large variance when the expected values of such probabilities are equal. As an example, imagine two urns containing red and white balls only. The color mixture in the first urn is 50-50; in the second urn, it is unknown. If a red ball would yield a prize of \$100 (in either urn), from which urn would you prefer to draw a ball at random? Of course, according to EU theory, the only relevant aspect of the probability distribution of the chance of winning is its expected value, no matter what its general shape. Since the expected probability of winning is 1/2 for both urns, the value of each is $\frac{1}{2}U(10) + \frac{1}{2}U(0)$. However, most people prefer the first urn, which suggests a dislike for ambiguity. A reply to the Ellsberg paradox can be found in Raiffa (1961). A discussion of the Ellsberg experiments and similar ones, including the Allais (1953) paradox, and of their implications for decision theory is contained in Fellner (1961); Becker and Brownson (1964); MacCrimmon (1968); MacCrimmon and Larsson (1975); and Slovic and Tversky (1974).

Another interesting set of EU violations was reported by Becker, DeGroot, and Marschak (1963). In their experiment, subjects could choose one of the following three lotteries:

A: x_1 or x_4 with equal chances.
B: x_2 or x_3 with equal chances.
C: x_1, x_2, x_3, or x_4, each with probability 1/4.

If $x_1 < x_2 < x_3 < x_4$, an EU maximizer can choose only *A* or *B*, as *C* implies a contradiction. That is, choosing *C* over both *A* and *B* implies that

$$\frac{1}{4}[u(x_1) + u(x_2) + u(x_3) + u(x_4)] > \frac{1}{2}[u(x_1) + u(x_4)],$$

with the left-hand side at the same time being greater than $\frac{1}{2}[u(x_2) + u(x_3)]$. Adding up these two inequalities yields the contradictory result that

$$\sum_{i=1}^{4} u(x_i) > \sum_{i=1}^{4} u(x_i).$$

In testing twenty-five different sets of such questions, sixty out of sixty-two students preferred lottery *C* at least once, with two subjects preferring *C* as often as nineteen out of twenty-five times. The size of the payoffs (pennies or dollars) did not seem to affect the extent of this type of EU violation.

Similar results were obtained by Coombs (1975). In his experiments, subjects were asked to rank, in order of attractiveness, three gambles, *A*, *B*, and *C*, where *C* constituted a probability mixture of *A* and *B* (as in the above experiment). For example, if *A* offers even chances at \$7 or \$0 and *B* even chances at \$5 or \$3, then a 40-60 mixture of *A* and *B*, called gamble *C*, would offer outcomes of \$7, \$5, \$3, and \$0 with probabilities .2, .2, .3, and .3, respectively.

As shown above, EU theory is violated if gamble *C* is either more preferred or less preferred than both gambles *A* and *B*. In general, there are six possible rankings of this triplet, which can be partitioned into three classes called monotone orderings (*ACB* or *BCA*), folded orderings (*CAB* or *CBA*), and inverted orderings (*ABC* or *BAC*). The last two of these orderings (i.e., folded and inverted) violate EU theory.

In the experiment reported by Coombs (1975), twenty-six subjects were given 20 different triplets in each of which the *C* gamble was a 50-50 probability mixture of the *A* and *B* gambles. Of the 520 triplets thus rank ordered, 283 (or 54 percent) were monotone, 139 (or 27 percent) folded, and 98 (or 19 percent) inverted. Hence, almost half of all rankings violated EU theory, with the majority being of the folded type (i.e., the mixture being preferred to its components).

To account for such behavior, Coombs suggested a theory of risk preference (called portfolio theory), which assumes that risk-preference functions are single-peaked for fixed levels of EV. This theory will be discussed further in the next chapter.

Regarding the probability side of EU, many studies have shown that people are poor intuitive statisticians. Tversky and Kahneman (1973) showed that people tend to overestimate the probability of conjunctive events and to underestimate the probability of disjunctive ones. Studies on Bayesian revision have revealed a conservatism bias in which posterior probabilities are underestimated when new information is provided (Edwards, 1968; Slovic and Lichtenstein, 1971). On the other hand, there also exists a base-rate ignorance phenomenon in which the diagnosticity of new information is overvalued by ignoring prior probabilities (Slovic and Lyon, 1976; Bar-Hillel, 1980). We shall return to these phenomena in Chapter 3 when discussing prevalent heuristics and biases in human judgments.

Finally, an important set of experiments by Tversky (1969) shows lawful and predictable violations of the transitivity axiom. Since this research is associated with an alternative decision model, it will be described in that context in the next chapter.

Additional experimental studies showing violations of EU theory are reported in Edwards (1953, 1954a, 1954c); Slovic (1966b); Wallsten (1968); Tversky (1967a); Hershman and Levine (1970); Lichtenstein and Slovic (1971, 1973); Lindman (1971); Fryback, Goodman, and Edwards (1973); and Grether and Plott (1979).

2.3.2 Field Studies

In 1954, Johnson et al. (1961) conducted a large survey of 1,075 midwestern and western farm managers regarding their decision processes. About half the farmers were presented with hypothetical choice situations involving probabilistic monetary gains and losses from which utility functions could be constructed. The resulting utility functions were classified according to their degree of relative marginal utility to see if risk-taking attitudes related to the farmers' characters, dispositions, and managerial behavior (see Halter, 1956).

Those farmers who accepted both unfair gambles and unfair insurance schemes were generally older and had more experience, fewer dependents, higher net worth, and less debt relative to those not exhibiting this response pattern. Those who would not accept fair gambles on gains also tended to have high net worth, but at the same time they possessed the highest debt positions. Very few farmers would not accept fair bets on the loss side, which suggests risk-taking tendencies for losses.

Regarding preferences for risk and type of farming, an interesting relationship was observed. Farmers with high relative marginal utilities for gains were most frequently found in the more risky farming enterprises (e.g., cash crops or fat-stock feeding). Those with intermediate marginal utility levels were often involved in dairying or tobacco farming, while those least risk-taking (on the gain side) were primarily involved in general farming.

A similar relationship was found on the loss side, where the relative marginal disutilities for losses correlated with the type of farming in which farmers were engaged. For example, farmers who showed a relatively large marginal disutility for losses of wealth were typically engaged in low-risk farming. Interestingly, farmers with low gross incomes and low net worths showed a greater marginal disutility per dollar of loss than farmers who were better off. Their risk aversion may have kept them from entering into more profitable farming.[5]

Another farming study, involving wool producers in Australia, was conducted by Officer (1967). Utility functions were constructed via three different methods for six farmers who represented various farm sizes (see Officer and Halter, 1968). The utility functions were used to predict the amounts of fodder reserves the farmers had stocked in protection against drought. The predictions from EU theory were generally better than those derived from a model of minimization of expected cost. The NM functions predicted best if they were constructed from 50-50 lotteries, thereby avoiding probability distortions. The findings showed the existence of nonlinear utility functions (even for small amounts), which were rather stable over the period of study (one year).

An interesting study by Katona (1965) on the effects of private pension plans on individual savings uncovered behavior that is difficult to account for in an expected utility framework. Katona raised the question of whether working people who expect retirement income from pension plans would put more or fewer funds into private savings (e.g., deposits with banks and savings institutions, bonds, or stocks) than would working people who are not covered by such pension plans. Private pension plans, which were relatively unimportant in 1945, expanded so much that by 1965 almost half of all privately employed workers in the United States were covered (in addition to there being almost universal social security coverage). This development presented a unique opportunity to study the effect of private pension plans on discretionary savings, since coverage by these pension plans was more a function of type of employment than the result of voluntary action resulting from differential predispositions toward thriftiness.

At the outset, Katona formulated two alternative hypotheses regarding the effect of pension plan coverage on discretionary savings. The first hypothesis, derived from traditional economic theory, suggests that increased "forced savings" (via private pension plans) reduces voluntary savings, other economic things being equal. An alternative to this "substitution effect" hypothesis is that increased forced savings will lead to *increased* voluntary savings because of changes in aspiration level and goal gradient effects. The level of aspiration theory, as formulated by Kurt Lewin (see Marrow, 1969, pp. 44–46), essentially holds that people raise their sights (i.e., aspirations) with success and lower them with failure. The goal gradient effect refers to a well-known phenomenon in which the closer one gets to a goal, the greater one's effort.

Comparisons between "the average savings ratios of the people covered and people not covered under a private pension plan — paired so as to make them similar in many [socioeconomic] characteristics — indicated that the former saved more than the latter" (Katona, 1965, p. 6). This finding supports an aspiration level and goal gradient hypothesis rather than traditional economic theory. Katona (1975) discusses other examples of psychological phenomena counter to economic principles.

Another field study suggesting the inappropriateness of expected utility theory as a descriptive model was conducted by Kunreuther (1976) and Kunreuther et al. (1978) on insurance coverage against floods and earthquakes. This insurance decision can be viewed as a "contingent claim" problem consisting of the following parameters (see Kunreuther, 1976).[6] Let

c = cost per dollar of insurance;
p = probability of a disaster occurring;
L = dollar loss resulting from the disaster;
t = percentage of tax write-off on uninsured loss;
A = current wealth of decision maker;
I = amount of insurance taken out; and
$U(x)$ = concave NM utility function.

If a disaster occurs, the final asset position will be $f(I) = A - L + (1 - c)I + (L - I)t$. If no disaster occurs, the final asset position will be $g(I) = A - cI$. If there are no restrictions on the fraction covered, and assuming proportional recovery, the optimal amount of insurance (I^*) can be determined from the following constrained optimization problem:

$$\max E[U(I)] = pU[f(I)] + (1 - p)U[g(I)]$$

subject to

$$0 \leq I \leq L.$$

Using the standard Kuhn and Tucker (1951) criteria, we find that if $0 < I^* < L$, the optimal amount is determined by the following first-order condition:

$$pU'[f(I)][(1 - c) - t] + (1 - p)U'[g(I)](-c) = 0$$

or

$$k = \frac{(1 - p)c}{p(1 - c - t)} = \frac{U'[f(I^*)]}{U'[g(I^*)]}.$$

The left-hand side of the above equation can be viewed as a contingency price ratio (k). It represents the ratio of the "expected" cost of insurance should no disaster occur to the "expected" net gain in assets from insurance after a disaster has occurred. The higher this ratio, the more expensive the insurance is. For actuarially fair insurance, $k = 1$. For life insurance, it is typically around 2.

To understand the boundary cases of maximum coverage ($I^* = L$) and no coverage ($I^* = 0$), let us write out the contingency price ratio:

$$k = \frac{U'[f(I^*)]}{U'[g(I^*)]} = \frac{U'[A - L + (1 - c)I^* + (L - I^*)t]}{U'[A - cI^*]}.$$

If $I^* = L$, we get $\{U'[A - cL]\}/\{U'[A - cL]\}$, or $k = 1$. Hence, for $k \leq 1$, the optimal decision is to purchase maximum coverage. Similarly, if $I^* = 0$, we get $k = \{U'[A - L(1 - t)]\}/\{U'[A]\}$. Hence, if the loading charge (i.e., the cost of insurance above its actuarial expected loss) is so high that it equals or exceeds the ratio of the marginal utilities of postdisaster to predisaster wealth, the optimal choice is to remain uninsured.

Through face-to-face interviews, Kunreuther assessed homeowners' subjective values of p, c, and L. The sample included 2,000 floodplain homeowners and 1,000 living in earthquake areas. By design, about half of each group was insured. The survey showed that half of the uninsured homeowners in floodplains and about two-thirds of the uninsured group in earthquake areas were unable to estimate the insurance cost, the damage, or the probability of a future disaster. Hence, these individuals were not in a position to evaluate the attractiveness of insurance by utilizing an expected utility model. Interestingly, a smaller, but still significant, proportion of the insured homeowners fell into this category as well. For those who did provide usable estimates, the contingency price ratio (k) was computed and related to their insurance actions. The results are shown in Table 2.2.

Although traditional economic theory postulates risk aversion on the loss side (e.g., Friedman and Savage, 1948; Arrow, 1971, 1973), Table 2.2 contains much evidence to the contrary. It shows that 39 percent of the uninsured homeowners (under the assumption that they were risk-neutral or risk-averse) violated EU theory because their value of k was less than or equal to 1, in which case they should have taken full coverage. On the other hand, if k exceeds 10 (a conservative figure), one would not expect even

Table 2.2. Kunreuther's Study on Flood and Earthquake Insurance

	Flood Survey		*Earthquake Survey*	
Contingency Price Ratio	*Insured (%)*	*Uninsured (%)*	*Insured (%)*	*Uninsured (%)*
Less than .05	20	12	21	13
.05–.1	15	13	14	9
.11–1	15	14	17	17
1.1–10	11	13	19	16
10.1–30	4	2	5	10
Over 30	35	46	24	35

Note: The table shows contingency price ratios (k) for insured and uninsured individuals who had positive estimates of the premium (c), the probability (p), and the loss (L). Each percentage column totals 100 percent. A tax rate (t) of .3 was assumed.

highly risk-averse individuals to purchase insurance. Nevertheless, 39 percent of the insured homeowners did buy insurance against floods when they should not have, and 29 percent did so in the case of earthquake insurance.

The general conclusions of Kunreuther's study are that people seldom have enough information to abide by EU theory and that if they do, their decisions are often not consistent with the assumption of risk aversion or even more relaxed EU interpretations.

Other field studies provide further evidence that EU theory provides little insight into decisions involving low-probability and high-loss events. Eisner and Strotz (1961) concluded that air accident or flight insurance is less attractive economically than regular life insurance. The value of k equals about 3.3 for flight insurance and 2 for regular life insurance. Nevertheless, there exists a great demand for flight insurance. Furthermore, flight insurance is typically "bought" (i.e., the consumer initiates the purchase), whereas most regular life insurance is "sold" (i.e., the insurance salesman initiates the contact).

In a similar vein, Pashigian, Schkade, and Menefee (1966) studied the widespread preference for the lowest deductible in the purchase of automobile insurance. Although this can always be rationalized by assuming a sufficiently risk-averse exponential utility function (see Gould, 1969), it does raise questions as to whether people maximize expected utility.

Contrary to the revealed risk-averse preferences referred to in the above paragraph, other studies suggest considerable risk taking (when viewed from an EU perspective). Examples of such risk taking are the low sales of highly subsidized insurance (see Anderson, 1974, for a discussion of flood insurance and the Federal Insurance Administration, 1974, for a discussion of crime insurance), as well as people's reluctance to wear seatbelts in automobiles despite their proven value (see Robertson, 1974). These examples suggest that people either ignore low-probability events or have difficulty making rational decisions about them.

2.4 CONCLUSIONS

In its early beginnings, expected utility maximization was suggested as a descriptive model to explain the so-called St. Petersburg paradox. Being a measure of intrinsic value (i.e., its measurement did not rely on trade-offs with other commodities), it assumed an important role in classical economics. Later, the utilitarian perspective in economics was replaced by an ordinal preference theory in which worth was measured only in terms of trade-offs with other commodities. In its cardinal form, EU maximization revived when Von Neumann and Morgenstern (1947) proposed it as a normative theory. Since then, EU maximization has been used both as a prescriptive and descriptive model.

Early experimental tests found the Von Neumann-Morgenstern utility measure to be operational and capable of predicting choice behavior. Somewhat later, however, there appeared formulations of choice situations in which people systematically violated the axioms. Although an EU defender may note that most of these "paradoxes" and violations involve the probability side, not the value side, the two are so intractably mixed in the NM utility function that distortions in either would invalidate the model. At the level of field studies, the findings were also mixed; although several studies on farming supported EU theory, other studies involving insurance behavior questioned its descriptive validity. Of course, EU's adequacy depends to a considerable extent on the level at which behavior is examined (e.g., individual vs. aggregate), as well as the nature of the task and the type of response mode. Given the limited empirical support for EU theory, however, various researchers formulated alternative descriptive models. These models will be discussed in the next chapter.

3 ALTERNATIVE DESCRIPTIVE MODELS

This chapter will discuss several alternative descriptive models, as well as their underlying theoretical premises. The first section offers an overview of the various classes of models, while the second discusses the so-called holistic judgment models, most of which are modifications of EU theory and fall into the category of "as-if" models. Rather than claiming to offer descriptions of the decision process, these models purport to predict behavior by assuming that people act as if they followed the model. Section 3.3 outlines the tenets of the so-called information-processing view of decision making in which the aim is a better understanding of the decision process itself. In this context, we shall discuss Simon's bounded rationality theory (1955), as well as some heuristics and biases researched by Tversky and Kahneman (1974). Section 3.4 examines several of the non-holistic judgment models, together with their relationship to the information-processing view.

3.1 SCHEMATIC OVERVIEW

Figure 3.1 offers a schematic overview of the various classes of descriptive models that have been proposed.[1] The first distinction concerns holistic

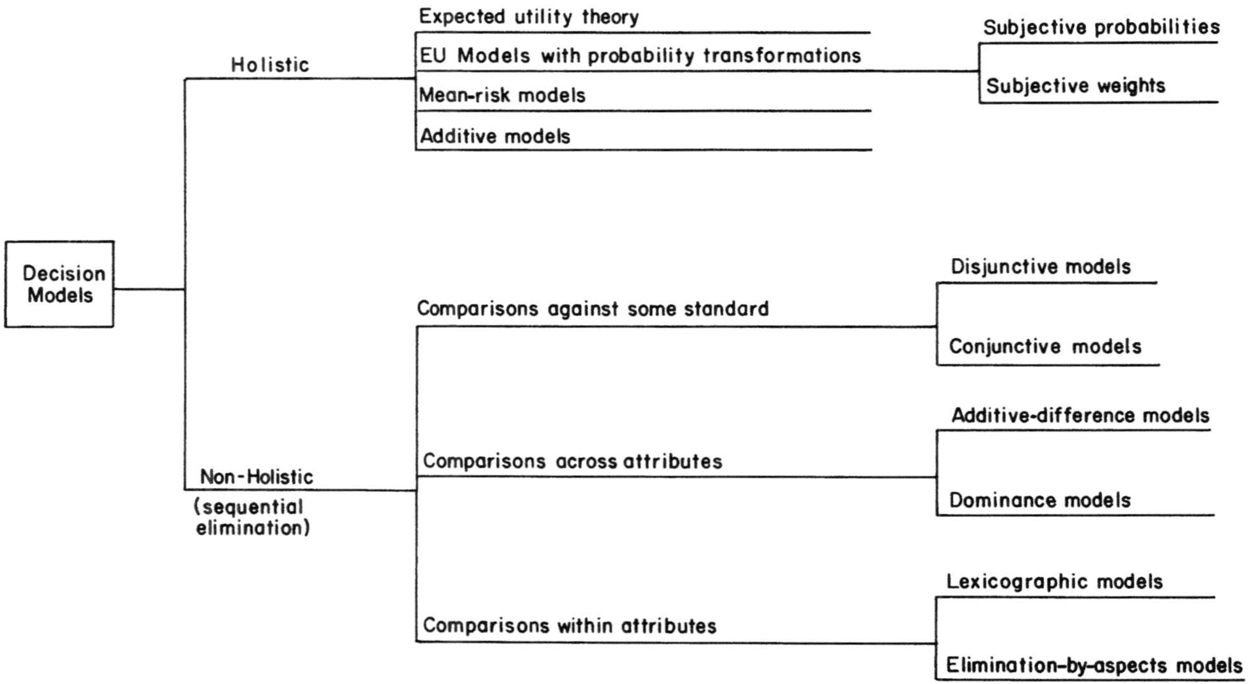

Figure 3.1. Classification Scheme for Descriptive Models

versus non-holistic judgments. In the holistic approach, each alternative, $\bar{x}$, is assessed independently of the others and assigned a value, $U(\bar{x})$, so that $U(A)$ is greater than $U(B)$ if, and only if, A is preferred to B.[2] In the non-holistic judgment models, an alternative is never evaluated just by itself. Instead, the optimal choice is filtered out by making comparisons, usually within attributes, vis-à-vis other alternatives. The latter approach is therefore also referred to as sequential elimination.

Before providing some representative examples of the various model types, we will briefly define each one. Within the holistic group, as shown in Figure 3.1, reside four subgroups. The first of these is the traditional expected utility model in which $U(\bar{x}) = \Sigma p_i U(x_i)$ (assuming a discrete outcome space). In the second subgroup, the probabilities are replaced by $f(p_i)$ so that $U(\bar{x}) = \Sigma f(p_i) U(x_i)$. If the $f(p_i)$ behave as mathematical probabilities (e.g., $\Sigma f(p_i) = 1$), the models belong to the subjective expected utility (SEU) category. Otherwise, they will be referred to as subjectively weighted utility models. The third subgroup contains models for which $U(\bar{x})$ is a function of the mean of $\tilde{x}$ — that is, $E(\tilde{x})$ — and its risk. The models within this subgroup differ primarily on how risk is measured. Finally, there are the additive models, in which $U(\bar{x})$ is an additive function of probabilities and outcomes.

In the non-holistic group, three subgroups are distinguished. In the first, alternatives are compared against some standard and eliminated if they fail to measure up. If the criteria require that all attributes meet certain minimum standards, the model is conjunctive. If satisfaction of one of several conditions is sufficient, the model is a disjunctive one.[3]

In the second subgroup, comparisons are made across attributes within a pair of alternatives. The domination rule, for example, is aimed at eliminating options that are not superior in at least one attribute when compared to another alternative. The additive-difference model sums the within-attribute differences (after appropriate transformations) across all attributes to arrive at an index of relative pairwise attractiveness.

Finally, comparisons can be made across alternatives, attributes being compared one at a time. In the lexicographic method, the alternatives are first compared on their most important dimension. If one alternative is clearly superior to the others, that alternative will be the optimal choice. In case of a tie, the second dimension is considered, and so forth. In the method of elimination by aspects, alternatives not meeting some standard are eliminated. This process also considers one attribute at a time; however, the attributes are ordered according to their stochastic discrimination power (Tversky, 1972a).

3.2 HOLISTIC JUDGMENT MODELS

Since the EU model was discussed in detail in Chapter 2, we shall start with the second subgroup. The subjective expected utility (SEU) models usually assume (1) independence between utility and subjective probability, (2) risk invariance of utility, and (3) $\Sigma f(p_i) = 1$. Reviews can be found in Edwards (1959, 1961); Luce and Suppes (1965); Coombs and Huang (1970b); Břicháček (1970); and Lee (1971). In the beginning, SEU models encountered measurement difficulties. DeFinetti (1937) and Preston and Baratta (1948) had developed subjective probability measures based on a person's willingness to bet.[4] For example, let us say that the maximum acceptable odds favorable to an event *E* occurring are 5 to 1. The interpretation would then be that event *E* is perceived to be 5 times as likely to occur as not *E*, or a subjective probability of 5/6 for the occurrence of *E*. Since these procedures were developed outside a utility framework, they implicitly assumed linear utility for money.

In an earlier, but at the time unrecognized, essay, Ramsey (1931) had realized this measurement difficulty. He therefore suggested that one should first construct a utility function using bets with known subjective probabilities and then measure subjective probabilities for unknown events using that utility function and maximum betting-odds ratios. To find an event with known subjective probabilities, equal likelihood was used (e.g., indifference between heads and tails in coin tossing) as this can be established psychologically without knowledge of the underlying value function. The procedure outlined by Ramsey (1931) was elaborated on by Davidson, Suppes, and Siegel (1957), who provided the first empirical data on independent, simultaneous measurement of subjective probabilities and utilities. Subsequent developments led to the theories of conjoint measurement (Luce and Tukey, 1964; Tversky, 1967b; Krantz and Tversky, 1971) and functional measurement (Anderson, 1970). A comprehensive review of various measurement systems is contained in Krantz et al. (1971).

The general findings of SEU research are that subjective probabilities often relate nonlinearly to objective ones. Typically, the subjective probability curves overestimate low probabilities and underestimate high ones (Lee, 1971, p. 61). However, the evidence seems inconclusive with respect to the general nature of probability misperceptions — in particular, its stability across tasks and its dependence on outcomes. For example, Marks (1951), Irwin (1953), and Slovic (1966b) found that subjective probabilities are higher when the outcomes are more desirable (i.e., wishful thinking).

The SEU model has also been used outside the context of monetary bets or gambles. Vroom (1964) formulated a theory of motivation in which effort expended on possible alternatives is a multiplicative function of the desirability of various outcomes (called valences) and the beliefs (called expectancies) that the outcomes will materialize. This so-called expectancy theory shows formal parallels to SEU, as do various theories in learning, attitude formation, and personality development (see Lawler, 1973). Hence, SEU models are widely used. In most versions, the utility function concerns the attribute's value under conditions of certainty (e.g., Edwards, 1955); however, in some versions, it also measures a person's risk-taking attitude (e.g., Ramsey, 1931).

The next subgroup to be discussed consists of models in which the probability transformations do not lead to quantities that possess characteristics of mathematical probabilities (e.g., $\Sigma p_i = 1$).[5] We will consider three models of such subjectively weighted utility: Handa's (1977) certainty equivalence theory, Karmarkar's (1978) subjectively weighted utility model, and Kahneman and Tversky's (1979) prospect theory.

Handa (1977) proposed a theory in which $U(x)$ is linear and $f(p_i)$ exhibits overweighting of low probabilities and underweighting of high ones. This certainty equivalence (CE) theory is based on axioms similar to NM utility theory, except that the axioms and transformations are defined on the probability component. Schneeweiss (1974) had earlier developed this approach (including axioms) in his discussion of the dual nature of probabilities and outcomes. Handa showed that the Allais paradox can easily be explained by the CE theory and suggested that it agrees with other experimental findings as well. Fishburn (1978), however, has noted that Handa's theory reduces to the expected value model (i.e., $f(p) = p$) for sufficiently rich prospects (e.g., three outcomes).

Karmarkar (1978) suggested a model that can be viewed as a special case of Anderson and Shanteau's (1970) information-integration model in that the decision weights are normalized as follows:

$$f(p_i) = \frac{w_i(p)}{\Sigma w_i(p)} .$$

Karmarkar proposed the specific weighting function:

$$w_i(p) = \frac{p_i^\alpha}{p_i^\alpha + (1 - p_i)^\alpha} ,$$

for which $w(0) = 0$, $w(1/2) = 1/2$, and $w(1) = 1$. For $\alpha = 1$, $w(p)$ is linear; for $\alpha > 1$, it is S-shaped; and for $\alpha < 1$, it is counter S-shaped. In another article, Karmarkar (1979) showed that the Allais paradox can readily be explained with his subjectively weighted utility model, assuming $\alpha < 1$. Note that in this model, the weight associated with probability p_i will depend on the levels of the other probabilities as $\Sigma f(p_i) = 1$. This dependency has psychological meaning in that certain probabilities can "intimidate" others.

A very elaborate subjectively weighted utility theory was proposed by Kahneman and Tversky (1979). Their so-called prospect theory was motivated by the following empirically observed tendencies:

1. People generally do not weight the utilities of outcomes by their respective probabilities (as is assumed in EU theory). Instead, they tend to overweight outcomes they consider certain relative to those they consider merely probable. This tendency is referred to as the *certainty effect.*
2. When a choice between two positive prospects (i.e., gains only) is compared with its mirror-image choice between two corresponding negative prospects (i.e., losses only), individuals typically reverse their preferences. This tendency is termed the *reflection effect.*[6]
3. To simplify decision making, people typically disregard common components between alternatives, focusing instead on elements that distinguish the alternatives. This phenomenon is called the *isolation effect.*

Although prospect theory shows similarities to EU theory in that it is an expectation theory, it differs in the following ways:

1. Unlike the Von Neumann-Morgenstern utility function, which is unique up to positive linear transformations, prospect theory defines a value function that is unique up to positive ratio transformations. Furthermore, this value function does not measure attitudes toward risk, but only the value of outcomes under conditions of certainty. It is concave for gains and convex for losses.
2. Instead of the objective probabilities used in EU theory, prospect theory utilizes decision weights, $\pi(p_i)$, that reflect the outcomes' impact on the prospect's attractiveness. Kahneman and Tversky suggested that low probabilities are generally overweighted and high ones underweighted.
3. Prospect theory treats choice situations involving strictly positive or negative outcomes differently than those involving zero and/or both positive and negative outcomes. In the former case, the sure gain or loss is factored out.

4. In a related vein, prospect theory proposes an editing phase prior to the evaluation of the gambles. Various editing operations are suggested (e.g., coding, combining, segregation, and cancellation), which organize and reformulate the options so as to simplify choice.
5. Finally, the value function in prospect theory measures the subjective value of outcomes relative to some reference point that may vary as a function of problem presentation. The emphasis is on *changes* in wealth or assets, not on final asset positions (as in utility theory).

The probability weighting function, $\pi(p)$, exhibits the following properties:

1. $\pi(0) = 0$ and $\pi(1) = 1$.
2. Subadditivity for small p (i.e., $\pi(rp) > r\pi(p)$ for $0 < r < 1$).
3. Overweighting of small p (i.e., $\pi(p) > p$).
4. Subcertainty: $\pi(p) + \pi(1 - p) < 1$ for $0 < p < 1$.
5. Subproportionality: $\dfrac{\pi(pq)}{\pi(p)} \leq \dfrac{\pi(pqr)}{\pi(pr)}$ for $0 < p, q, r \leq 1$.

Although its predictions are somewhat indeterminate for low p, assuming a $v(x)$ and $\pi(x)$ as given, prospect theory has made a substantial contribution by offering a framework from which to understand well-documented, lawful violations of EU theory.

The best known in the subgroup of mean-risk models is probably the mean-variance or mean-standard deviation model underlying Markowitz's (1952, 1959) portfolio theory. It is used both normatively and descriptively and has been researched extensively in finance, economics, and psychology. Various references to this model can be found in Libby and Fishburn's review (1977, p. 277). As shown earlier, the model is only strictly compatible with EU maximization if $U(x)$ is quadratic. More detailed discussions on its exact and approximate congruencies with EU maximization can be found in Baron (1977) and Levy and Markowitz (1979).

Apart from variance, other moments have been proposed in the measurement of risk, most notably skewness and kurtosis (Lichtenstein, 1965). Additionally, various measures of risk have focused on the negative, or loss, side of the distribution, leading to mean-semivariance or mean-negative outcome models. The negativeness of outcomes is judged either against zero or against some aspiration level. An example of the latter type is a model recently proposed by Fishburn (1977). In his theory, risk is defined by the following two parameter function:

$$\int_{-\infty}^{t} (t - x)^{\alpha} dF(x),$$

where t is a target return and α a measure of how deviations below t are to be weighted; and x and $F(x)$ denote the gamble's outcomes and cumulative density function, respectively. This so-called α-t model predicts choice by EV alone if all x_i are above t, and by a dominance relation involving risk and EV if $x_i < t$ for some i.

The α-t model is only congruent with EU for limited shapes of $U(x)$ — namely, $U(x) = x$ for all $x \geq t$, and $U(x) = x - k(t - x)^{\alpha}$ for all $x \leq t$, with $k + 1 = [U(t) - U(t - 1)]/[U(t + 1) - U(t)]$. Clearly, this condition is very restrictive, which makes the α-t model generally incompatible with the EU criterion.

Pruitt (1962) proposed another mean-risk model, in which risk is defined as the sum of negative outcomes weighted by their probabilities.

A very general mean-risk model coming out of mathematical psychology was proposed by Coombs and Huang (1970b). In this so-called portfolio theory, an optimal risk level is assumed for every level of expected value (i.e., single-peaked risk-preference function).[7] Gambles of equal expected value are judged in terms of their deviations from this optimal risk level. Hence, if two gambles, A and B, which have equal expected values, are combined into a probability mixture called gamble C, the new gamble may well be closer to the optimal risk level than either A or B, leading to the types of inverted orderings (i.e., EU violations) discussed in Chapter 2.

Pollatsek (1971) has shown formally that EU is inconsistent with single-peaked preference functions on either skewness or variance (provided the utility function is continuous and increases monotonically with money) and that SEU is inconsistent with single-peaked preference functions on either skewness or range (assuming that the subjective probability function is continuous and increases monotonically with objective probabilities).

In general, portfolio theory leaves the definition of risk unspecified since it needs to be inferred and modeled from preferences. The theory's only assumptions are (1) after EV is held constant, choice is governed by a risk-preference function; (2) this function is single-peaked; (3) preferences among gambles follow a partial ordering by dominance; and (4) risk is invariant under translations (i.e., adding a constant sum to all outcomes). The first three of these assumptions are sufficient to prove that preferences among gambles can be represented as a set of indifference curves in an EV-risk space. For a proof of this result, see the appendix in Coombs (1975).[8]

Finally, within the holistic group, we are left with models in which the basic stimuli are combined additively (either linearly or nonlinearly) into an overall judgment. The best example of this subgroup is Slovic and Lichtenstein's (1968a) study of duplex gambles (see Appendix IV). It was assumed that $U(\bar{x}) = w_0 + w_1 A_w + w_2 P_w + w_3 A_\ell + w_4 P_\ell$, where the w_i are regression weights, A and P amounts and probabilities, respectively, and w and ℓ subscripts standing for winnings and losses. As will be explained in more detail in Chapter 6, this additive model was used to examine the relative importance of various risk dimensions.

Outside the context of risk, there is additional evidence that additive linear models provide good approximations to multiattribute decision behavior. Such psychologists as Hoffman (1960), Goldberg (1968, 1970, 1971), Slovic (1972c), and Dawes and Corrigan (1974) used additive linear models (inferred from past decisions) to predict the judgments of clinical diagnosticians, university admission officers, and stockbrokers. In business contexts, similar applications were studied by Bowman (1963), Kunreuther (1969), and Armstrong (1978). In these studies, it was often found that substituting the additive linear model for the human decision maker led to improved decision making because of the elimination of human error. This effect, known as bootstrapping, would apply even if the actual decision process of the person being modeled contained known nonlinearities, interactions among attributes, or sequential decision components. The robustness of the additive linear model (for exceptions, see Libby, 1976) attests to its considerable approximation ability, as well as to the unreliability with which humans execute their intuitive decision rules.

3.3 THE INFORMATION-PROCESSING PERSPECTIVE

As noted before, holistic models are generally "as-if" models in which the evaluation criteria (e.g., expected utility) relate in mathematically complex ways to the basic stimuli. An exception to this generalization is the additive linear model, which postulates a simple mathematical transformation of the basic variables. This latter approach is characteristic of the information-processing perspective, in which decision making is viewed as transforming stimuli. By way of introduction, we shall consider some of the theoretical stages of the human information-processing system as proposed by Klatzky (1975).

In the first stage following a stimulus presentation, a certain amount of information enters sensory registers, where it is briefly stored in sensory form and is subject to decay. While the information is thus stored, pattern recognition — a process involving a complex interaction between the stored information and previously acquired knowledge — occurs. A second process, called attention, occurs at the same time and serves to focus or tune in on relevant information while filtering out the rest (see Bruner, Goodnow, and Austin, 1956).

After information has been recognized and attended to, it can be briefly stored in short-term memory. However, in this stage, it is no longer stored in raw sensory form; rather, it is stored as a meaningful chunk. Short-term memory is limited in the number of chunks it can hold simultaneously (around seven) and the length of time it can hold a chunk without rehearsal (see Miller, 1956). Finally, information can be stored almost permanently in long-term memory, where it can be coded acoustically, visually, or semantically (i.e., in terms of meaning). Generally, information in long-term memory can be retrieved in several ways, which suggests a highly complex and well-organized content-addressing system.

Newell, Shaw, and Simon suggested the following formal characteristics of man as an information-processing system:[9]

1. A control system consisting of memories, which contain symbolized information and are interconnected by various ordering relations. . . .
2. A number of primitive information processes, which operate on the information in the memories. Each primitive process is a perfectly definite operation for which physical mechanisms exist. . . .
3. A perfectly definite set of rules for combining these programs into whole programs of processing. From a program it is possible to deduce unequivocally what externally observed behaviors will be generated. At this level of theorizing, an explanation of an observed behavior of the organism is provided by a program of primitive information processes that generate this behavior. [1958, p. 151]

Research on perception, recognition, information storage and retrieval, conducted mostly in the area of problem solving (Simon and Newell, 1971), suggests various limitations for the above system. First, at the perceptual (as opposed to sensory) level, it seems to be a sequential, rather than a parallel, information-processing system (Simon and Barenfeld, 1969), with the elementary processes requiring from tens to hundreds of milliseconds. Second, short-term memory capacity is very limited (around seven symbols), as suggested by immediate recall experiments. (For a review, see Newell and Simon, 1972.) Finally, long-term memory, although having fast retrieval and essentially infinite storage capacity, requires long storage time, on the order of seconds or tens of seconds.

Bounded Rationality. At the microscopic level, research on relatively simple tasks has raised questions about people's ability to behave rationally (i.e., as defined in traditional economic theories) in more complex tasks. In response to such questions, Simon (1957) proposed an alternative theory, called bounded rationality, which holds that all intendedly rational behavior occurs within constraints, including cognitive ones. Most decision rules that people use are sensible when viewed in the presence of these constraints, but not otherwise.

The basic tenets of the theory of bounded rationality are developed in Simon's articles on a behavioral model of rational choice (1955) and the structure of the environment (1956). In the former, the decision maker is depicted as having limited knowledge of alternative courses of action and limited awareness of possible consequences. Furthermore, knowledge about the mapping of actions onto outcomes is fuzzy, as is the value function defined on those outcomes. Given this situation, it is a reasonable procedure to partition the outcome space into acceptable, neutral, and unacceptable consequences and then to explore the mapping of a subset of acceptable outcomes back into the domain of actions. Since the value function thus proposed implies a partial ordering of outcomes, with satisfactory levels (i.e., aspirations) specified for each dimension, goals can be viewed as constraints (see Simon, 1964). Hence, the classical optimization problem is reduced to a search for acceptable or feasible solutions. In this search, the goal constraints are adjusted as a function of the ease of finding feasible solutions (i.e., adaptive aspiration levels).

In his article on the structure of the environment (1956), Simon examined whether the approximate rationality discussed above (approximate given the cognitive limitations of humans) is conducive to survival under various characteristics of the environment. Simon described a simpleminded organism that rests, explores, and consumes food. Its search is random until it sees food, which it then approaches and consumes. Assuming that it has a limited-vision horizon, a random distribution of food heaps, and the simple choice mechanism that we have described, the organism's survival chance will be much higher than under conditions of totally random behavior (as, e.g., without vision). Furthermore, in the presence of multiple goals (i.e., various food types), an interesting economy of goal numerality occurs. Assuming all heaps of food types are randomly distributed in the environment, the probability of not finding at least one need-satisfaction point decreases as the number of goals (i.e., food heaps) increases. Thus, a first-come, first-served model of need satisfaction will be conducive to survival under various structures of the environment, which supports (theoretically) the viability of choice models that are considerably simpler than those found in traditional economic theory.

In sum, the theory of bounded rationality suggests that a distinction be made between objective rationality (as assumed in economics) and subjective rationality. At best, we can expect people to behave rationally within the framework of their knowledge and subgoals. However, to act optimally in a subjective manner may still require above-capacity information processing, leading to the view that humans "satisfice" rather than optimize. "Most human decision making, whether individual or organizational, is concerned with the discovery and selection of satisfactory alternatives; only in exceptional cases is it concerned with the discovery and selection of optimal alternatives" (March and Simon, 1958, p. 141).

The notions of bounded rationality and satisficing behavior led Cyert and March (1963) to develop a behavioral theory of the firm. They argued that most organizations "exist and thrive with considerable latent conflict of goals. Except at the level of nonoperational objectives, there is no internal consensus" (p. 117). Most conflict is resolved by having goals as independent constraints and by dealing with subgoals and a limited set of problems only (called "local rationality"). Although inconsistencies among subgoals prevail, their visibility is minimized by using acceptable-level decision rules and sequential goal attention, both of which are manifestations of bounded rationality as described above.

Lindblom (1964), who arrived at a similar view of organizational decision making, suggested that administrators make "successive limited comparisons" in order to search in the neighborhood of existing solutions and thus avoid the necessity of having to look at all aspects of a problem and to weigh the pros and cons of a solution.

The theory of bounded rationality depicts the firm and its decision makers as attempting to survive in a complex environment by reacting to problems as they present themselves. This "muddling-through" approach falls far short of the economic assumption of a maximizing entity that anticipates the future with great rationality. Hence, organizations, as well as individuals, experience cognitive strain in making decisions and thus exhibit considerable satisficing behavior.[10]

Heuristics and Biases. The information-processing view suggests that people simplify problems and use mental shortcuts to arrive at solutions. However, these so-called heuristics often lead to systematic biases (Tversky and Kahneman, 1974). For example, a common judgmental heuristic is a person's anchoring onto an initial value or reference point from which he or she then makes adjustments to arrive at some final judgment. This particular heuristic, however, may lead to biases because of insufficient adjustment. It may, for example, lead to overestimation of the probability of some conjunctive event and to underestimation in the case of disjunctive events.

To illustrate, in one of her experiments, Bar-Hillel (1973) presented subjects with three bets (or events) from which they had to choose the one with the highest probability. If the event were to happen, they would receive a certain prize. The three events were:

1. A simple event — drawing a red marble from a bag containing 50 percent red and 50 percent white marbles.
2. A conjunctive event — drawing a red marble seven times in succession, with replacement, from a bag containing 90 percent red marbles and 10 percent white marbles.
3. A disjunctive event — drawing a red marble at least once in seven successive tries, with replacement, from a bag containing 10 percent red marbles and 90 percent white marbles.

In this experiment, a significant majority preferred the second bet over the first. Subjects also preferred the first bet over the third. The probabilities of each event for the three bets are .50, .48, and .52, respectively. These biases can be explained as effects of anchoring. The stated probability of the elementary event provides a natural starting point from which insufficient adjustment is made.

Another heuristic concerns subjective probability judgments on the basis of representativeness (Kahneman and Tversky, 1972, 1973). Often these judgments are biased because of ignorance of base rates, insensitivity to sample size, or misconceptions of chance. Another way to estimate probabilities is on the basis of availability (Tversky and Kahneman, 1973). Here, however, a prevalent bias might be the differential ease with which relevant instances are retrieved from memory. For example, after hearing a list of names of well-known female personalities and male personalities who are less well known, one may judge the list to have more female names than its actual percentage because the females' names stood out more than the males'.

In Chapter 2, we noted that base rates or prior probabilities are often ignored in probabilistic judgments and that subjective posterior probabilities usually differ systematically from those based on Bayes's theorem. One psychological explanation for some of these findings may be that people's heuristic in assessing the relevance of information is based on it causal quality (Tversky and Kahneman, 1977). This theory would explain why people may consider the probability of a daughter's having blue eyes, given that her mother has blue eyes, to be higher than the probability of a mother's having blue eyes, given that her daughter has blue eyes. Assuming that successive generations have approximately the same incidence of blue eyes, such a belief is erroneous. Causal quality might similarly explain insensitivity to base rates, the causality of which is often unclear. Tversky and Kahneman (1977) suggest that data can be perceived as causal (e.g., the mother's having blue eyes), diagnostic (e.g., the daughter's having blue eyes), or incidental, in which case no relationship is perceived between the provided datum and the quantity to be assessed. The hypothesis is that these three psychological perceptions (causal, diagnostic, incidental) represent decreasing levels of data influence on probability revisions. In the incidental case, the datum may have no impact at all.

The information-processing perspective has led to an identification and examination of common heuristics employed by humans in simplifying cognitive tasks. Because many of these heuristics involve probability judgments, they directly concern the fifth axiom of EU theory, which states that probabilities are combined in accordance with mathematical probability theory. However, people also tend toward cognitive simplification in other areas of judgment. The non-holistic models discussed in the next section provide an example of such simplification in the context of multiattribute choice (e.g., gambles).

3.4 NON-HOLISTIC JUDGMENT MODELS

We will now turn our attention to the second major group of models shown in the classification scheme of Figure 3.1 — those involving non-holistic judgments. These models generally reflect the information-processing perspective in that they propose mental shortcuts that are considerably easier, cognitively, than holistic judgments. The shortcuts are often sequential, eliminating options that do not meet certain preset standards. As a result, these models may be noncompensatory in that "surpluses" on subsequent dimensions cannot compensate for deficiencies uncovered at an early stage of the evaluation process since the alternative will already have been eliminated.

The first subgroup provides a good example of the various noncompensatory models as initially identified by Coombs and Kao (1955) and Coombs (1964). In accordance with Simon's satisficing principle, alternatives are partitioned into an acceptable or nonacceptable group on the basis of a conjunctive or disjunctive criterion. The criterion is then tightened for a next go-around, thereby further partitioning the acceptable set. This process is repeated until only one alternative is left, which is then considered optimal.

Empirical support for such a model is cited in Shepard (1964), Einhorn (1971), and Libby and Fishburn (1977). In business decisions, for example, it is quite common (see Reder, 1947) to eliminate certain investment proposals because the probability of failure exceeds some critical level (i.e., a disjunctive rejection rule).[11] Similarly, in purchasing a house or an automobile, initial screening rules are often disjunctive (e.g., the price is not to exceed a certain amount).

Einhorn (1970) conducted an empirical test of conjunctive and disjunctive models versus the linear (i.e., a holistic) model. Because of the difficulty of testing the former when only responses (y) and input (x_i) data are available, Einhorn first developed compensatory approximations to the conjunctive and disjunctive models. These were a parabolic function

$$y = \prod_{i=1}^{n} x_i^{w_i}$$

and a hyperbolic function

$$y = \prod_{i=1}^{n} [1/(a_i - x_i)]^{w_i},$$

respectively, which after log transformation can be directly regressed on the available data. The judgmental task involved hypothetical applicants for graduate school, with information given on three independent variables. The approximate conjunctive and disjunctive models offered better fits to the data than did the linear model, suggesting the use of noncompensatory strategies.

The second subgroup of models concerns comparisons across attributes. A good example is Tversky's (1969) model of additive differences in which a multidimensional alternative $\bar{x} = [x_1, \ldots, x_n]$ is preferred to $\bar{y} = [y_1, \ldots, y_n]$ if, and only if, $\Sigma\phi_i[u_i(x_i) - (u_i(y_i)] \geq 0$. The u_i functions measure the subjective values of the various attributes, and ϕ_i is an increasing continuous function that determines the contribution of the particular subjective difference on dimension i to the overall evaluation of the alternatives. For all i, it is assumed that $\phi_i(-\delta) = -\phi_i(\delta)$. Tversky proved that this additive-difference model is very prone to intransitive rankings in multiple paired comparisons. For $n \geq 3$, transitive rankings are only guaranteed if the ϕ_i are linear — a rather severe restriction.

Empirical evidence for additive-difference models comes from several marketing studies involving binary product choices. Russo and Dosher (1976) used eye-fixation sequences and verbal protocols to demonstrate that subjects estimate dimensional utility differences and combine these estimates across dimensions. Small differences are often ignored. Similar results were reported by Van Raaij (1977), who examined consumer information-processing strategies under various task structures.

The final subgroup to be discussed contains models in which alternatives are compared primarily within dimensions. A good example of within-attribute comparisons using a lexicographic decision rule was provided by Tversky's study of the transitivity axiom (1969). It can be easily seen that for certain evaluation models in which intradimensional comparisons take place, intransitivities can result. Using Tversky's (1969) example, consider the three two-dimensional alternatives in Table 3.1. Suppose the following decision rule is used for pairwise comparisons: If the difference between the two alternatives on dimension I in Table 3.1 is larger than 1, choose on the basis of the first dimension only; if the difference is less than or equal to 1, choose on the basis of the second dimension only. This lexicographic semiorder will yield intransitive rankings in that $x \succ y$, $y \succ z$, but $z \succ x$.

Another quasi-lexicographic model was proposed by Payne and Braunstein in their study of pairs of duplex gambles (1971). In this model, comparisons are first made within the probability dimension, after which dollar dimensions are considered. A detailed review of lexicographic models can be found in Fishburn (1974).

In the last model type to be discussed — the elimination-by-aspects (or EBA) rule — the ranking of alternatives corresponds essentially to a random utility model:

> Suppose that each alternative consists of a set of aspects or components, and that each aspect possesses a weight. Suppose further that at each stage in the process one selects an aspect (from those included in the available alternatives) with probability that is proportional to its weight. The selection of an aspect eliminates all the alternatives that do not include the selected aspect and the process continues until all alternatives, save one, are eliminated.
>
> In contemplating a dinner at a restaurant, for example, the first aspect selected may be sea food: this eliminates all restaurants that do not serve acceptable sea food. Given the remaining alternatives, another aspect — say a price level — is selected, and all restaurants that exceed the selected price level are eliminated. The process continues until only one restaurant that includes all the selected aspects remains. [Tversky, 1972a, p. 349]

The EBA model differs from lexicographic or conjunctive models in that, because of its probabilistic nature, the criteria (or aspects), as well as their order, may vary from one occasion to the next. The axiomatic foundation of the EBA rule is discussed in Tversky (1972a) and its psychological meaning in Tversky (1972b).

Table 3.1. Choices among Two-Dimensional Alternatives

	Dimensions	
Alternative	*I*	*II*
x	2	6
y	3	4
z	4	2

3.5 CONCLUSIONS

This chapter discussed, briefly and incompletely, some of the major descriptive models proposed as alternatives to EU theory. The holistic judgment models should generally be viewed as "as-if" models, concerned more with questions of prediction (under the principle of parsimony) than with description. The non-holistic models are more concerned with information processing per se; hence, they strive for greater cognitive realism.

Compared to the holistic models, the non-holistic ones more adequately reflect the importance of the number of alternatives, the number of attributes, and the nature of the response mode. Even mathematically simple lotteries are often sufficiently complex cognitively to induce mental shortcuts and adaptation of one's decision rule to the problem presentation and the response mode. Important evidence of this tendency comes from the so-called preference-reversal phenomenon, in which subjects switch preference as a result of a change in the response mode (Lindman, 1971; Grether and Plott, 1979). It was found that in a pairwise choice gamble A may be preferred to B, whereas in stating selling-limit prices the reverse preference would result. Of course, such phenomena are more difficult to account for in holistic judgment models than in non-holistic ones.

Another important element of adaptive behavior is that people often use different models at different stages of the decision process (Payne, 1976). A prescriptive case for this approach was made by Etzioni (1967) in his mixed scanning model. (See also Janis and Mann, 1977, pp. 35–39.)

In sum, the holistic models are primarily goal-oriented, whereas the non-holistic models are mostly process-oriented. A simple example by Simon (1969) provides a good illustration of the issues involved. Suppose we wanted to model the decision behavior of an ant that moves from one goal (i.e., prey) to the next. If the surface on which it lives (e.g., a beach) is relatively flat, then the ant will approach its goal in a straightforward fashion. To predict behavior in such a simple environment requires only knowledge of the ant's location and of its goal, since its path will be a straight line. However, if the environment is hilly, relative to the ant's ability to climb, then its path will be highly curved, reflecting obstacles in the ant's way. Furthermore, the end position may change as the ant discovers other preys. To model behavior in this more complex environment, one must know the ant's limiting factors in covering terrain, the magnitudes of the obstacles, and the distribution of preys. The latter approach is characteristic of the information-processing perspective, which seeks to model people's objectives, as well as their search and evaluation strategies.

4 A POSITIVISTIC TEST OF EU THEORY: *Preferences for Information*

The previous two chapters suggested that EU theory is often inadequate as a descriptive model. The evidence cited in Chapter 2 showed either that some of the EU axioms were directly violated or that predictions from the theory did not hold. However, how damaging is this evidence when viewed from a positivistic economic perspective?

4.1 THE POSITIVISTIC VIEW

According to Friedman (1935) and Machlup (1967), two leading exponents of the positivistic view, a descriptive theory should be tested, not on the validity of its assumptions or axioms, but on its predictive power. Hence, the direct evidence reviewed in Chapter 2 (e.g., the various paradoxes) is not particularly disturbing within the positivistic view. What counts is whether the theory predicts behavior not used in the construction of the theory (i.e., behavior not yet observed). The evidence from field studies or richer laboratory studies would thus be of relevance. However, in these studies the evidence counter to EU theory can often be refuted precisely because it is indirect.

For example, in field studies some assumptions need to be made about the values of certain parameters (such as costs, tax rates, probabilities, etc.), as well as the shape of $U(x)$. Even if the data are inconsistent with certain of these prior assumptions, another set of parameters can often be found, ex post facto, to fit the data. Thus, in answer to Pashigian, Schkade, and Menefee's (1966) conclusions that consumers do not act in accordance with EU theory when selecting deductibles for collision in automobile insurance, Gould (1969) countered that the data were in fact consistent with certain subsets of exponential utility functions. The incompatibilities only applied to quadratic or logarithmic functions.

The question therefore arises, To what extent, within the positivistic view, can the EU hypothesis be falsified? The most irrefutable evidence— that which directly concerns the axioms — is discounted in positive economics. On the other hand, the evidence that is admissible has limited refutation power exactly because it is indirect evidence. Given this high immunity to falsification, the present chapter aims at a strong experimental positivistic test of the EU hypothesis. At the outset of the research, an attempt was made to design an experimental paradigm that satisfies the following conditions:

1. Subjects must choose from a small number of alternatives.
2. The optimal alternative can be determined from $U(x)$.
3. Various preference patterns can be proved to be either consistent or inconsistent with a large class of $U(x)$.
4. The preferences are sufficiently far removed from the EU axioms for the experiment not to be viewed as directly testing specific axioms.

As we will explain in the next section, an urn paradigm involving preferences for information was selected.

4.2 THE BASIC PROBLEM

Consider a choice situation involving two nontransparent urns, one of which must be chosen. It is known that each urn contains 1 million balls, with each ball being either red or white. The number of red balls in each of the two urns has been determined at random and independently of the other urn. Each number from zero to 1 million (including the limits) is equally likely to be the actual number of red balls for a given urn. It is important to realize that the numbers of red balls are almost certainly different in the two urns because they were determined independently of each other.

After an urn has been selected, the experimenter will draw one ball at random from the chosen urn. If the ball is white, an amount of \$$a$ will be won. If the ball is red, the payoff is an amount of \$$x$, which is anywhere from \$$a$ to \$$b$, with $b > a$. For each urn, it was predetermined — through a random device — what the amount of \$$x$ would be. Each amount in the range from a to b is equally likely to be the true amount for a given urn. Once again, the amounts are almost certainly different for the two urns as they were determined independently of each other.

So far the urn problem is quite simple because there is no reason to prefer one urn over the other. However, before asking which urn one prefers, the experimenter offers a choice between two types of information: (1) what the probabilities are of drawing a red ball for each of the urns or (2) what the payoffs are for each of the two urns. The basic problem is which information one should prefer. Of course, once either the probabilities or the payoffs are known, the choice of which urn to prefer is trivial (i.e., the one with the higher probability of winning or the one with the higher payoff).

The urn problem can also be formulated on the loss side. In that case, a white ball implies a sure loss of –\$$a$ and a red one a probabilistic loss of $-\$\tilde{x}$, with $-b \leq -x \leq -a$, and $-\tilde{x}$ uniformly distributed on $[-b, -a]$. It will be shown that risk-neutral decision makers should be indifferent between either type of information on both the gain and the loss side. Risk-averse decision makers should prefer to know the probabilities on the gain side and the amounts on the loss side. The reverse preferences hold for risk takers. The generality of these findings makes this problem particularly suited for a positivistic test of the EU hypothesis.

In a later section of this chapter, the analysis will be extended to the case in which the decision maker can choose from n urns. The choice is then between knowing the probabilities of drawing a red ball for all n urns and knowing the payoffs for all n urns. It will be shown that the conclusions described above generalize to the case of n urns.

The analysis that follows is restricted to three cases in which the utility function over the range of relevant outcomes is either strictly concave, strictly convex, or linear. Throughout the analysis, it will be assumed that the random variables representing the chances of winning or losing and the amounts to be won or lost are uniformly distributed, as well as continuous (the latter for mathematical convenience).

4.2.1 Mathematical Structuring

In the ensuing analysis, the following symbols will be used to represent constants, variables, and functions:

Constants:

a is the payoff to be received if a white ball is drawn.

b is the upper limit on payoff if a red ball is drawn ($b > a > 0$).

n is the number of urns from which to choose, with $n \geq 2$.

p_i^* is the true probability of drawing a red ball from urn i, for i going from 1 to n.

x_i^* is the true amount to be received from urn i if a red ball is drawn from urn i ($a \leq |x_i| \leq b$).

Variables:

$\tilde{p}_i$ is a random variable representing the possible values that p_i^* can assume for urn i.

$\bar{p}_i$ is the expected value of the random variable $\tilde{p}_i$.

$\tilde{x}_i$ is a random variable representing the possible value that x_i^* can assume for urn i.

$\bar{x}_i$ is the expected value of the random variable $\tilde{x}_i$.

$\max(x_1, \ldots, x_n)$ is the maximum value of $\tilde{x}_1$ through $\tilde{x}_n$.

$\tilde{R}$ is a random variable representing the possible outcomes (or results) of the experiment, assuming that correct decisions are made with respect to the types of information and the urns from which to choose.

Functions:

$g_i(t)$ is a prior density function on the random variable $\tilde{p}_i$.

$f_i(t)$ is a prior density function on the random variable $\tilde{x}_i$.

$U(x)$ is a continuous, monotone, twice-differentiable, Von Neumann-Morgenstern (1947) utility function defined on $[a, b]$ and $[-b, -a]$; x refers to changes in current wealth, rather than final wealth, levels.

$E[\bullet]$ is a mathematical expectation operator. For example, $E[U(x_1)]$

$$= \int_a^b f_1(x_1)U(x_1)dx_1.$$

The Expected Utility of Information. In determining the value of knowing the probabilities or the payoffs (i.e., the expected utility of information), one must first compute the certainty equivalent of the experiment without information. The next step is to compute the value of the experiment with various types of information. The difference between these two computations will be the monetary value of having that additional information. To simplify matters, this section makes direct use of the uniformity of g_i and f_i. In Appendix I, the problem is solved more generally, without assuming that $g_i = g_j$ and $f_i = f_j$.

In the first case, when we have no information about the true probabilities or the true payoffs, the expected utilities of the two urns will be equal — that is,

$$E[U(\tilde{R})] = E(p)E[U(x)] + E[1 - p]U(a) = \frac{1}{2}E[U(x)] + \frac{1}{2}U(a). \tag{4.1}$$

In the second case, when the experimenter discloses the values of p_1^* and p_2^*, the expected utility of the experiment, averaged over all p_i^*, becomes:

$$E[E[U(\tilde{R}|p_1^*, p_2^*)]] = E[\max(p_1, p_2)]E[U(x)] + E[1 - \max(p_1, p_2)]U(a).$$

Since the distribution of $\max(p_1, p_2)$ equals $2G(p)g(p)$, where $G(p)$ is the cumulative density function (c.d.f.) of p, the above result, assuming uniformity, reduces to

$$E[E[U(\tilde{R}|p_1^*, p_2^*)]] = \frac{2}{3}E[U(x)] + \frac{1}{3}U(a). \tag{4.2}$$

In the third case, when the experimenter discloses the values of x_1^* and x_2^*, the expected utility of the experiment, averaged over all x_i^*, becomes

$$\begin{aligned} E[E[U(\tilde{R}|x_1^*, x_2^*)]] &= E(p)E[U(\max(x_1, x_2))] + E[1 - p]U(a) \\ &= \frac{1}{2}E[U(\max(x_1, x_2))] + \frac{1}{2}U(a) \\ &= \frac{1}{2}\int_a^b 2F(x)f(x)U(x)dx + \frac{1}{2}U(a) \\ &= \frac{1}{2}\int_a^b \frac{2(x - a)}{(b - a)^2}U(x)dx + \frac{1}{2}U(a). \end{aligned} \tag{4.3}$$

In the above equation, $F(x)$ is the c.d.f. of $\tilde{x}$. The value of knowing p_i^* equals the difference in certainty equivalents of Equations (4.2) and (4.1). The value of knowing x_i^* equals the difference in certainty equivalents of (4.3) and (4.1).

Before analyzing what information should be preferred under various shapes of $U(x)$, an important result can be stated immediately. Suppose that p_i^* is defined, not on [0, 1], but on [0, u] where $0 < u < 1$; what consequence will this have? In that case, $E[\max(p_1, p_2)]$ will be equal to (⅔)u, assuming the p_i^* are uniform on [0, u], and $E(p)$ will equal (½)u. Hence, Equations (4.2) and (4.3) will both be multiplied by a factor u, which vanishes when comparing the two. Therefore, an important result is that narrowing the probability range from [0, 1] to [0, u] should never, according to EU theory, be the cause of a change in preference for information, regardless of the shape of $U(x)$.

4.2.2 The Preference for Information

Earlier it was hypothesized that the preference for the type of information depends only on the general shape of $U(x)$ on $[a, b]$ or $[-a, -b]$. Table 4.1 summarizes these hypotheses for both the gain and the loss side.

Table 4.1. Optimal EU Preferences for Information

	Gain Side	*Loss Side*
Risk-seeking	Amounts (x_i^*)	Probabilities (p_i^*)
Risk-averse	Probabilities (p_i^*)	Amounts (x_i^*)
Risk-neutral	Indifferent	Indifferent

The easiest case to prove is that of indifference for risk neutrality. If $U(x) = x$, Equations (4.2) and (4.3) will both reduce to $(\frac{1}{3}b + \frac{2}{3}a)$. For Equation (4.2):

$$\frac{2}{3}E(x) + \frac{1}{3}U(a) = \frac{2}{3}\int_a^b \left(\frac{1}{b-a}\right)xdx + \frac{1}{3}a = \frac{2}{3}\left(\frac{1}{b-a}\right)\frac{1}{2}x^2\Big|_a^b + \frac{1}{3}a$$

$$= \frac{2}{3}\left(\frac{1}{b-a}\right)\frac{1}{2}(b^2 - a^2) + \frac{1}{3}a = \frac{1}{3}(b + a) + \frac{1}{3}(a)$$

$$= \frac{1}{3}\,b + \frac{2}{3}\,a.$$

For Equation (4.3):

$$\frac{1}{2}\int_a^b 2F(x)f(x)U(x)dx + \frac{1}{2}U(a) = \frac{1}{2}\int_a^b \frac{2(x-a)}{(b-a)^2}(x)dx + \frac{1}{2}(a)$$

$$= \frac{1}{(b-a)^2}\int_a^b x(a - x)dx + \frac{1}{2}\,a$$

$$= \frac{1}{(b-a)^2}\left[\frac{(x-a)^3}{3} + \frac{a(x-a)^2}{2}\right]\Bigg|_a^b$$

$$+ \frac{1}{2}(a)$$

$$= \frac{(b-a)^3}{3(b-a)^2} + \frac{a(b-a)^2}{2(b-a)^2} + \frac{1}{2}\,a$$

$$= \frac{1}{3}b + \frac{2}{3}a.$$

Regarding the other cases, only one will be proved explicitly as the others follow similar proofs. It will be proved that if $U(x)$ is concave, knowledge of p_i^* should be preferred over knowledge of x_i^* on the gain side. The following is to be proved:

$$\frac{2}{3}E[U(x)] + \frac{1}{3}U(a) > \frac{1}{2}E[U(\max(x_1, x_2))] + \frac{1}{2}U(a) \text{ for}$$

$a \leq x \leq b$, with $U' > 0$, $U'' < 0$ and uniform f_i.

Proof. Rewrite the above inequality as

$$\frac{2}{3}E[U(x)] - \frac{1}{2}E[U(\max(x_1, x_2))] > \frac{1}{2}U(a) - \frac{1}{3}U(a)$$

or

$$\frac{2}{3}\int_a^b \frac{1}{(b-a)}U(x)dx - \frac{1}{2}\int_a^b \frac{2(x-a)}{(b-a)^2}U(x)dx > \frac{1}{6}U(a)$$

or

$$\frac{2}{3}\int_a^b (b-a)U(x)dx - \int_a^b (x-a)U(x)dx > \frac{1}{6}U(a)[(b-a)^2]$$

or

$$I \equiv \int_a^b [\frac{2}{3}(b-a) - (x-a)]U(x)dx > \frac{1}{6}U(a)[(b-a)^2].$$

Note that $[⅔ (b - a) - (x - a)]$ decreases monotonically with x; it is positive on the interval $[a, t)$ and negative on $(t, b]$ where

$$t = \frac{1}{3}a + \frac{2}{3}b.$$

If we substitute a function $s(x)$ for $U(x)$ so that

$$s(x) < U(x) \text{ for } a \leq x < t$$

and

$$s(x) > U(x) \text{ for } t < x \leq b,$$

then $I > I_s$ where

$$I_s \equiv \int_a^b [\frac{2}{3}(b-a) - (x-a)]s(x)dx.$$

If it can be shown that $I_s \geq ⅙\, U(a)[(b-a)^2]$, the proof will have been completed as $I > I_s$.

To find a suitable $s(x)$ function, consider Figure 4.1.[1] Let $s(x)$ be a linear function passing through $[a, U(a)]$ and $[t, U(t)]$. Note that $s(x) < U(x)$ on $[a, t)$ and that $s(x) > U(x)$ on $(t, b]$. The equation of $s(x)$ is $s(x) = m(x - a) + U(a)$, with $m = [s(t) - U(a)]/[t - a]$. Using $s(x)$ as defined above, let us evaluate I_s:

$$I_s = \int_a^b [\frac{2}{3}(b - a) - (x - a)][m(x - a) + U(a)]dx$$

$$= \int_a^b \{\frac{2}{3}m(b - a)(x - a) - m(x - a)^2 + \frac{2}{3}U(a)(b - a) - U(a)(x - a)\}dx$$

$$= \frac{2}{3}m(b - a)\frac{1}{2}(x - a)^2 - \frac{1}{3}m(x - a)^3 + \frac{2}{3}U(a)(b - a)x - U(a)\frac{1}{2}(x - a)^2 \Big|_a^b$$

$$= \frac{1}{3}m(b - a)^3 - \frac{1}{3}m(b - a)^3 + \frac{2}{3}U(a)b(b - a) - U(a)\frac{1}{2}(b - a)^2 - [\frac{2}{3}U(a)(b - a)a]$$

$$= \frac{2}{3}U(a)(b - a)^2 - \frac{1}{2}U(a)(b - a)^2$$

$$= \frac{1}{6}U(a)[(b - a)^2].$$

Since $I > I_s$, it follows that $I > \frac{1}{6}U(a)[(b - a)^2]$, Q.E.D. (See the fourth inequality of the proof.)

An alternative proof could have been constructed using Hadar and Russell's (1969) theorems on second order stochastic dominance. This proof, which is of similar complexity, is left to the reader.

4.2.3 Generalization to *n* Urns

To analyze the general case of n urns, it is helpful to state first the density of a random variable defined as the maximum of n independent random variables. Algebraically, let

$$y_{max} = \max[y_1, \ldots, y_n],$$

where the y_i are independently distributed random variables on $[a, b]$ with density functions $h_i(y)$. The c.d.f. of y_{max}, called $H_{max}(y)$, will be

$$H_{max}(y) = \prod_{i=1}^{n} H_i(y),$$

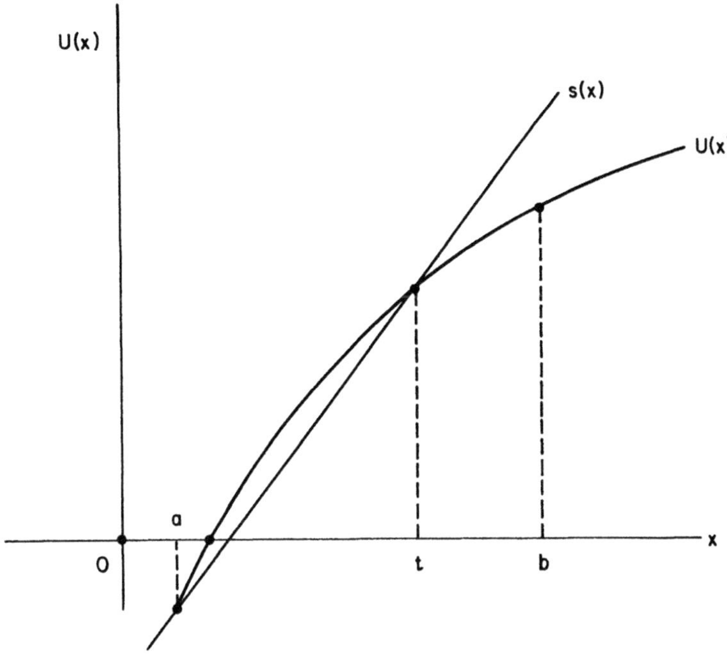

Figure 4.1. Graphic Illustration of the Proof of Preference for Information

where $H_i(y)$ is the c.d.f. of y_i. To find the density function $h_{\max}$, we must differentiate (with respect to y), which yields

$$h_{\max}(y) = \sum_{j=1}^{n} [h_i(y) \prod_{\substack{i \neq j \\ i=1}}^{n} H_i(y)].$$

For uniform h_i, this reduces to

$$h_{\max}(y) = \frac{n}{(b-a)^n}(y-a)^{n-1}. \qquad (4.4)$$

If we are presented with n urns, a disclosure of the true values of all p_i will yield a maximum p value whose distribution follows directly from (4.4) — namely,

$$g_{\max}(p) = np^{n-1} \text{ (assuming uniformity).}$$

The expected value of $p_{\max}$ will be

$$E[p_{\max}] = \int_0^1 p g_{\max}(p) dp = \frac{n}{n+1}.$$

Hence, the expected utility of the experiment, conditional on knowing all p_i^*, averaged over all p_i^*, is

$$E[E[U(\widetilde{R}|p_1^*, \ldots, p_n^*)]] = \frac{n}{n+1} E[U(x)] + \frac{1}{n+1} U(a). \tag{4.5}$$

Similarly, disclosure of all x_i^* will yield an $x_{\max}$ whose density function is as follows:

$$f_{\max}(x) = \frac{n}{(b-a)^n}(x-a)^{n-1}.$$

The average value of $x_{\max}$ can thus be computed as

$$\begin{aligned} E[x_{\max}] &= \int_a^b \frac{n}{(b-a)^n}(x-a)^{n-1} x\,dx \\ &= \frac{n}{(b-a)^n}\int_a^b x(x-a)^{n-1}dx \\ &= \frac{n}{(b-a)^n}\left[\frac{(x-a)^{n+1}}{n+1} + \frac{a(x-a)^n}{n}\right]_a^b \\ &= \frac{n}{(b-a)^n}\left[\frac{(b-a)^{n+1}}{n+1} + \frac{a(b-a)^n}{n}\right] \\ &= n\left[\frac{b-a}{n+1} + \frac{a}{n}\right] = a + \frac{n}{n+1}(b-a). \end{aligned}$$

The expected utility with knowledge of x_i^*, averaged over all x_i^*, equals

$$E[E[U(\widetilde{R}|x_1^*, \ldots, x_n^*)]] = \frac{1}{2}\int_a^b U(x)\frac{n(x-a)^{n-1}}{(b-a)^n}dx + \frac{1}{2}U(a). \tag{4.6}$$

Note that for $n = 2$, Equations (4.5) and (4.6) indeed reduce to (4.2) and (4.3), respectively.

If n goes to infinity and all p_i^* are known, one would always expect to find an urn for which $p_i^* = 1$. Indeed,

$$\lim_{n\to\infty} E[(p_{\max})] = \lim_{n\to\infty}\frac{n}{n+1} = 1.$$

In the limit case, the expected utility of the experiment with knowledge of p_i^* is

$$\lim_{n\to\infty} E[E[U(\widetilde{R}|p_1^*, \ldots, p_n^*)]] = E[U(x)].$$

Similarly, if n goes to infinity, and all x_i^* are known, one would always expect to find an urn for which $x_i^* = b$. Indeed,

$$\lim_{m \to \infty} E[x_{\max}] = \lim_{n \to \infty} [a + \frac{n}{n+1}(b - a)] = a + b - a = b.$$

Hence, the expected utility of the experiment with knowledge of x_i^* is

$$\lim_{n \to \infty} E[E[U(\tilde{R}|x_1^*, \ldots, x_n^*)]] = \frac{1}{2} U(b) + \frac{1}{2} U(a).$$

In comparing the limiting values $E[U(x)]$ and $\frac{1}{2} U(a) + \frac{1}{2} U(b)$, it is clear that if $U(x)$ is concave, knowledge of p_i^* should be preferred over knowledge of x_i^* in case $n \to \infty$ — that is, $E[U(x)] > \frac{1}{2} U(a) + \frac{1}{2} U(b)$ if $U(x)$ is concave and $f(x)$ is nondegenerate.

Up to this point, we have proved the hypotheses of Table 4.1 for $n = 2$ and $n \to \infty$. In the case of finite n, with $n > 2$, we will sketch the proof for one case only, as the others follow similar proofs. Consider the case in which $U(x)$ is concave on the gain side. To prove that knowing p_i^* should be preferred to knowing x_i^*, it must be shown that Equation (4.5) is larger than (4.6), or

$$\frac{n}{n+1} E[U(x)] + \frac{1}{n+1} U(a) > \frac{1}{2} \int_a^b U(x) \frac{n(x-a)^{n-1}}{(b-a)^n} dx + \frac{1}{2} U(a).$$

As before, collect $U(x)$ terms on the left and $U(a)$ terms on the right. Writing out the $E[U(x)]$ term and multiplying through by $(b - a)^n$ will then yield

$$I \equiv \int_a^b [\frac{n}{n+1}(b-a)^{n-1} - \frac{n}{2}(x-a)^{n-1}] U(x) dx$$

$$> \frac{n-1}{2(n+1)} (b-a)^n U(a).$$

The portion in brackets decreases monotonically with x for $x > a$. It is positive on $[a, t)$ and negative on $(t, b]$, where

$$t = a + (b - a) \sqrt[n-1]{\frac{2}{n+1}}\,.$$

Again define a linear function $s(x)$ passing through $[a, U(a)]$ and $[t, U(t)]$ so that $s(x)$ is a lower bound for $U(x)$ on $[a, t)$ and an upper bound on $(t, b]$. With $I > I_s$, it is sufficient to prove that

$$I_s \geq \frac{n-1}{2(n+1)} (b-a)^n U(a).$$

The equation of $s(x)$ will again be

$$s(x) = m(x - a) + U(a), \text{ with } m = \frac{s(t) - U(a)}{t - a}.$$

Evaluating I_s for the general case yields

$$I_s \equiv \int_a^b [\frac{n}{n+1}(b-a)^{n-1} - \frac{n}{2}(x-a)^{n-1}][m(x-a) + U(a)]dx$$

$$= \int_a^b [m(\frac{n}{n+1})(b-a)^{n-1}(x-a) - \frac{n}{2} m(x-a)^n$$

$$+ U(a)\frac{n}{n+1}(b-a)^{n-1}$$

$$- \frac{n}{2}(x-a)^{n-1}U(a)]dx$$

$$= m(\frac{n}{n+1})(b-a)^{n-1}\frac{1}{2}(x-a)^2 - \frac{n}{2} m(\frac{1}{n+1})(x-a)^{n+1}$$

$$+ U(a)\frac{n}{n+1}(b-a)^{n-1}x$$

$$- \frac{1}{2}(x-a)^n U(a) \Big|_a^b$$

$$= \frac{m}{2}(\frac{n}{n+1})(b-a)^{n+1} - \frac{m}{2}(\frac{n}{n+1})(b-a)^{n+1}$$

$$+ U(a)\frac{n}{n+1} b(b-a)^{n-1}$$

$$- \frac{1}{2}(b-a)^n U(a) - U(a)(\frac{n}{n+1})a(b-a)^{n-1}$$

$$= U(a)(\frac{n}{n+1})(b-a)^{n-1}(b-a) - \frac{1}{2}(b-a)^n U(a)$$

$$= (\frac{n}{n+1} - \frac{1}{2})(b-a)^n U(a) = \frac{n-1}{2(n+1)}(b-a)^n U(a), \text{ Q.E.D.}$$

Hence, the proof for $n = 2$ generalizes to $n > 2$. The other cases of Table 4.1 follow similar proofs, which are left to the reader.

4.3 THE EXPERIMENT

The urn paradigm developed in the previous sections was tested experimentally with sixty-two Wharton M.B.A. students.[2] The first part of the experiment established each subject's risk-taking attitude over four different intervals. The second part contained several urn questions to ascertain subjects' preferences for information. The design was aimed at a direct test of the hypotheses of Table 4.1, as well as the presumed irrelevance of narrowing the probability range. Appendix II contains a copy of the questionnaire.

Design. The $[a, b]$ and $[-b, -a]$ intervals examined were [\$10, \$20], [\$500, \$1,000], [−\$20, −\$10], and [−\$1,000, −\$500]. For each interval, four questions were used to establish the subject's risk-taking attitude. The first three of these four questions offered a choice between a lottery offering \$$a$ with probability p and \$$b$ with probability $(1 - p)$ and a sure amount $(pa + (1 - p)b)$. The p values used were .5, .3, and .7, respectively. The fourth question was the same as the first one (i.e., $p = .5$), but the ranges were narrowed to [±\$12, ±\$18] and [±\$600, ±\$900], respectively. (See the first sixteen questions in Appendix II.)

The second part of the questionnaire concerned the urn problem described earlier in this chapter. The questions on the preference for information were presented for each of the four intervals. They were repeated for three probability ranges: [0, 1], [0, .4], [0, .1]. The last question in this part of the questionnaire increased the number of urns to ten. The payoff interval in this case was [10, 20], with a probability range of [0, 1]. The third and final part of the questionnaire contained some socioeconomic questions dealing with age, sex, and financial status.

To control for an order effect in the questions that assessed the subjects' risk-taking attitudes, the sequence of the four blocks (one per interval) of four questions was varied. If A, B, C, and D represent questions for the intervals [10, 20], [500, 1,000], [−20, −10], and [−1,000, −500], respectively, the four sequence orders used were: ABCD, BADC, CDAB, and DCBA. Subjects were randomly assigned to one of these four sequences.[3] With respect to the urn questions, the sequence was the same for all subjects (see Appendix II).

4.4 RESULTS

The first issue examined was whether the sequence order affected subjects' risk-taking attitudes for a given lottery question. It was found that the order of administering the small-amount (10–20) and large-amount (500–1,000) lottery questions had no significant ($p < .05$) effect. Neither did it matter whether the win questions preceded or followed the loss questions, which suggests an absence of a carry-over or contrast effect. It was therefore decided to pool the data across questionnaire type in order to have a larger sample size for testing the two sets of EU hypotheses.

Subjects were classified as risk-seeking, risk-averse, or mixed for a given interval $[a, b]$ on the basis of both a strict and a weak criterion. Under the strict classification, a subject was considered risk-taking (averse) if he or she exhibited risk-taking (averse) preferences for all four lottery questions concerning that interval. The weak classification required only three out of four responses to be risk-taking (averse). This latter classification was included because of the low percentages of subjects (around one-fourth) meeting the strict criterion.

Table 4.2 shows how many risk-averse or risk-seeking subjects (under both classifications) exhibited information preferences in accordance with EU theory. The table concerns only the interval [\$10, \$20], but includes both the gain and loss sides. Table 4.3 shows the same data for the interval [\$500, \$1,000]. The preferences are shown for progressively narrower probability ranges $[0, u]$ — namely, [0, 1], [0, .4], and [0, .1]. According to EU theory, the level of u should not affect preferences, provided $0 < u \leq 1$.

Tables 4.2 and 4.3 show for each cross classification the percentage of subjects who behaved in accordance with EU theory. On the gain side, these are the entries on the main diagonal (ignoring the "mixed" row), and on the loss side, they are the off-diagonal entries (see also Table 4.1). For example, on the interval [\$10, \$20] with $0 \leq p_i^* \leq .4$, only 35 percent (or 7/20) of the subjects stated preferences for information in Question 21 as predicted by EU theory. Under the strict classification, none of the EU predictions was significantly better than 50 percent (the benchmark for a two-by-two table).[4] The only significant ($p < .05$) departures from chance occurred in Question 22 (Table 4.2) and Question 23 (Table 4.3) under the strict classification; in both cases, however, the findings were exactly opposite of what EU theory would predict.

Under the weak classification, similar results were obtained. Only for Question 19 did EU theory predict significantly ($p < .05$) better than chance; for Questions 26 and 27 it did significantly worse than chance. It must therefore be concluded that in this problem situation, EU theory failed seriously in predicting subjects' preferences for information.

With respect to the narrowing of the probability ranges, a strong effect was found on the gain side (contrary to EU theory). For both small and large amounts, there was a dramatic increase in preference for x_i^* as u was lowered from 1 to .4. This increase was on the order of a factor of 2 or 3 in all four cases. For example, in comparing Questions 17 and 21, we see that the preference for x_i^* went from 9 to 18 and from 13 to 37 under the strict and weak classifications, respectively. Lowering u to .1 did not induce additional increases. On the loss side, the "u effect" was much weaker on [−20, −10] and absent on [−1,000, −500].

Table 4.2. Risk Attitude and Information Preference: The Case of Small Amounts ($10–$20)

	Gain Side						*Loss Side*					
	Ques. 17 $u=1$		*Ques. 21* $u=.4$		*Ques. 22* $u=.1$		*Ques. 19* $u=1$		*Ques. 25* $u=.4$		*Ques. 26* $u=.1$	
Risk-Taking Attitude	x_i^*	p_i^*	x_i^*	p_i^*	x_i^*	p_i^*	x_i^*	p_i^*	x_i^*	p_i^*	x_i^*	p_i^*
Strict classification												
Risk-seeking	2	1	6	1	4	2	7	10	10	5	11	5
Risk-averse	7	6	12	1	14	1	1	1	1	1	2	0
Mixed	9	26	26	13	29	9	15	26	21	18	34	6
Percentage correct	50%		35%		24%(*)		58%		35%		37%	
Weak classification												
Risk-seeking	4	12	17	2	15	4	11	26	20	13	28	7
Risk-averse	9	14	20	7	25	4	3	2	5	1	6	0
Mixed	5	6	7	6	7	4	9	9	7	10	13	4
Percentage correct	46%		52%		40%		69%(*)		46%		28%(**)	

Note: The entries are numbers of subjects (except for percentages). Asterisks in parentheses denote whether the percentage of correct EU predictions differed from 50 percent at the .05(*) or .01(**) levels of significance.

Table 4.3. Risk Attitude and Information Preference: The Case of Large Amounts ($500–$1,000)

	Gain Side						*Loss Side*					
	Ques. 18 $u=1$		*Ques. 23* $u=.4$		*Ques. 24* $u=.1$		*Ques. 20* $u=1$		*Ques. 27* $u=.4$		*Ques. 28* $u=.1$	
Risk-Taking Attitude	x_i^*	p_i^*	x_i^*	p_i^*	x_i^*	p_i^*	x_i^*	p_i^*	x_i^*	p_i^*	x_i^*	p_i^*
Strict classification												
Risk-seeking	0	4	1	3	4	0	7	1	7	1	5	3
Risk-averse	4	10	13	1	11	3	5	3	4	4	4	3
Mixed	19	25	27	15	31	10	31	12	31	13	36	9
Percentage correct	56%		11%(**)		39%		38%		31%		47%	
Weak classification												
Risk-seeking	6	16	17	5	21	1	22	10	25	8	27	6
Risk-averse	15	18	22	10	22	9	13	5	10	9	11	7
Mixed	2	5	2	4	3	3	8	1	7	1	7	2
Percentage correct	44%		50%		57%		46%		35%(*)		33%	

Note: The note of Table 4.2 applies here as well.

The above analyses included only subjects who were risk-averse or risk-taking on [a, b]. However, as noted earlier, lowering u should not lead to changes in preferences for any shape of $U(x)$. Table 4.4 offers a direct cross classification of subjects' preferences between $u = 1$ and $u = .4$, $u = 1$ and $u = .1$, and $u = .4$ and $u = .1$ for each of the four [a, b] intervals. Below each matrix is listed what percentage did not change preference (i.e., subjects along the main diagonal). The table also indicates whether the predictions from EU theory differed from chance at the .05(*) or .01 (**) levels of significance.

In comparing $u = 1$ with $u = .4$, we see that none of the EU predictions did better than chance on any of the four intervals. Comparing $u = 1$ with $u = .1$ reveals predictions significantly ($p < .05$) worse than chance for the interval [500, 1,000] and better than chance for the interval [−1,000, −500]. The best predictions were found for $u = .4$ versus $u = .1$, where for three of the four intervals EU theory did significantly ($p < .01$) better than chance. However, since the $u = .4$ and $u = .1$ questions were presented in pairs (see Appendix II), this finding could also reflect an anchoring or carry-over effect.

Table 4.4 also suggests, as did Tables 4.2 and 4.3, that lowering u induces a shift in information preference in favor of x_i^*. The effect is strongest on the gain side. For example, on [10, 20], twenty-four subjects switched preference toward x_i^* when u was lowered to .4, compared to only five subjects reversing the other way. On [500, 1,000], these numbers were twenty-seven subjects versus eight subjects for $u = .4$, and thirty-one versus six subjects for $u = .1$. The effect also exists on [−20, −10], but seems absent on [−1,000, −500], possibly because of the high percentages preferring x_i^*. Note that the findings of Table 4.4 confirm those of Tables 4.2 and 4.3.

In sum, lowering u induces changes in preferences contrary to EU theory. The deviations from EU are large and cannot be explained from random error or random preferences. The effect generally seems to be that lowering u increases the preference for information about the true payoffs, which suggests that subjects do not combine probabilities and utilities multiplicatively in choosing between the two types of information.

The last issue to be examined is that of multiple urns, which, according to EU theory, should be the same as the case of two urns for concave or convex $U(x)$. Of the twenty-two subjects who were either strictly risk-taking or strictly risk-averse on [10, 20], about 55 percent did not exhibit the same preference in Question 29 as in Question 17. These two questions differed only in that Question 17 involved two urns and Question 29 ten urns (see Appendix II). Under the weak classification, this percentage was the same (55 percent, or twenty-six out of forty-seven subjects).

Table 4.4. Narrowing the Probability Range

Range			*Ques. 21* $u=.4$ x	p	*Ques. 22* $u=.1$ x	p			*Ques. 22* $u=.1$ x	p
[10, 20]	*Ques. 17* $u=1$	x	12	5	14	4	*Ques. 21* $u=.4$	x	36	7
		p	24	7	25	6		p	8	5
	Correct prediction:		40%		41%				73%(**)	
			Ques. 23 $u=.4$ x	p	*Ques. 24* $u=.1$ x	p			*Ques. 24* $u=.1$ x	p
[500, 1,000]	*Ques. 18* $u=1$	x	14	8	15	6	*Ques. 23* $u=.4$	x	34	7
		p	27	11	31	7		p	11	5
	Correct prediction:		42%		37%(*)				68%(**)	

Table 4.4. *(Continued)*

			Ques. 25 $u = .4$		*Ques. 26* $u = .1$				*Ques. 26* $u = .1$	
			x	p	x	p			x	p
[−20, −10]	*Ques. 19* $u = 1$	x	12	9	19	2	*Ques. 25* $u = .4$	x	25	5
		p	19	14	27	9		p	17	6
	Correct prediction:		48%		49%				58%	
			Ques. 27 $u = .4$		*Ques. 28* $u = .1$				*Ques. 28* $u = .1$	
			x	p	x	p			x	p
[−1,000, −500]	*Ques. 20* $u = 1$	x	28	14	32	10	*Ques. 27* $u = .4$	x	36	6
		p	13	3	11	5		p	8	9
	Correct prediction:		53%		64%(*)				76%(**)	

Note: Asterisks in parentheses denote predictions significantly different from 50 percent at the .05(*) and .01(**) levels.

Under both classifications, the discrepancies were larger for risk seekers (86 and 67 percent, respectively) than for risk averters (40 and 50 percent, respectively). In the case of ten urns (Question 29), the figures for correct prediction were 40 and 42 percent under the strict and weak classifications, respectively. These figures do not differ significantly from those for Question 17. Hence, changes in preferences between Questions 17 and 29 appeared to be random. For both questions, however, there existed no significant relationship with risk-taking attitude, which is contrary to what EU theory would predict.

4.5 CONCLUSIONS

Under the positivistic view, the EU hypothesis is difficult to falsify. Direct evidence regarding its assumptions is usually deemed irrelevant since the theory is an "as-if" model. Indirect evidence, however, has seldom been shown to falsify the theory irrefutably because of considerable degrees of freedom in specifying the shape of $U(x)$, as well as the values of various economic parameters (the latter particularly in field studies). The present study aimed to design an experimental choice situation for which EU theory, if indeed incorrect, could be falsified on the grounds of failure to predict the general direction of preference, using very weak assumptions about the shape of $U(x)$ on the relevant interval. The resulting choice situation was an urn problem involving preferences for information. A major part of the study concerned the mathematical analyses of this problem, including some proofs that the concavity or convexity of $U(x)$ on an interval $[a, b]$ is sufficient to predict preference of one type of information over another.

An experiment was conducted to test EU's predictions about preferences for information, as well as EU's prediction that narrowing the probability range should not lead to changes in preferences. Both sets of predictions were found to be false. In most cases, EU's predictions did not do better than pure chance.

Given this serious failure of the theory to predict, let us consider some defenses of EU that might be invoked. First, there are the issues of the hypothetical nature of the choice situation and the lack of competition, both of which were addressed in Chapter 1 (Section 1.3.3). Second, it might be argued that the dollar values of the two types of information were too close to be of any real import. To examine this issue, consider the interval [500, 1,000] and a logarithmic utility function (i.e., $U(x) = \log_e(x)$). The expected utility of the urn experiment without information is 6.40776 utiles, or a certainty equivalent of \$606.53 (computed from Equation [4.1]). With knowledge of p_i^*, the certainty equivalent becomes \$646.86 (Equation [4.2]); with knowledge of x_i^*, it becomes \$632 (Equation [4.3]). The difference in the values of information is thus \$14.86, which is not a trivial sum for most student subjects.

As a last objection, it might be argued that even though the problem clearly states that p_i^* and x_i^* have uniform prior density functions on their respective intervals (see Appendix II), subjects in fact used nonuniform priors either because of distrust or because of psychological distortions of probabilities. Although such SEU defenses are often powerful, it can be shown that the EU predictions of Table 4.1 also hold if $g_i(p)$ and $f_i(x)$ are not uniform, provided their functional forms are identical.[5]

Finally, it should be noted that the choice between knowing p_i^* or x_i^* underlies various real-world decision situations. For example, before selecting research projects, a research and development department may spend money either on ascertaining the probability that a patent for each project will result or on assessing the profits from each patent. Of course, there are many other instances in which one must choose between better knowledge of the probabilities of success or better knowledge of the associated reward structure. Often, however, the choices will not be mutually exclusive, nor will statistical independence hold between probability and payoffs, which makes the decision yet more complex.

5 AN EXPERIMENTAL STUDY OF INSURANCE DECISONS

This chapter describes an insurance study that was aimed at a better understanding of people's preferences for so-called pure risk alternatives (Williams, 1966). Unlike speculative risk choices, pure risk alternatives offer no chance of gain. The present study ran parallel to another research effort, also based at the Wharton School of the University of Pennsylvania. This other effort consisted of field studies (Kunreuther et al., 1978) and laboratory experiments (Slovic et al., 1977) on insurance behavior, particularly decisions involving low-probability, high-loss events. Relationships with this parallel research will be highlighted later in this chapter.

The basic experimental design of the present study consists of a questionnaire completed by 202 undergraduate students and 101 clients of an insurance agency (see Appendix III). The questionnaire contains hypothetical insurance choices, some representative of those found in the real world. The study investigates only the last stage of the decision process. Respondents were asked to focus on a specific hazard and to make a choice when all relevant information was readily available. It should be noted that the subjects were of above average intelligence and of above average education, all of which favors EU theory.

Parts of this chapter were published in Schoemaker and Kunreuther (1979) in the *Journal of Risk and Insurance*. Reprinted by permission.

5.1 ISSUES TO BE EXAMINED

Both field studies and laboratory experiments provide a puzzling and conflicting picture of insurance behavior when viewed from an expected utility standpoint. Eisner and Strotz's (1961) investigation of the demand for flight insurance; Pashigian, Schkade, and Menefee's (1966) study of low deductibles in automobile insurance; Anderson's (1974) study of the low demand for subsidized flood insurance; Robertson's (1974) investigation of seat-belt usage in automobiles; and Kunreuther et al.'s (1978) study of subsidized flood and earthquake insurance — all present findings that would be difficult to reconcile with expected utility theory's assumption of risk aversion. At the experimental level also, controlled studies by Greene (1963, 1964); Williams (1966); Neter and Williams (1971); Murray (1971, 1972); and Slovic et al. (1977) show that people's preferences often run counter to expected utility theory, particularly in regard to the assumption of risk aversion.

Of course, the existence of a prosperous and expanding insurance industry appears to favor the view that people are generally risk-averse. Even though not all insurance carried by individuals is obtained voluntarily (some insurance being required by law or mortgage contracts, and some obtained from group coverage through employment), the vast majority of people carry more insurance than is minimally required. Hence, in this regard, people appear to be risk-averse.

On the other hand, it is a well-known fact in the industry that insurance is "not bought but sold." It is therefore of interest to examine to what extent insurance decisions are influenced by economic parameters and hazard perceptions, as opposed to psychological factors and social norms.

The present chapter addresses four main issues relevant to insurance. The first issue concerns people's desire to protect themselves against high-probability, low-loss events versus low-probability, high-loss events when expected values are equal. The assumption of risk aversion in traditional utility theory implies that people would most prefer protection against low-probability, high-loss hazards.

The second issue deals with the role of context and problem presentation in insurance decisions. Empirical evidence suggests that people often prefer the lowest deductibles (Pashigian, Schkade, and Menefee, 1966), perhaps because they think it increases the chances of collecting on a policy. We will refer to this preference for low deductibles as the deductible effect. Several questions in the experiment examined whether a deductible effect is indeed discernible and whether it vanishes when the same decision situation is presented without reference to deductibles or insurance. Of course, EU theory would not predict such an effect, nor would it predict different behavioral responses if the problem were presented in a different manner. In this same vein, we will examine an illegitimate portfolio effect, in which statistically identical choices are judged differently.

The third issue involves the effect of comprehensive insurance (i.e., providing protection against several hazards under one policy). Expected utility theory would predict that people's maximum bid for a comprehensive policy would equal (on average) the sum total of their maximum bids for insurance against the hazards separately. It is assumed here that all policies have zero deductibles and provide full coverage. The maximum bids for the individual hazards must be determined simultaneously because of portfolio and wealth effects. It can be shown that according to EU theory, the sum of the individual maximum bids (each being conditional on having coverage at the maximum acceptable prices against the other hazards) will equal the maximum bid for the comprehensive policy.

The final issue studied concerns the effect of scale (or magnitude) of the loss and the premium on insurance purchase decisions. Suppose an insurance policy costing c dollars offers complete protection (with zero deductible) against a potential loss of $\$L$, which has a probability p of occurring. What will be the effect on people's preference for insurance if both c and L are increased by a factor of $k > 1$ (assuming p is constant)? If the insurance is reasonably priced, utility theory would predict an increased preference for insurance as k increases.[1] The real-world analogue of this question is whether people would rather pay a fraction of a premium to cover against a proportionate fraction of the loss than pay the full premium.

Hence, the present study specifically examines EU theory's assumption of risk aversion for losses. Although Slovic et al. (1977) also addressed this issue, their experiments involved abstract loss points and simultaneous evaluations of hazards (i.e., multiple urns) rather than dollars and single questions. However, in view of their strong results, which run counter to the risk-aversion hypothesis, it is useful to examine briefly some general reasons why people may be risk-seeking in the domain of losses.

The findings of Slovic et al. (1977) suggest that there may be some critical probability threshold below which people ignore the threat that a large loss may occur. This threshold may exist because people have limited attention capacity and must be selective about the problems to which they allocate their scarce "attention resources." The notion of a probability threshold also gives insight into the field-study findings of Kunreuther et al. (1978), which showed that the perceived probability that a loss may occur is greater among insured homeowners than among uninsured homeowners. It further suggests that the perceived probability of loss, rather than being a rationalization after the fact, indeed plays a role in insurance decisions.

Another reason for risk seeking in the loss domain might be the so-called certainty effect (Tversky, 1975), which states that consequences obtained with certainty loom larger than those that are uncertain. It is interesting to note in this context that Sir Robert Mark, head of London's Scotland Yard, in an interview with *U.S. News and World Report* (May 10, 1976), stressed that the "best deterrent to deliberate, and therefore preventable, crime is not so much the severity of punishment as the likelihood of being caught and if caught, the near certainty of being convicted if guilty." This certainty effect suggests that people focus more on the probability of a loss (e.g., imprisonment) than on its magnitude.

5.2 THE EXPERIMENT

The questionnaire shown in Appendix III was given to two distinctly different groups of respondents. For each group, the questionnaire involved a within-subject and between-subject design. The following question pairs are part of the within-subject design: 4-5; 4-8; 4-12; 6-10; 7-11. The between-subject design concerns a treatment effect for Question 3, as well as checks on order biases for Questions 4, 6, and 9. The last part of the questionnaire shows the other versions of these four questions. The remaining questions were the same. The rationale behind the design will become apparent when discussing the results.

Subjects. The first group of subjects consisted of 240 students who were taking an introductory management course. They were asked (as part of their course) to complete the questionnaire anonymously. Both groups were informed that the questions did not have right or wrong answers. Of the 240 students sampled, 84 percent provided usable responses.

The second group surveyed (by mail) consisted of 630 clients of an independent Philadelphia insurance agency that wrote property and casualty insurance. Compared to the clientele of other such insurance agencies, the respondents of this study were overrepresented in educators and underrepresented in blue-collar workers. Professionals, white-collar workers, and self-employed persons were represented in average proportion. The vast majority of the clients (98 percent) carried more insurance (homeowners or automobile) than required by law (frequently ten times more than minimum legal requirements), suggesting risk aversion. A 16 percent response rate was achieved with this client group, which is about average for a questionnaire of twenty-five minutes (as measured from pretests) and no monetary compensation (Kanuk and Berenson, 1975). Table 5.1 compares the rather different socioeconomic characteristics of the student and client groups.

Table 5.1. Socioeconomic Profiles of Student and Client Respondents

	Age			Sex			Marital Status				
	$\bar{x}$	*SD*	*N*	*Male*	*Female*	*N*	*Single*	*Married*	*Divorced*	*Widowed*	*N*
Students	20.1	3.3	194	77%	23%	199	97%	2.5%	.5%	0%	194
Clients	40.1	15.3	98	85%	15%	98	25%	69.0%	3.0%	3%	100

	Nationality			Religion				
	American	*Other*	*N*	*Jewish*	*Catholic*	*Protestant*	*Other or None*	*N*
Students	97%	3%	191	39%	27%	14%	20%	174
Clients	91%	9%	97	13%	20%	41%	26%	92

	Yearly Income				Wealth			
	$\bar{x}$	*SD*	*Median*	*N*	$\bar{x}$	*SD*	*Median*	*N*
Students	$ 3,654	$ 6,135	$ 2,000	191	$ 6,728	$22,888	$ 3,000	191
Clients	$24,111	$16,215	$20,000	99	$48,545	$69,199	$28,000	99

	Occupation							
	Student	*Professional*	*Blue-Collar*	*White-Collar*	*Academic, Teacher*	*Self-Employed*	*Retired, Housewife, Other*	*N*
Students	97%	1%	2%	0%	0%	0%	0%	195
Clients	8%	13%	5%	37%	22%	10%	5%	82

	Highest Education			
	High School	*College*	*Graduate School*	*N*
Students	0%	100%	0%	197
Clients	17%	34%	49%	100

Note: In this table, $\bar{x}$ denotes the arithmetic average (i.e., mean), *SD* the standard deviation around the mean, and *N* the sample size.

These statistics were obtained from responses to questions at the end of the insurance questionnaire in Appendix III, which also contains definitions for the variables of income and wealth.

Response Biases. To check whether the 101 client respondents were a representative sample of the population of 630 clients we compared the sample and population distributions of such variables as sex, geographical location, age, occupation, and marital status.[2] (Because of its high response rate of 82 percent, it was not deemed necessary to analyze response biases for the student group.) No response biases within the client group were observed (as measured from chi-square tests for goodness of fit) with respect to sex, age, occupation, and marital status. However, there was an overrepresentation of respondents from within the city of Philadelphia, as measured from the postmarks on the return envelopes. Of course, this may reflect mailing habits — for example, a respondent living outside Philadelphia who posts his or her mail from within the city before, during, or after work. Disregarding this geographical bias, it seems reasonable to consider the sample as representative of the agency at large.

5.3 RESULTS

Because of the distinctly different socioeconomic profiles of the student and client groups (i.e., the danger of hiding important differences), it was decided not to pool the data of the two groups, but to report them separately. A second argument against data pooling is Simpson's paradox.[3] According to that paradox, a relationship that is observed in two independent studies may reverse when the data are aggregated (Blyth, 1972; Bickel, Hammel, and O'Connell, 1975).

5.3.1 Pure Risk Alternatives

The first part of the survey presented subjects with several binary choices involving losses only. For example, Question 2 involved a choice between two alternatives, the first (A) offering a 6 out of 10 chance of losing $100, and the second ($B$) a 1 out of 100 chance of losing $6,000. According to expected utility theory, risk-averse individuals should prefer alternative A since the expected losses are equal and since A has less variance or risk. However, only 33 percent of the students and 58 percent of the clients chose that alternative. A set of similar questions produced findings on the same order of magnitude as shown in Table 5.2.

Table 5.2 shows that on average for Questions 1, 2, and 3, 60 percent of the students preferred the risky alternative, as compared with 37 percent of the clients. The students were significantly more risk-taking than clients

Table 5.2. Preferences for Safe and Risky Alternatives with Equal Expected Losses

	Binary Choice to Be Made by Subject					*Preferred Alternative*			
	Safe Alternative		*Risky Alternative*						
Question Number	P_ℓ	A_ℓ	P_ℓ	A_ℓ	*Respondent Group*	*Safe*	*Risky*	*Indifferent*	*N*
1	.9	$ 20	.002	$ 9,000	Students	44%	49%	7%	202
					Clients	67%	29%	4%	100
2	.6	$100	.01	$ 6,000	Students	33%	55%	12%	200
					Clients	58%	37%	5%	100
3	.5	$400	.02	$10,000	Students	42%	47%	11%	193
					Clients	63%	35%	2%	97
	Weighted averages for all three questions:				Students	40%	50%	10%	
					Clients	63%	34%	3%	

Note: The left side of Table 5.2 shows the alternatives for three questions. P_ℓ stands for the probability of losing and A_ℓ for the amount to be lost. The right side of the table lists for each question the percentage of students and clients preferring the safe, the risky, or neither alternative. The last column (N) lists sample sizes.

($z = 3.8$, $p < .0003$), which may have been due to differences in financial status. Furthermore, students may have had difficulty in imagining the loss of large amounts of money (which students usually do not have).[4]

The relatively poor student group (with an average yearly income of $3,650 and an average wealth of $6,700) could probably well imagine, but ill afford, the very likely loss associated with the safe alternatives and hence were willing to gamble on the risky alternative.[5] However, the relatively affluent client group (with an average yearly income of $24,000 and an average wealth of $48,500) probably considered the small loss to be negligible, but the large loss quite real, and hence chose the safe alternative. These contentions are borne out by the reasons stated by the students and clients. Those preferring the safe alternative typically remarked that the small loss was no comparison to the large loss, whereas those preferring the risky alternative typically remarked that the probability of a loss was so low that they preferred to take their chances.

A within-group analysis revealed that the students who preferred the risky alternative for Question 2 had lower means of income and wealth ($3,000 and $5,100, respectively) than the students who preferred the safe alternative (who had a mean income of $4,900 and a mean wealth of $9,200). These within-group differences in mean income and wealth are significant at the .01 and .07 levels, respectively.

However, the within-group analysis for the clients did not yield such strong findings. Even though the average income of the clients who preferred the safe alternative (for both Questions 1 and 2) was higher, their mean wealth was lower. Although this finding also suggests that financial status plays a role and that income is more important than wealth, the differences were not statistically significant ($p > .2$).

A within-group comparison of the reasons given for either choice provided the same breakdown as the between-group analysis. Risk takers tended to focus on odds and risk averters on losses.

5.3.2 Other Factors Affecting Risk Preferences

Question 3 was used to test if people could be made more risk-averse by "forcing" them to focus on the large loss associated with the risky alternative. To accomplish this, a subsample of randomly selected respondents was asked to provide a brief description of what a $10,000 loss would mean to them. This description was requested before they evaluated the choice in Question 3 (see Appendix III).

Of those in the student group who received this vividness treatment, 42 percent preferred the safe alternative, as compared to 38 percent in the control group. (The latter group did not provide a description). For the client group, the results were opposite of what had been hypothesized; the figures for this group were 58 percent and 63 percent, respectively. The differences in each group, however, were not statistically significant, z being close to .5 for both groups.

The next issue examined was whether socioeconomic and self-assessment variables showed any relationship to subjects' preferences for the risky or the safe alternative. As a first approach, the preferences in Questions 1 and 2 were subjected to discriminant analyses (Press, 1972), with the socioeconomic and self-assessment data at the end of the questionnaire being used as predictor variables. Most discriminatory in this regard were the variables of prudence-adventuresomeness, age, locus of control, and optimism-pessimism (listed in order of importance). However, because of high multicollinearity, it was decided to assess the various influences on a univariate basis as well. Table 5.3 shows the means, standard deviations (SD), and t-values associated with the differences in means between those preferring the risky versus the safe alternative in Question one. Statistically significant ($p < .1$) differences are marked with an asterisk.

The table shows that age and income are the most important socioeconomic variables. However, as these variables are highly correlated ($r = .6$, $p < .0001$ for students, and $r = .23$, $p < .02$ for clients), the effect of age may reflect spurious correlation. With respect to the self-assessment variables, there appeared to be no strong and systematic effects regarding people's preference for the safe or risky alternative in Question 1, except for the prudent-adventuresome variable.

Preference and Use of Intuition. For most questions, subjects were asked to indicate the strength of their preferences on a seven-point scale (see questionnaire). An analysis of these responses reveals that for both Questions 1 and 2, students, as well as clients, who preferred the safe alternative had a stronger mean preference for their choice than those who preferred the risky alternative. For Question 1 these differences are significant at the .08 and .11 level for students and clients, respectively ($t = 1.38$ with 184 df., and $t = 1.25$ with 94 df., one-tailed tests). For Question 2, the differences are significant at the .005 and .015 levels, respectively ($t = 2.6$ with 174 df., and $t = 2.23$ with 93 df., one-tailed tests).

Table 5.4 reveals that clients who preferred the safe alternatives based their choices more on intuition than did clients who preferred the risky alternative. This held true for both Questions 1 and 2, and the differences were significant at the .1 and .16 levels, respectively ($t = 1.64$ with 94 df., and $t = 1.44$ with 93 df., two-tailed tests).

Table 5.3. Differences between Risk Seekers and Risk Averters

Variable	Students					Clients				
	Risk Seekers		*Risk Averters*			*Risk Seekers*		*Risk Averters*		
	Mean	*SD*	*Mean*	*SD*	*t-Value*	*Mean*	*SD*	*Mean*	*SD*	*t-Value*
Age	19.60	1.10	20.40	4.50	1.66	38.00	14.70	42.70	15.60	1.36
% female	22%		25%		0.48	14%		16%		0.25
Income	3.33	5.90	3.99	6.60	0.70	23.30	15.00	26.20	16.60	0.25
Wealth	6.42	23.00	7.18	24.50	0.21	53.60	61.40	46.70	73.70	0.44
Adventurous	4.64	1.55	4.07	1.62	2.40*	4.52	1.50	3.44	1.77	2.86*
Follower	2.60	1.16	2.73	1.45	0.67	2.76	1.30	2.94	1.58	0.54
Low control	2.77	1.29	2.97	1.51	0.96	3.41	1.48	2.85	1.49	1.69*
Sociable	4.02	1.67	3.86	1.80	0.62	4.00	1.65	4.06	1.85	0.15
Nonreligious	4.45	1.96	4.36	2.00	0.30	4.66	2.02	4.45	2.12	0.45
Generous	4.56	1.53	4.27	1.50	1.28	4.17	1.71	4.24	1.63	0.19
DM—hard	3.47	1.66	3.94	1.90	1.78*	3.45	1.62	3.24	1.66	0.57
DM—others	2.37	1.53	2.40	1.44	0.14	2.62	1.45	2.91	1.56	0.85
Pessimistic	3.00	1.68	3.19	1.86	0.71	3.07	1.73	2.73	1.79	0.86
Sample size	95		85			29		66		

Note: "DM" in the left-hand column refers to decision making. The last nine, self-assessment variables in that column correspond to the last part of the questionnaire (Appendix III), where the scale goes from 1–7, from left to right. Sample sizes are approximate (±2) as some variables had missing data. All t-values correspond to differences in means; an asterisk denotes statistical significance ($p<.1$). A z-test was used for the "% female" variable.

Table 5.4. Strength of Preference and Use of Intuition

Choice of Alternatives	Students					Clients				
	N	Strength of Preference		Use of Intuition		N	Strength of Preference		Use of Intuition	
		$\overline{x}$	(SD)	$\overline{x}$	(SD)		$\overline{x}$	(SD)	$\overline{x}$	(SD)
Question 1										
Safe	88	5.68	(1.72)	5.14	(2.26)	67	5.87	(1.81)	4.69	(2.69)
Risky	98	5.33	(1.73)	5.59	(1.91)	29	5.34	(2.07)	3.71	(2.68)
Neutral	14	0.00	(0.00)	1.88	(1.96)	4	0.00	(0.00)	2.50	(3.00)
Question 2										
Safe	66	5.41	(1.64)	5.47	(1.91)	58	5.67	(1.72)	4.74	(2.48)
Risky	110	4.64	(2.02)	5.42	(1.95)	37	4.78	(2.30)	3.97	(2.66)
Neutral	24	0.00	(0.00)	2.92	(2.56)	5	0.00	(0.00)	1.00	(0.00)

Note: $\overline{x}$ denotes mean; standard deviations are shown in parentheses. The seven-point scales on which the variables were measured are shown in Appendix III. The strength of preference for those who were neutral was, by definition, zero.

For the student group, the findings were opposite. With respect to Question 1, students who preferred the risky choice were more intuitive in their decision making. This difference is significant at the .14 level (t = 1.53 with 184 df., two-tailed). However, for Question 2, there was no significant difference in the use of intuition between those who preferred the risky alternative and those who preferred the safe.

Table 5.4 also shows that respondents who were indifferent made significantly more calculations than did those who preferred either the safe or the risky alternative. The decision to be indifferent, however, may have been more the result of an erroneous understanding of normative decision principles (i.e., the misconception that one should be indifferent between alternatives when expected values are equal) than of a true inner preference. Indeed, the most frequent explanation given for the indifference answer was "equal expected values" (which subjects wrote on the line labeled "Comment on Why"; see Appendix III).

A final point of interest concerns the effect of statistical knowledge on the use of intuition. Table 5.5 lists the mean intuition use of the respondents knowing none, one, two, or all three of the statistical concepts listed under the section for personal data in the questionnaire. The table lists these mean intuition scores for Question 1, as well as the means for CIAVER, which is an average calculation-intuition (CI) score based on all nine calculation-intuition scales of the questionnaire.[6]

Table 5.5. Effect of Statistical Knowledge on the Use of Intuition

Statistical Concepts Known	*CIQ1*			*CIAVER*		
	$\bar{x}$	*SD*	*N*	$\bar{x}$	*SD*	*N*
			Students			
0	4.40	2.61	5	4.60	1.82	5
1	5.02	2.37	51	4.71	1.33	51
2	5.25	2.25	64	4.72	1.46	64
3	4.83	2.36	59	4.32	1.34	59
			Clients			
0	4.58	2.78	65	4.78	1.46	67
1	4.20	2.90	10	5.00	1.05	10
2	4.46	2.54	13	4.29	1.38	14
3	2.33	1.94	9	3.67	1.41	9

Note: CIQ1 is the intuition score for Question 1; CIAVER is the average intuition score of all nine calculation-intuition scores in the questionnaire.

Table 5.5 shows that in all four cases those who knew all three concepts were the least intuitive. The differences in means between those who knew one concept and those who knew three were significant at the .4 level and .07 level for Question 1 (t = .42, 108 df., for students; t = 1.63, 17 df., for clients) and at the .1 level and .02 level for CIAVER (t = 1.52, 108 df., for students; t = 2.35, 17 df., for clients).[7] Hence, the data suggest that statistical knowledge affects the use of intuition. Those who were familiar with statistics tended to be more analytic than those less familiar with statistics.

5.3.3 Insurance Preferences

To investigate the hypothesis that insurance is viewed more as an investment (Slovic et al., 1977) than as a protective mechanism against large losses (as EU theory suggests), subjects were asked to rank four different insurance policies in order of attractiveness.[8] Table 5.6 provides a summary of this question.

The premiums for each policy are considerably less than the corresponding expected loss (as would be the case in subsidized insurance). Hence, EU theory would have predicted that all of the policies should have been attractive; yet many individuals found some of the policies unattractive, as shown in Table 5.7. The table shows that substantial portions of the respondents (from 30 percent to 77 percent) judged each policy as neutral or unattractive, which is contrary to expected utility theory. The findings also raise

Table 5.6. Summary of the First Insurance Question (A 1 Out of 100 Chance of Losing Somewhere between $10,000 and $30,000)

Policy Number	*Premium (Cost)*	*Amount You Pay if Loss Occurs (Deductible)*
P1	$20	$500
P2	$70	$200
P3	$80	$100
P4	$90	$ 0

Answer											
	10	9	8	7	6	5	4	3	2	1	0
Very attractive					Neutral						Very unattractive

Note: Respondents were asked to rank all four policies by placing the policy numbers in the above boxes.

Table 5.7. Frequencies of Absolute Rankings

	Students				*Clients*			
(Policy) *(Premium)*	*P1* *$20*	*P2* *$70*	*P3* *$80*	*P4* *$90*	*P1* *$20*	*P2* *$70*	*P3* *$80*	*P4* *$90*
Attractive (7–10)	56%	32%	23%	49%	70%	29%	36%	46%
Neutral (4–6)	11%	41%	36%	23%	6%	29%	28%	21%
Unattractive (0–3)	33%	27%	41%	28%	24%	42%	26%	33%
	100%	100%	100%	100%	100%	100%	100%	100%
Mean rank	5.97	5.16	5.66	5.96	6.91	4.69	5.25	5.43
SD	3.89	2.59	2.62	3.44	3.91	2.99	2.65	3.80
Sample size	192	177	177	182	91	87	85	89

questions about people's ability to focus on two dimensions simultaneously (i.e., premiums and deductibles) and to weigh trade-offs appropriately. *P*1, having the lowest premium, was the only policy that was judged to be attractive by a majority of students and clients. With respect to the other policies, the majority did not behave as risk averters.

Because many respondents may have considered some policies unattractive relative to others on the list, rather than unattractive in general, Table 5.8 depicts the *relative* rankings of the policies. The evidence of Tables 5.7 and 5.8 shows that the policies with the highest deductible (*P*1) and the lowest deductible (*P*4) were more attractive than the two policies with intermediary deductibles. The preference for the lowest deductible (in this case $0) suggests a type of certainty effect. By paying an extra $10 (relative to *P*3), an individual is certain not to lose $100, even though the chance of this happening would be only .01 (i.e., an EV of − $1). Apparently the psychological certainty of total repayment is well worth the extra $10. In this sense, insurance may have been viewed as an investment aimed at maximizing claim payments in case the hazard should occur. On the other hand, strong preferences for the highest deductible do not lend support to the investment theory. It is interesting to note that only 29 percent of the students and 40 percent of the clients provided the rank order $P1 > P2 > P3 > P4$. EU theory would predict this preference order for risk-taking, risk-neutral, and moderately risk-averse decision makers.

To study the effect of the probability of loss on the attractiveness of the insurance policies, Question 4 was repeated (as Question 5) with a slight

Table 5.8. Frequencies of Relative Rankings

(Policy)	*P1*	*P2*	*P3*	*P4*
(Premium)	*$ 20*	*$ 70*	*$ 80*	*$ 90*
(Deductible)	*$500*	*$200*	*$100*	*$ 0*
		Students		
Attractiveness				
Most	46%	9%	10%	33%
Second	7%	38%	36%	20%
Third	8%	32%	48%	8%
Least	39%	21%	6%	39%
	100%	100%	100%	100%
Sample size	166	171	169	167
		Clients		
Attractiveness				
Most	60%	4%	8%	30%
Second	6%	46%	31%	13%
Third	5%	25%	60%	9%
Least	29%	25%	1%	48%
	100%	100%	100%	100%
Sample size	82	80	77	82

variation: the probability of loss was reduced from .01 to .001. Since the premiums and deductibles remained unchanged, one would expect a decline in the attractiveness of every policy. The format and response mode of Question 5 were identical to those of Question 4; the questions differed only in their probability levels (see Appendix III). Table 5.9 contains a tabulation of the responses to Question 5.

A comparison of Tables 5.7 and 5.9 reveals that *P*1 increased in attractiveness as the probability of loss decreased. Since *P*1 should have decreased in attractiveness, a likely explanation is that many respondents viewed the scale more as one for relative rankings than for absolute rankings. Indeed, the spread between *P*1 and *P*4 (in mean ranks, as well as percentages of attractiveness) increased between Questions 4 and 5. This explanation is also borne out by Table 5.10, which lists the percentages of respondents for whom the attractivenes of a given policy decreased as they went from Question 4 to Question 5. These percentages would have been 100 percent had all respondents made rational choices.

Table 5.9. Question 5: Frequencies of Absolute Rankings

	Students				*Clients*			
(Policy)	*P1*	*P2*	*P3*	*P4*	*P1*	*P2*	*P3*	*P4*
Attractive	75%	30%	25%	24%	78%	30%	23%	30%
Neutral	10%	30%	31%	39%	5%	27%	38%	20%
Unattractive	15%	40%	44%	54%	17%	43%	39%	50%
	100%	100%	100%	100%	100%	100%	100%	100%
Mean rank	7.84	4.60	4.27	3.56	7.78	4.55	4.45	3.82
SD	3.25	2.89	2.74	3.34	3.44	3.18	2.85	3.71
Sample size	190	172	172	177	92	83	82	84

Table 5.10. Effect of a Reduction in the Probability of Loss

Policy	*Premium*	*Students*	*Clients*
*P*1	$20	10% (N=192)	11% (N=91)
*P*2	$70	44% (N=177)	28% (N=87)
*P*3	$80	55% (N=177)	38% (N=85)
*P*4	$90	65% (N=182)	40% (N=89)

Note: Table shows percentages of respondents who gave a lower rank to a policy when the probability decreased tenfold.

The data of Table 5.10 fully support the "spread" or anchoring explanation. *P*1 (whose relative attractiveness increased most between Questions 4 and 5) was least lowered in absolute ranking, and *P*4 (whose relative attractiveness decreased most) was most lowered in absolute ranking. Furthermore, the percentages in Table 5.10 exhibit "connectedness" (i.e., monotone increases as premiums increase).

5.3.4 Context and Format Effects

In the insurance problem, *P*4 has the attractive feature of complete repayment whenever a loss is suffered, even though it has a relatively high contingency price ratio.[9] To determine whether the preference for *P*4 was invariant to its presentation, subjects were given the following choice (see Question 8), which is mathematically equivalent to the *P*4-*P*1 choice of Table 5.6: alternative *A*, a certain loss of $90; or alternative *B*, a certain loss of $20 *and* a 1 out of 100 chance of losing $500. This question was stripped of its insurance context so that no deductible effect could operate. If present, the deductible effect may be viewed as an evoking process (March and Simon, 1958, p. 10) that leads the decision maker to utilize a different psychological (or evoked) set when the problem is presented with an insurance context. This evoking process may introduce into the psychological set exogenous parameters (e.g., societal norms) that would not otherwise be present.

Without the insurance context, only 13 percent of the students preferred the zero deductible policy (alternative *A*), whereas 45 percent of these *same* students preferred this policy when it was presented with an insurance context (see Table 5.11). This increase from 13 percent to 45 percent is highly significant ($z = 7.2, p < .0001$) and suggests a strong context or deductible effect. The effect was also very significant for the client group, for which the increase went from 16 percent to 36 percent ($z = 3.1, p < .0007$).

These findings indicate that people's preferences can be reversed by changing the context and/or format of a problem. The data suggest that respondents focused more on the deductible when the choice was presented in an insurance context.[10] Further support for this finding was obtained by analyzing how often respondents individually reversed preference. The data revealed that 39 percent of the students and 24 percent of the clients reversed their preferences when the choice between *P*1 and *P*4 was presented without the insurance context. Of those students reversing preference, 88 percent ($N = 73$) reversed away from *P*4 and now chose the option with the highest deducible (*P*4). This figure was 83 percent in the client group. These

Table 5.11. The Deductible Effect

Ranking	*Students*	*Clients*
	With the Insurance Context	
Prefer *P*4	45%	36%
Prefer *P*1	55%	64%
Indifferent	0%	0%
	100% (N=177)	100% (N=85)
	Without the Insurance Context	
Prefer *A* (*P*4)	13%	16%
Prefer *B* (*P*1)	83%	82%
Indifferent	4%	2%
	100% (N=198)	100% (N=98)

Note: Table shows percentages of students and clients preferring *P*4 (no deductible) to *P*1 ($500 deductible) when presented with and without an insurance context.

percentages differ from a 50–50 reversal at the .0003 and .002 levels of significance, respectively; thus, noise or stochastic preferences are not a likely explanation for the preference reversals.

In addition to having different contexts the choice situations described above involved different formats. In the insurance formulation, the emphasis was on paying an extra \$70 to avoid a .01 chance of losing \$500. The second formulation, however, emphasized a certain loss of \$90 (*P*4) or of \$20 with a .01 chance of losing an additional \$500 (*P*1). The insurance formulation stressed that something is to be gained (i.e., protection), while the other formulation stressed the certainty of being in a losing situation.

5.3.5 An Illegitimate Portfolio Effect

Another type of context effect was studied in Questions 11 and 7. In Question 11, respondents were asked to state their preferences for two insurance policies. The decision maker was faced with two independent potential losses against which he or she could purchase insurance. The two insurance policies were as follows:

Policy *A*: \$8 premium to protect against a .001 chance of losing \$10,000.
Policy *B*: \$40 premium to protect against a .01 chance of losing \$5,000.

Note that the ratios of premium to expected loss are equal for these two policies and that both premiums are less than the expected loss. Question 11 further informed respondents that they had four alternatives from which to choose:

Alternative 1 (*A*1): Buy neither policy.
Alternative 2 (*A*2): Buy policy *A* and not policy *B*.
Alternative 3 (*A*3): Buy policy *B* and not policy *A*.
Alternative 4 (*A*4): Buy both policies.

The question then asked respondents to provide an absolute and relative ranking of all four alternatives by using a scale identical to that used in Questions 4 and 5.

Table 5.12 summarizes how often members of the client group judged each alternative as attractive, neutral, and unattractive.[11] As expected (on the basis of expected utility theory), the majority of the clients found it attractive to buy both policies. Oddly enough, however, the majority did not find it attractive (in an absolute sense) to buy only one policy. This

Table 5.12. Question 11: Absolute Preferences for Insurance Portfolios

	Alternatives			
	A1	*A2*	*A3*	*A4*
Attractive	18%	41%	37%	74%
Neutral	9%	32%	34%	13%
Unattractive	73%	27%	29%	13%
	100%	100%	100%	100%
Mean rank	2.47	5.47	5.23	7.55
SD	3.31	2.88	2.77	3.19
Sample size	91	92	91	96

puzzling finding may well have been due to people's difficulty in providing absolute and relative rankings simultaneously (as was suggested earlier in regard to Questions 4 and 5).

With respect to relative rankings, expected utility theory would predict that risk averters should most prefer *A*4 and least prefer *A*1. The reverse would hold for risk takers, who should most prefer *A*1 (provided they are at least moderately risk-taking). The relative ranking of *A*2 and *A*3 depends on the relative degrees of risk taking and risk aversion. Table 5.13 provides a breakdown of four reasonable preference orders and lists the percentages of clients who provided such rankings.

The findings of Table 5.13 show little agreement with earlier data, which suggested that around 63 percent of the clients were risk averters and that around 37 percent were risk takers (see Questions 1, 2, and 3). Since only 10 percent stated risk-taking preferences in Question 11, it appears that revealed risk-taking attitudes vary as a function of the context and situation, and not only, as EU theory suggests, as a function of the probability distribution over final wealth positions and the shape of the utility function.

Table 5.13. Rank Orderings of Joint Insurance Alternatives

Preference Order	*Percentage*	
$A4 > A3 > A2 > A1$	31%	Risk averters
$A4 > A2 > A3 > A1$	25%	Risk averters
$A1 > A2 > A3 > A4$	8%	Risk takers
$A1 > A3 > A2 > A4$	2%	Risk takers
Other preference orders	34%	
	100% ($N = 89$)	

To assess whether the presence of the other choice affected people's judgment of the \$8 policy, a comparison was made with the responses to Question 7. The choice in Question 7 was identical to part of Question 11. The clients were first asked to imagine that they had just lost \$40 (as if they had bought policy *B* and thus eliminated any risk resulting from that potential loss). They were then presented with a choice between alternative *A*, which offered a certain loss of \$8, and alternative *B*, which offered a .001 chance of losing \$10,000. This choice is identical to deciding whether to buy policy *A* in Question 11 after having been forced to buy policy *B*. If one prefers *A* to *B* in Question 7, then consistency requires that one also prefer *A*4 to *A*3 in Question 11 (for any shape of the NM utility function).

The finding was that 23 percent ($N = 92$) did not have consistent preferences, which suggests that people may judge a proposition differently when it is presented singly than when it is presented along with several other choices. It is important here to distinguish between a legitimate portfolio effect as the cause for preference changes and the illegitimate (or psychological) one that was observed in Questions 7 and 11. Of course, one can legitimately change preference for a gamble *X* if a second one — gamble *Y* — is also suddenly presented. However, Questions 7 and 11 were designed (by means of the \$40 loss) to eliminate legitimate portfolio considerations as a cause for preference change so that a preference reversal would be counter to the normative theory.

The vast majority (88 percent) preferred to lose \$8 rather than be exposed to a .001 chance of losing \$10,000 (after having lost \$40). However, only 79 percent preferred buying both policies over buying policy *B* or policy *A* in Question 11. This decrease is significant at the .05 level ($z = 1.69$) and suggests the existence of an illegitimate portfolio effect. What should be irrelevant alternatives do, in fact, influence choices.

5.3.6 Comprehensive Insurance

To investigate context and format effects further, respondents were asked several questions relating to comprehensive insurance. In Question 6, respondents were asked to state the maximum amounts they would be willing to pay for protection against each of three independent potential losses (considered simultaneously).[12] In another question (10), respondents were asked to state *one* maximum amount they would pay for a comprehensive policy covering all three losses. According to utility theory, individuals should bid so that the comprehensive bid equals the sum of the three individual bids. Table 5.14 lists the frequencies with which people indicated they would be willing to pay less, the same, or more for the comprehensive

Table 5.14. Preferences for Comprehensive Insurance

Preference	*Students*	*Clients*
Pay less	49%	53%
Pay the same	23%	16%
Pay more	28%	31%
	100%	100%
Sample size	158	68

Note: Table shows percentages of students and clients whose maximum bids for a comprehensive insurance plan was less, the same, or more than the sum total of their maximum bids for the individual policies of that plan.

plan in relation to their willingness to pay for the three policies individually. The table shows that 49 percent of the students and 53 percent of the clients indicated they would pay less for the comprehensive plan than they would if each component policy were offered separately. These percentages are significantly higher than the percentages of those saying they would pay more ($p < .005$ and $p < .05$, respectively).

This finding suggests that grouping policies together may lead to less total coverage than does the individual presentation of policies. It is interesting to note here that Slovic et al. (1977) found that they could "sell" more insurance (in their urn experiments) in a situation in which coverage against a likely small loss was combined with coverage against an unlikely large loss than they could in a situation in which insurance was offered separately for each event. The present study did not present such choices, and its findings cannot therefore be said to be inconsistent with those of Slovic et al. Taken together, the two findings suggest that combined plans, depending on the type of policies involved, may either increase or decrease total insurance sales.[13]

5.3.7 Scale Effects

A final set of questions (Question 9) revolved around assessing the impact of a scale effect on people's decisions. Respondents were presented with two independent potential losses against which they could buy subsidized insurance separately.[14] Policy *A* involved a $100 premium to protect against a 1 out of 4 chance of losing $500, while policy *B* involved a $1 premium to protect against a 1 out of 4 chance of losing $5. It should be noted that *A* and *B* are symmetrical as they differ only in scale.

According to expected utility theory, both policies should be attractive (as both are subsidized); furthermore, policy *A* should be more attractive than policy *B* if respondents are risk-averse. Subjects were asked two separate questions: (1) which policy they would prefer if they had to make a choice; and (2) how many policies they would buy if they could do as they wished. Table 5.15 presents a cross tabulation of answers to these two questions. The table shows that when forced to choose, 49 percent of the students and 47 percent of the clients preferred the $1 policy or were indifferent between the two — behavior that is inconsistent with utility theory. In the same spirit, when free to do as they wished, 44 percent of the students and 72 percent of the clients preferred to buy neither policy. Only a minority of both the student and client groups (13 percent and 7 percent, respectively) expressed choices consistent with expected utility theory by preferring to buy both policies.

Table 5.15 also shows that of those whose forced preference was policy *A* ($100), which suggests risk aversion, around 87 percent (in both groups) would not buy both policies voluntarily, which suggests they were risk-seeking. Another puzzling finding is that of those preferring neither policy, about 65 percent (of both groups) did not pick *B* when forced to choose. Conversely, of those students who preferred both policies, only 52 percent preferred policy *A* when forced to choose. Clearly, EU theory offers no easy explanations for these results.

5.4 CONCLUSIONS

The findings of this study generally lend support to the findings of Kunreuther et al. (1978), Slovic et al. (1977), and Kahneman and Tversky (1979), all of which highlight people's limited abilities to process information (particularly probabilities) and suggest risk-taking preferences in the domain of losses. The prevalence of this risk-taking attitude (which is contrary to traditional utility theory) may be rooted in people's limited sensitivity to low-probability events (i.e., below a certain threshold, people are no longer sensitive to changes in probabilities). It also suggests a psychological phenomenon in perception and judgment, whereby sensitivity to changes diminishes as one moves further away from a neutral point (i.e., diminishing marginal disutility). Both explanations, however, question EU theory's traditional assumption of risk aversion for losses.

The influence of context was very strong in the insurance questions in which the policy with a low deductible was perceived as more attractive (relative to other policies) than when the same choice was presented in a

Table 5.15. Responses to the Scale-Effect Question

	Students				*Clients*			
	Preference if Forced to Choose	*Breakdown by Preferred Number of Voluntary Policies*			*Preference if Forced to Choose*	*Breakdown by Preferred Number of Voluntary Policies*		
		0	*1*	*2*		*0*	*1*	*2*
$100 Policy (*A*)	93 (51%)	27	54	12	46 (53%)	25	15	6
$1 Policy (*B*)	51 (28%)	30	19	2	22 (25%)	19	3	0
Indifferent	37 (21%)	24	4	9	19 (22%)	19	0	0
	181 (100%)	81 (44%)	77 (43%)	23 (13%)	87 (100%)	63 (72%)	18 (21%)	6 (7%)

Note: Table shows respondents' answers as to what they would prefer if forced to choose between policies *A* and *B* and how many policies they would purchase voluntarily. (The answers are cross-tabulated.)

purely mathematical fashion without reference to insurance and deductibles. Format and context effects seem symptomatic of people's tendency to resort to simplifying strategies or to derive cues from the larger context of the problem. Usually the simplifying strategies consist of focusing more on certain parts of the problem than on others, which may lead to inconsistent preferences. The contextual cues sought might involve such factors as the justifiability of one's choice and its social acceptability.

In trying to identify some of the determinants of people's preference for the risky or safe alternative, it was found that respondents who were better off financially were more inclined to choose the safe alternative. Regarding personality factors, respondents who perceived themselves as prudent were significantly more risk-averse than those who viewed themselves as adventuresome. None of the other self-assessment variables, however, showed systematic relationships to risk-taking preferences.

In general, research on determinants of risk-taking attitudes is inconclusive. For example, Slovic (1966a) and Slovic, Weinstein, and Lichtenstein (1967) found females to be more risk-averse than males, whereas such a sex effect (for monetary payoffs) was absent in the present study and in that of Kogan and Wallach (1967). Reviews of other influences on risk-taking attitudes can be found in Kogan and Wallach (1974) and Greene (1963); both of these reviews attest to the complexity and multifaceted nature of the construct of "risk-taking attitude." The low convergence in risk taking across different settings and contexts (see, e.g., this study; Weinstein, 1969; Slovic, 1972a) raises serious questions about the adequacy of a single utility function in representing people's attitudes toward monetary risks across different contexts.

It was interesting to observe that students and clients did not differ substantially in their risk-taking attitudes or in their abilities to provide consistent evaluations of alternatives. The clients, all of whom participated voluntarily, probably devoted more time to the survey than did the students, who were required to participate. This could account for the client group's somewhat higher degree of consistency and lower degree of reliance on intuition. It is, however, reassuring that in this type of study, student subjects are representative of the larger population and that experimental findings with student subjects may well generalize to this larger population.

Although the present study was primarily designed to test EU theory, it also has several implications for prospect theory (Kahneman and Tversky, 1979). According to prospect theory, people would prefer a high-probability, low-loss event over a sure loss of equal expected value, and a sure loss over a low-probability, high-loss event (of equal expected value). By implication, prospect theory would predict that people would prefer insurance against low-probability, high-loss events over insurance against high-probability, low-loss events (assuming equal expected losses). That prediction is contrary to the findings of this study.

On the issue of context influences, prospect theory, because it recognizes the importance of problem presentation, might predict deductible and illegitimate portfolio effects. For example, prospect theory's isolation effect suggests that people focus on components that distinguish the alternatives and that they disregard components that the alternatives share. This tendency may have led to a limited focus on the (common) probability of loss in evaluating the insurance policies of Questions 4 and 5. Similarly, in Question 7 it might have led to a disregard of the outright (common) loss of $40, which may underlie the illegitimate portfolio effect observed between Questions 11 and 7. With respect to the issue of comprehensive insurance, prospect theory, in its current form, does not make a clear prediction either way; how the problem would be structured is a matter of interpretation.

On the issue of scale effect, prospect theory would predict the opposite of EU theory because of the convexity of the value function over losses, unless the probability were so low that overweighting would induce risk aversion. As for the specific values examined in Question 9, prospect theory would predict that neither coverage would be attractive because of the certainty effect. Indeed, 72 percent of the clients had the preferences that prospect theory would predict; however, only 44 percent of the students expressed such preferences. Prospect theory would also predict that policy *B* would be more attractive than *A*. However, that was the case for only 28 percent of the students and 25 percent of the clients.

In summary, it seems that additional research is needed to modify EU theory and prospect theory so that they can account for the various factors explored in this study. These factors include the effects of financial status (income and wealth versus other measures), the influence of statistical knowledge and decision-making style, and, most important, the impact of context and format effects on choice behavior.

6 STATISTICAL KNOWLEDGE AND GAMBLING DECISIONS: *Moments vs. Risk Dimensions*

In the previous chapter, we analyzed insurance decisions and found that the nature of the decision rule (i.e., whether it is intuitive or calculative) affects choices. We also found that statistical knowledge has an effect on whether people base their decisions on intuition or calculation. Those who were familiar with statistics (particularly such concepts as expected value, random variable, and expected utility theory) were significantly more calculative (i.e., less intuitive) than were those who did not know any of these concepts.[1]

This chapter's study provides a more detailed analysis, using different and more refined measures than the insurance study, of the effect of statistical knowledge on decision rules. The task was changed from choosing among pure risk alternatives to evaluating speculative risks. Specifically, the task involved bidding on four-outcome gambles offering stochastic gains and losses. This different task was chosen because several previous

Parts of this chapter were published in P. J. H. Schoemaker, "The Role of Statistical Knowledge in Gambling Decisions: Moment vs. Risk Dimension Approaches," *Organizational Behavior and Human Performance* 24 (1979):1–17. Reprinted by permission of Academic Press, Inc.

studies utilized these gambles, which are called duplex bets, and because the conflicting research findings of these studies might be reconciled by focusing on the role of statistical training.

The present chapter specifically examines (1) whether statistically trained subjects differ from untrained subjects in their assessment of risk; (2) if so, the ways in which they differ; and (3) whether these differences can be explained by differential information-processing ability. Previous research on decision making in betting settings has identified two general strategies for risk assessment. The first strategy suggests that people are most sensitive to expected values, variances, and other moments in evaluating gambles. This moment approach is in contrast to the risk-dimension approach; in the latter, payoffs and probabilities are viewed as separate stimuli. Experimental evidence exists for both models, even though they are theoretically incompatible, one being multiplicative and the other additive.

6.1 LITERATURE

Edwards (1954c), Coombs and Pruitt (1960), Lichtenstein (1965), and Slovic and Lichtenstein (1968b), who provided some of the first studies of moments, found that the expected values and/or variances had significant effects on choices. More recent work (Anderson and Shanteau, 1970), using functional measurement, also suggests that multiplicative models work quite well in comparison to additive ones.

Slovic and Lichtenstein (1968a), Payne and Braunstein (1971), Ranyard (1976), and others, however, examined models in which the risk dimensions themselves were central. In the Slovic and Lichtenstein study (1968a), subjects were asked to rank and bid on gambles in which the probability of losing could be varied independently of the probability of winning. (See Appendix IV for an analysis of a duplex bet.) The responses of each subject were analyzed with a multiple regression model in which the four risk-dimensions of the duplex gamble were the independent variables. The linear regression model thus provided a way of measuring the relative importance of each of the four risk dimensions.

Slovic and Lichtenstein found that the weights associated with these dimensions varied as a function of the response mode (i.e., whether subjects had to rank the gambles or to bid on them). The researchers interpreted the changes in weights as adaptations of the subject's information-processing strategy to the response mode, with the aim of reducing the information load. They further suggested that differences among weights may reflect a subject's belief that some of the risk dimensions are more important than others for the task at hand. Slovic and Lichtenstein reported substantial individual differences in the relative importance of risk dimensions.

Slovic and Lichtenstein's findings on the effect of the response mode were replicated by Sjöberg (1968) and Andriessen (1971). The latter found that probabilities derived from pure chance processes are assessed differently from those based on skill processes. In the skill setting, subjects were betting on their ability to stop a dot that suddenly moved from left to right on the screen of an oscilloscope, after having been told their average probability of success on previous tries. Andriessen concluded that the relative performance of the additive model versus the EV model (in terms of correlation coefficients) was even higher in the skill setting than in the chance setting.

Additional evidence for the additive model was provided by Slovic's (1969b) study on maximizing a bet's attractiveness while keeping its expected value (EV) constant. The majority of subjects behaved as if the probability of a compounded event exceeded its true value, which suggests non-multiplicative ways of combining probabilities. Ronen (1973) and Tversky and Kahneman (1973) reported related display effects.

In a direct test of the role of EV, Lichtenstein, Slovic, and Zink (1969) concluded that EV was an irrelevant decision guide, even when explained and shown explicitly. Additional support for a risk-dimension view comes from the phenomenon of preference reversal. Lichtenstein and Slovic (1971, 1973), Lindman (1971), Slovic (1975), and Grether and Plott (1979) obtained such reversals as a function of changes in response mode; the interpretation is that decision strategies are adapted to the response mode in order to reduce cognitive strain.

Payne and Braunstein (1971) explicitly explored the relative merits of risk-dimension versus moment approaches to decision making. They used specially constructed duplex games in which the explicit (displayed) probability values differed for each gamble in a pair, but for which the underlying probability distributions were identical. It was found that preferences among gambles were related to the explicitly stated probability values, which supports Slovic and Lichtenstein's view that a gamble is perceived as a multidimensional stimulus.[2] Payne and Braunstein presented an information-processing model of choices between paired gambles that is lexicographic in nature (comparing risk dimensions).

A more complete review of the literature on moment and risk-dimension approaches is offered by Payne (1973), who suggests that there is little consensus on how subjects judge duplex bets or other gambles of low complexity. One possible explanation for some of the conflicting research findings is that individual differences are confounding variables that must be controlled for. As Anderson and Shanteau (1970) suggested, it may be that the additive model works better for untrained subjects and that the multiplicative model is more suitable for trained subjects. Conflicting findings can then be explained as the result of sampling from different subject populations. The experiment described in this chapter offers an empirical test of this conjecture by comparing information-processing strategies between statistically trained and untrained subjects.

6.2 HYPOTHESES

It is well known from cognitive psychology (Bower, 1975) that one's ability to process information (perceiving, coding, storing, recognizing, retrieving, etc.) is a function of past experiences and can be improved through learning. The manner in which information is processed is a function of the structure and organization of the human mind, which is dynamic and adaptive in nature.

It is hypothesized that statistical training constitutes a form of mental training and programming that (1) reduces the cognitive strain associated with probabilistic information processing; (2) increases the quality of risk assessment; and (3) affects the nature of the decision rule in the direction of multiplicative models. Essentially, the view is that people attempt to strike a balance between the quality of a decision and the cost (including the cognitive strain) of arriving at it.[3] Statistical training makes it easier to use more complex, normative strategies, such as evaluating moments, and therefore reduces the cost of a decision of higher quality.[4]

6.3 THE EXPERIMENT

The core of the experiment consisted of the evaluation of thirty-one duplex bets, a type of gamble first used by Slovic and Lichtenstein (1968a). Figure 6.1 shows a duplex bet, which is played by independently spinning the win-and-lose pointer. The payoff is the difference between the amount won and lost. Each bet was projected on a screen for thirty seconds, and subjects were asked to evaluate each bet by providing a hypothetical bid from −10 to +10. Positive bids were used for attractive bets, and negative bids for unattractive ones. For attractive bets, the magnitude of the bid represents the maximum dollar amount the subject would pay to play the bet. For unattractive bets, it represents the minimum amount the subject would have to be paid to play the bet. These definitions were also provided to the subjects.

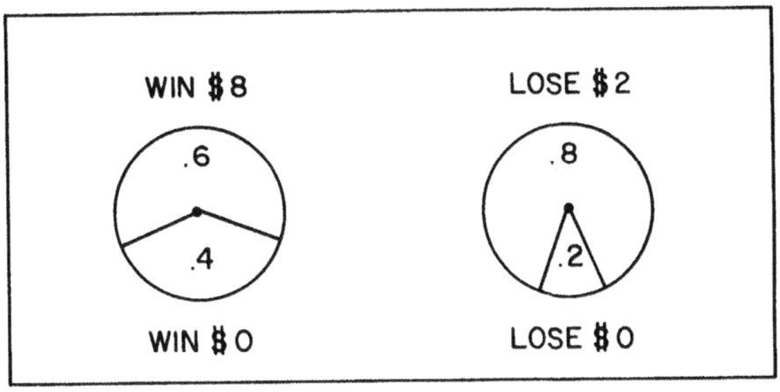

Figure 6.1. Example of a Duplex Gamble

In contrast to the methodology of the Slovic and Lichtenstein (1968a) study, the response mode was kept constant throughout this experiment (i.e., the focus was on bids only), and four, rather than three, levels were used for each of the risk dimensions. The possible probability levels were .2, .4, .6, or .8, and the possible gains or losses were $2, $5, $8, or $10.

The set of gambles used in this experiment is not factorially complete. (Such completion would require 256 gambles.) The subset was selected on the basis of its difficulty; thus, symmetrical bets, which are easier to judge, appear less frequently than their base rates in the factorially complete set. All levels of each factor appear with the same frequency (seven times) in the first 28 bets (see Table 6.1). The last 3 bets are repeats of earlier bets (8, 13, and 6, respectively). The sequence of the first 28 bets was random and the same for all subjects.

Before subjects evaluated the duplex gambles, some control questions were asked to establish each subject's risk-taking attitude and "dimension preference." Risk-taking attitudes for the interval from –$10 to +$10 were measured by asking whether or not subjects world flip a fair coin (i.e., chances of getting heads or tails are equal) for $10, $5, or $2 (three separate questions; see Appendix V).

"Dimension preference" was measured by presenting the subject with a "win" urn of unknown content. Before having to judge the worth of this urn, the subject could know either the probability of winning something from this urn or how much would be won if a "winning" ball was drawn. The subject was given the general range of the payoff ($0 to $10), as well as the probability range (0 to 1). A preference for either of these two types of information was used as a measure of dimension preference.[5] The urn question was then repeated with a "loss" urn having a payoff range of $0 to –$10.

Table 6.1. Listing of the 31 Duplex Gambles

Gamble	P_w	A_w	P_ℓ	A_ℓ
0	.2	10	.4	−8
1	.4	10	.2	−10
2	.2	8	.8	−2
3	.6	2	.8	−2
4	.4	8	.2	−10
5	.8	2	.6	−5
6	.6	8	.8	−5
7	.8	8	.4	−10
8	.8	8	.6	−10
9	.4	5	.8	−5
10	.6	5	.6	−8
11	.8	2	.2	−5
12	.4	5	.6	−8
13	.8	2	.6	−8
14	.2	10	.8	−10
15	.2	10	.2	−2
16	.6	5	.2	−2
17	.6	5	.4	−10
18	.6	5	.6	−2
19	.6	2	.4	−5
20	.2	10	.2	−8
21	.2	8	.4	−8
22	.8	5	.2	−10
23	.4	8	.6	−2
24	.4	10	.8	−2
25	.8	2	.4	−5
26	.2	10	.6	−8
27	.4	2	.4	−5
28	.8	8	.6	−10
29	.8	2	.6	−8
30	.6	8	.8	−5

Note: P_w and P_ℓ refer to the probabilities of winning and losing, respectively. A_w and A_ℓ refer to the amounts to be gained or lost, respectively, from each disk.

After subjects had answered the coin-flipping and urn questions and had evaluated the duplex bets, they were presented with several protocol-like questions aimed at assessing aspects of cognitive strain, decision quality, and decision strategy.

Cognitive strain (referring to the mental efforts expended in the process of making decisions) was measured indirectly through the subject's perception of the task difficulty and task boredom, and through the amount of time needed to develop an acceptable decision rule. The last two proxies vary only unidirectionally with cognitive strain over a limited range. It was assumed that task difficulty varied directly and boredom inversely with cognitive strain in this type of study. One indirect measure was the extent to which a subject processed all information, as opposed to focusing on only a few of the relevant risk dimensions.

Aspects of the quality of the decision were assessed subjectively by asking subjects how reliable they thought their bids were. Objective measures were the size of the difference between two bids for the same gamble and the frequency with which trained and untrained subjects made irrational bids. (Irrational bids are those exceeding the maximum amount to be gained or requiring minimum compensation in excess of the maximum amount to be lost.)

The nature of the decision rule was assessed by looking at the frequencies with which calculations were made and the extent to which bids could be explained from input variables via statistical models. Both goodness of fit and model type (i.e., additive versus multiplicative) were deemed relevant. Other measures were derived from subjects' descriptions of their decision rules.

Subjects. The general subject population of the experiment was the undergraduate student community at the University of Pennsylvania. Trained subjects were selected from a group of students taking an introductory management course in which elementary statistics had been covered. Untrained subjects were located via a sign-up sheet asking for subjects unfamiliar with statistics.[6] The experiments with these two groups of subjects were conducted in class (on separate occasions) under conditions that were as identical as possible. Neither group was told anything about the purpose of the experiment. The subjects of the management course, for example, were not told that they had been selected because of their knowledge of statistics. The subjects located via the sign-up sheet were compensated at normal hourly rates for their participation. (For further detail, see Schoemaker, 1977.)

Since statistical knowledge was the important blocking variable in this study, subjects were partitioned into a trained group and an untrained group on the basis of both an internal criterion and an external criterion. The internal criterion was the subject's ability to provide a proper definition or example of the concept of EV at the end of the experiment. The external criterion was whether the subject had been exposed to statistics through courses. The two criteria correlated so well that only one subject had conflicting credentials. He was classified as trained after having obtained additional information. The final classification resulted in fifty-one trained subjects (thirty-seven male and fourteen female) and thirty-seven untrained ones (sixteen male and twenty-one female). Because the percentage of females differed significantly between the trained and untrained groups (27 and 57 percent, respectively), and because a sex effect was observed, the findings were broken down by sex and group.

It should be noted that the groups identified as "trained" and "untrained" might well differ in ways other than statistical training — for example, quantitative ability. The ex-post-facto design, however, does not allow for easy control of variables that correlate with statistical training. Hence, "trained" and "untrained" are meant to refer to statistical knowledge and its covariates.

6.4 RESULTS

6.4.1 Cognitive Strain

This section will first evaluate whether statistically trained subjects experienced less cognitive strain as measured from protocol questions than did untrained subjects. Table 6.2 shows how subjects responded when asked (after having evaluated all thirty-one duplex bets) how difficult it was to develop a system or method by which to judge the bets. The only significant ($p < .05$) difference in the percentages of "no" answers occurred between trained and untrained males ($z = 2.47$, $p < .01$, one-tailed). Apparently, trained males found the task easier than did untrained males. The same effect, however, was not observed between trained and untrained females. It must be recognized that the answers may well contain a response bias as students may not like to admit that something is difficult. The direction of this bias would favor the null hypothesis of no difference due to statistical knowledge.

Table 6.2. Perceived Task Difficulty

	Males		*Females*	
Was the task difficult?	*Trained*	*Untrained*	*Trained*	*Untrained*
No	74%	38%	64%	63%
In between	9%	19%	14%	21%
Yes	17%	43%	22%	16%
	100%	100%	100%	100%
Sample size	35	16	14	19

Table 6.3. Perceived Boredom of Task

	Male		*Female*	
	Trained	*Untrained*	*Trained*	*Untrained*
Mean	3.17	2.62	3.57	3.00
SD	1.28	1.25	1.22	1.10
Sample size	36	16	14	21

Very interesting		Neutral		Very boring
1	2	3	4	5

Response scale

A related question asked subjects how boring or interesting they thought the task was. Of course, boredom is only inversely related to cognitive strain up to the point where the task becomes so difficult that it is no longer perceived as interesting.[7] If we assume that the duplex task is rather easy for trained subjects and challenging for untrained subjects, we would expect the findings to be as shown in Table 6.3. Trained subjects apparently found the task more boring than did untrained subjects. For males, the difference in means is significant at the .07 level (t = 1.49, one-tailed); for females, it is significant at the .08 level (t = 1.44, one-tailed).

When asked how many bets had passed by before they had developed some method by which to judge the duplex bets, subjects responded as shown in Table 6.4. The one-tailed test of trained subjects' needing fewer practice bets to develop a system than untrained subjects is accepted at the

Table 6.4. Time Needed to Develop a Decision Rule

	Males		*Female*	
No. of bets passed by	*Trained*	*Untrained*	*Trained*	*Untrained*
None	57%	13%	40%	5%
At least 1	43%	87%	60%	95%
	100%	100%	100%	100%
Average no.	2.19	5.13	3.29	4.71
SD	3.3	4.5	3.0	3.6
Sample size	37	15	14	21

.002 level for males ($z = 2.89$) and the .005 level for females ($z = 2.59$). This test was based on the percentages of subjects who said they needed no practice bets. The difference in the average number of bets is significant at the .005 level for males ($t = 2.61$, one-tailed) and .23 for females ($t = .76$).

Additional evidence that statistical knowledge provides an advantage in coping with duplex gambles derives from the question as to which part of the gamble subjects focused on most. Evaluation of duplex bets should involve processing of four independent risk dimensions. To the extent that this presents an information overload, we would expect people to focus more on certain dimensions than on others (in order to reduce the overload). Table 6.5 summarizes the frequencies with which each subgroup focused on different parts of the bet (as based on their answers to protocol questions).

Trained subjects of both sexes said they focused more equally on all parts of the gamble than did untrained subjects. The differences in the percentages (of the first row of Table 6.5) are significant at the .002 level for males ($z = 2.89$, one-tailed) and at the .02 level for females ($z = 2.27$, one-tailed), which is consistent with the hypothesis that untrained subjects tend to use simpler decision strategies. Note that for untrained subjects, Table 6.5 supports Slovic and Lichtenstein's (1968a) finding that probabilities are more important than payoffs. The findings are different, however, for the trained subjects, about half of whom ranked the dimensions equally.

Table 6.5. Parts of Bet on Which Subjects Focused

	Males		*Females*	
Focus	*Trained*	*Untrained*	*Trained*	*Untrained*
All parts equally	56%	13%	43%	10%
Amount of winning	3%	19%	7%	0%
Probability of winning	0%	19%	7%	24%
Amount of losing	8%	13%	0%	14%
Probability of losing	6%	0%	14%	19%
Dollar dimensions	8%	0%	7%	14%
Probability dimensions	11%	31%	14%	14%
Other	8%	5%	8%	5%
	100%	100%	100%	100%
Sample size	36	16	14	21

6.4.2 Decision Quality

We will now examine the regard in which trained subjects, other things being equal, made decisions of higher quality than did untrained subjects. At the end of the experiment, subjects were asked to estimate the maximum amount of dollars by which a second bid on a repeat gamble would deviate from an earlier bid. Trained males perceived themselves as significantly more consistent than untrained males ($t = 1.436, p < .08$, one-tailed). For the female group, the findings were in the same direction ($t = .65$); however, the difference was not statistically significant.

An objective test of the consistency of the decision rules is to measure by how much the bids, for each subject, actually differ between two identical bets. If a decision rule is executed without error, then identical bets will receive identical bids. The last three duplex gambles (*G*28, *G*29, and *G*30) were identical to three earlier ones (*G*8, *G*13, and *G*6, respectively). Since there were three pairs of identical bets, it was possible to assess each subject's consistency three times. The mean absolute differences of these repeat trials are listed in Table 6.6.

Table 6.6 shows clearly that for both sexes, the untrained subjects were less consistent than the trained ones on all three trials. This finding is statistically significant ($p < .02$) since we have six semiindependent tests in which all the deviations are in the hypothesized directions. A comparison of the average mean absolute deviations indicates that the difference in the male group is significant at the .0005 level ($t = 5.21$, one-tailed) and at the .01 level for the female group ($t = 2.51$). It was also found that males were significantly more consistent than females within both the trained and untrained groups ($p < .005$ and $p < .05$, respectively).

Table 6.6. Mean Absolute Differences in Bids of Repeat Gambles

	Males		*Females*	
	Trained	*Untrained*	*Trained*	*Untrained*
Mean absolute deviations				
*G*8–*G*28	1.11	4.13	3.57	4.90
*G*13–*G*29	1.03	1.44	.64	2.29
*G*6–*G*30	.95	3.06	2.50	4.90
Average	1.03	2.88	2.24	4.03
SD	.95	1.62	1.86	2.19
Sample size	37	16	14	21

Table 6.7. Frequencies of Irrational Bids

	Males		*Females*	
	Trained	*Untrained*	*Trained*	*Untrained*
Irrational Bids				
At least 1	24%	88%	36%	71%
Average no.	.43	2.31	1.21	2.38
SD	.96	2.09	2.12	3.11
Sample size	37	16	14	21

When we compared the subjects' perceptions with observed consistency, we found that the trained subjects (for both sexes) significantly underestimated their ability to provide consistent evaluations, whereas the untrained subjects overestimated their ability.

Another objective measure of a subject's ability to make high-quality decisions concerns the frequency of bids that exceed the maximum amount to be won or that imply compensation in excess of the maximum amount to be lost. Table 6.7 provides a frequency tabulation of such irrational bids for each subgroup. The table clearly shows that trained subjects had considerably fewer irrational bids that did untrained subjects. The difference in percentages is significant at the .00003 level for the male group ($z = 4.32$) and at the .03 level for the female group ($z = 2.05$, one-tailed). The difference in the average number of irrational bids is significant at the .0005 level for the male group ($t = 4.52$, one-tailed), but it is not significant for the female group ($t = 1.23$). These findings suggest that trained subjects better fit their decision rules to the actual meaning of the responses (as defined by the experimenter) than do untrained subjects. The use of EV as a proxy for quality is examined below.

6.4.3 Decision Strategy

So far we have presented evidence that trained subjects found the task cognitively less difficult than did untrained subjects and that their decision rules were more consistent. The third basic hypothesis concerns differences in the nature of the decision rules used by trained and untrained subjects.

Of the trained males, 89 percent claimed to have made some use of calculations, as compared to 81 percent of the untrained males. Although the difference is in the hypothesized direction, it is not statistically significant ($z = .79$). For the female group, the findings were also in the hypothesized

Table 6.8. Use of Expected Value

	Males		Females	
	Trained	Untrained	Trained	Untrained
% using EV	76%	19%	36%	5%
Sample size	37	16	14	21

direction (71 percent for the trained group and 67 percent for the untrained), but, again, they were not statistically significant ($z = .25$).[8] In addition to being asked whether they made calculations, subjects were asked to describe their decision rule(s). On the basis of these descriptions, trained and untrained subjects were compared in terms of the use of expected value (i.e., multiplying probabilities and outcomes). Table 6.8 indicates that trained subjects used expected values much more frequently than did untrained subjects. The percentage difference in the male group is significant at the .0005 level ($z = 3.87$, one-tailed) and at the .01 level for the female group ($z = 2.37$).

If we return to Table 6.5, which indicates the parts of the bets on which subjects focused most, we find that trained subjects (of both sexes) focused more equally ($p < .002$) on the gamble components than did untrained subjects. Hence, Table 6.5 also suggests that untrained subjects exhibit more differential dimension focus; they focused on risk dimensions rather than moments.

Another interesting insight into the nature of the decision rules was obtained from a comparison between the risk-taking attitude of the subject (as measured via the coin-flipping questions) and the parts of the gamble on which the subject said he or she focused. It can be derived from Table 6.5 that fourteen subjects said they focused solely on win dimensions, and sixteen subjects said they focused solely on loss dimensions (i.e., P_ℓ or A_ℓ). Of these fourteen, six subjects were risk-taking (as measured from the coin-flipping questions) and eight were risk-averse. However, of the sixteen subjects focusing on loss dimensions, only one was risk-taking and fifteen were risk-averse. Hence, those focusing on win dimensions were significantly more risk-taking ($X_1^2 = 3.73$, $p < .06$) than those focusing on loss dimensions.

However, no such relationship was found between the findings of Table 6.5 and subjects' answers to the urn questions described earlier. A likely reason is that subjects do not have a strong dimension orientation (i.e., they do not generally prefer information on payoffs over probabilities, or vice versa). In the urn questions, about 48 percent of the subjects changed preference for information (payoffs or odds) when the situation was changed from a "win" to a "loss" urn. This finding calls into question the validity of the construct of "dimension preference," as defined above across win and loss situations. It may well be, however, that the construct has validity in the win and loss domains separately. In either case, it appears that win situations are assessed differently (in terms of decision strategies) than loss situations. This observation merits further investigation.

A final comparison of decision rules was based on the subjects' descriptions of how they judged the duplex bets. These verbalizations were in general agreement with the above findings. Trained subjects usually computed expected values and then made adjustments upward or downward depending on their risk-taking attitude. Untrained subjects usually made comparisons between individual dimensions and tended to add or subtract, if they made calculations at all. Below are listed some illustrative descriptions given by *un*trained subjects:

> "I added up winnings and losses, and compared probabilities."
> "A small positive amount counted less than a small negative one."
> "My decisions were all based on the 'worst-case reasoning.' "
> "I madc it so that if I played four times and won once, I would be ahead."

The next section will use multiple regression analysis to provide further insight into the differences between the decision rules of trained and untrained subjects.

6.5 REGRESSION FINDINGS

Subjects' bids were analyzed via three different regression models as a way of examining differences in the decision strategies of trained and untrained subjects. The three models tested were:

1. An additive model with predictors A_w, P_w, A_ℓ, and P_ℓ.
2. A multiplicative model with predictors EV and var (variance).
3. A combined model with predictors A_w, P_w, A_ℓ, P_ℓ, and EV.

For definitions of the abbreviated predictors, see Table 6.1. These models were tested for each subject on both a full data set (thirty-one bids) and a restricted data set (twenty-four bids). In the restricted set, the first seven gambles had been eliminated because of a presumed learning phase. This number was decided upon on the basis of subjects' answers regarding the number of bets needed to develop a systematic decision rule.

The multiple regressions were used to examine two separate questions:

1. Are there differences between trained and untrained subjects in terms of the types of models that best explain their bids?
2. Are there differences in the degrees of programmability or predictability between a trained and an untrained subject when judging each subject by his or her best-fitting model?

Table 6.9 lists the mean *R*-squares of each of the three models (for both data sets) for trained and untrained subjects (broken down by sex). The table shows that, as hypothesized, trained subjects of both sexes have a higher mean *R*-square for the multiplicative model than for the additive model. For untrained subjects, the opposite is true.[9] The largest difference in means occurred for trained males (with the full data set). A *t*-test for difference in means using *adjusted* *R*-squares was highly significant ($p < .005$, $t = 2.93$).

To assess statistical significance in this way is questionable, however, given the dependence between samples (i.e., same subjects) and the complex, non-normal sampling distribution of *R*-square. As an alternative to *t*-tests, it was examined how frequently the *R*-squares of the combined model increased significantly (relative to the additive model) after the EV

Table 6.9. Degrees of Fit of Three Regression Models

	Males		*Females*	
	Trained	*Untrained*	*Trained*	*Untrained*
Regression type (31 bets)				
Additive	.698	.604	.628	.508
Multiplicative	.777	.540	.675	.480
Combined	.827	.654	.734	.583
Regression type (24 bets)				
Additive	.781	.678	.710	.610
Multiplicative	.815	.629	.721	.537
Combined	.872	.736	.787	.664
Maximum adjusted *R*-square (mean value)	.844	.682	.737	.594
Sample size	37	16	14	21

Note: Entries in the first six rows are mean *R*-squares.

term was included. In this analysis, the EV term was added as the fifth predictor to the additive model via stepwise regression. Of course, this test is conservative to the extent that EV correlates with P_w, A_w, P_ℓ, or A_ℓ. Nevertheless, the results were quite significant.

Using the appropriate *F*-test (Roscoe, 1975, p. 376) and a significance level of .01, it was found that 54 percent of the trained males had a significant improvement in *R*-square after the EV term was included, as compared to only 13 percent of the untrained males. This percentage difference was significant at the .002 level ($z = 2.78$, one-tailed). Of the trained female group, 36 percent had significant improvements in *R*-square, as compared to only 5 percent of the untrained females; this difference was also significant ($p < .05$). All these comparisons were based on the restricted data set, but similar percentage differences were found for the full data set. Hence, the *F*-tests were also consistent with the hypothesis that trained subjects use expected values (and multiplicative models in general) more frequently than do untrained subjects.

The second issue examined was whether the trained subjects were generally more predictable than the untrained subjects, using *R*-square as the relevant measure. Indeed, Table 6.9 shows that the trained subjects always had a higher mean *R*-square (unadjusted) than the untrained subjects, *regardless* of model type. Furthermore, when these two groups were compared on their best-fitting models only, the differences were larger still. After adjusting for differences in degrees of freedom, it was determined which of each subject's six *R*-squares was highest. The resulting maximum adjusted *R*-squares were then averaged for each subgroup (as shown in Table 6.9). For trained males, the mean maximum adjusted *R*-square (.844) significantly exceeded that of the untrained male group (.682) at the .001 level ($t = 3.6$, one-tailed). For the female groups, the difference was significant at the .002 level ($t = 3.2$). These findings strongly suggest that trained subjects (even thought they use mathematically more complex decision rules) are generally more predictable than untrained subjects. Of course, these findings also support the earlier observation that trained subjects are more consistent (i.e., have less noise in their decision rule).

As a final regression analysis, the regression equations of eight untrained subjects were compared with their answers to the question regarding the parts of the gamble on which they had focused most. (These untrained subjects were those who did clearly better on the additive model than on multiplicative or combined ones.) The analysis failed to reveal any statistically significant relationships between the regression weights and the parts of the gamble on which the subject said he or she had focused most. This finding suggests that (1) either regression equations cannot be used to infer the relative importance of risk dimensions or (2) subjects do not really know the dimensions on which they focus most, their own insights notwithstanding. Indeed, other studies (Slovic, Fleissner, and Bauman, 1972; Schmitt and Levine, 1977; Nisbett and Wilson, 1977) have shown that subjects' verbalizations of their cue utilizations often differ from the cue weights that are obtained statistically. These findings suggest that in terms of their descriptive validity, the regression equations themselves (as opposed to R-squares) must be interpreted with great caution, particularly when they are used on an individual level.

6.6 CONCLUSIONS

The results of this study are the product of two different investigative approaches: (1) protocol type of questions and (2) multiple regression analyses. Although each method has its limitations, each tends to compensate the other. For example, the widely used regression paradigm (see Slovic and Lichtenstein, 1971) has been criticized for several reasons: its robustness when wrong (Dawes and Corrigan, 1974); the paramorphic nature of the resulting models (Hoffman, 1960; Goldberg, 1971); its reliance on correlation as a measure of fit (Birnbaum, 1973); and its theoretical limitations in representing certain classes of decision models (Zeleny, 1976). These limitations of regression can be countered, however, by simultaneously using protocol types of investigation. This combination particularly reduces the chance of model misspecification and its associated fallacious inferences (Deegan, 1976). In this study, regression was primarily used to corroborate the protocol findings and analyses. Additionally, recognizing the paramorphic nature of the associated regression equations themselves, care was taken to limit regression analyses to aggregate comparisons of (adjusted) R-squares.

To summarize, the major conclusion of the present study is that variations in decision strategies as observed across previous studies (see Payne, 1973) can, in part, be understood in terms of individual differences, such as degree of statistical knowledge. Of course, the question remains as to whether the effect of statistical knowledge is due more to innate analytic ability or to the statistical training itself. This experiment does not provide a conclusive answer. However, the explicit use of expected values, as reported by the trained subjects themselves, strongly suggests that training itself plays an important role.

Future research might attempt to separate the effect of training from its covariates. Lichtenstein, Slovic, and Zink's (1969) study suggests, however, that this might not be easy. The present study did not attempt such a separation since previous studies (which the present study attempted to reconcile) did not include a focus on training effects. However, having established that statistical knowledge does have an influence, it now becomes important to explore its determinants further.

Other areas for future research suggested by this study concern the determinants and influences of cognitive style on risk assessment (e.g., intuitive versus analytical approaches). Another question is whether risk assessment differs in situations of pure win, pure loss, and mixed decisions.

In conclusion, the findings of this study are consistent with an information-processing view of decision making. Apparently, judging gambles is a cognitively difficult task. Untrained subjects tend to simplify this task by focusing more on certain risk dimensions than on others. The price of this strategy seems to be reduced consistency and less confidence in the resulting decisions. Statistically trained subjects appear to find the task considerably easier and to develop decision rules that come closer to normative rules (e.g., maximizing expected utility) than do untrained subjects. The findings support the hypothesis that subjects strike a balance between the quality of the decision rule and the cognitive strain associated with its execution. Recognition that trained and untrained subjects strike this balance differently may resolve, to some extent, the question of whether decision makers follow a moment or risk-dimension approach.

7 RISK TAKING AND PROBLEM CONTEXT IN THE DOMAIN OF LOSSES

The present chapter examines further two of the issues raised in the insurance study of Chapter 5. The first issue concerns the extent of risk taking in the loss domain. The second involves the influence that a gamble's context or presentation exerts on revealed risk-taking attitudes. These questions were examined through an experimental design in which probabilities, probabilistic losses, and premiums were systematically varied (see Table 7.1 and the questionnaire in Appendix VII). To assess the influence of context, each question was presented in both an "insurance" and a "gamble" format. Subjects randomly received questions in one of these two contexts. Only simple lotteries were examined.

The research presented here was conducted by J. C. Hershey and P. J. H. Schoemaker (1980b). The results were first published in "Risk Taking and Problem Context in the Domain of Losses: An Expected Utility Analysis," *Journal of Risk and Insurance* 47 (March 1980). The journal is acknowledged for its permission to reprint parts of the article.

Table 7.1. Questions Used in the Experiment

Question	*Probabilistic Alternative* *P*	*L*	*Sure Loss Alternative* *S*	*% Preferring Safe Alternative with Insurance Format (N=41)*	*% Preferring Sa Alternative wit Gamble Forma (N=41)*
1	.001	$ − 10,000	$ − 10	70.7%	56.1%
2	.005	− 2,000	− 10	75.6	61.0
3	.01	− 1,000	− 10	80.5	56.1
4	.05	− 200	− 10	56.1	58.5
5	.10	− 100	− 10	43.9	46.3
6	.20	− 50	− 10	36.6	43.9
7	.001	− 10,000	− 10	80.5	53.7
8	.01	− 10,000	− 100	65.9	46.3
9	.10	− 10,000	− 1,000	58.5	29.3
10	.50	− 10,000	− 5,000	39.0	31.7
11	.90	− 10,000	− 9,000	34.1	24.4
12	.99	− 10,000	− 9,900	26.8	22.0
13	.999	− 10,000	− 9,990	17.1	17.1
14	.01	− 100	− 1	68.3	63.4
15	.01	− 1,000	− 10	68.3	46.3
16	.01	− 10,000	− 100	63.4	39.0
17	.01	− 100,000	− 1,000	75.6	36.6
18	.01	− 1,000,000	− 10,000	61.0	29.3

7.1 BACKGROUND

As noted in several earlier chapters, the traditional assumption of risk aversion for losses (Friedman and Savage, 1948) has not been borne out by recent laboratory research. Slovic et al. (1977) and Kahneman and Tversky (1979), as well as Chapters 4 and 5 of this book, have all shown considerable risk taking for losses. Outside the laboratory, similar conclusions have been reached (for a review of pertinent studies, see Chapter 2).

With respect to context effects, several earlier studies on decisions under risk have reported presentation or format influences that are quite incompatible with EU theory. For example, Slovic and Lichtenstein (1968a) showed that the response mode affects the evaluation of gambles. In the same vein, Lindman (1971) and Grether and Plott (1979) showed that preference reversals can be induced by changing the way in which judgments are elicited (e.g., ranking versus selling price). Other display effects in violation of EU theory were observed by Ronen (1973), Payne and Braunstein

(1971), and Kahneman and Tversky (1979). Chapter 5 described yet another type of context effect: zero deductible policies were found to be less attractive when presented in a purely mathematical fashion than when presented in an insurance context, in spite of the mathematical equivalence of these two choice situations.

What are the implications of this research for EU theory, both descriptively and normatively? The risk-taking tendencies for losses can certainly be reconciled with EU theory provided the utility function, $U(x)$, contains some convex segments for $x < 0$. Hence, one question to be examined is whether people's preferences for losses can be explained through utility functions that are not strictly concave. If such an explanation is not possible, particularly when it concerns the simplest type of lotteries, the normative status of EU would be directly affected; that is, the preferences derived from standard reference lotteries must fit some reasonable utility function for the theory to be useful normatively.

The context effects cited above have very serious implications for EU theory as a descriptive model. Normatively, the implications are severe only if the effects also apply in the simple choice situations needed for the construction of $U(x)$. So far, however, the effects have been observed and studied only in more complex situations; other than highlighting its usefulness, such studies do not affect EU as a normative model — that is, the context effects would vanish if intuitive judgment were replaced by explicit EU calculations.

To assess the normative implications for EU theory, all the questions studied in this chapter involved basic or so-called reference lotteries. If subjects' preferences cannot be described by reasonably shaped utility functions or if significant context effects are discernible, both the normative and the descriptive status of EU will be affected. The shape of $U(x)$ and the role of context concern the hypotheses to be discussed next.

7.2 HYPOTHESES

The first hypothesis hence concerns the extent of risk taking in the domain of losses. The study by Slovic et al. (1977), as well as the study described in Chapter 5, revealed insurance preferences for high-probability, low-loss hazards over protection against low-probability, high-loss ones when expected losses were equal. In particular, Slovic et al. found an increased preference for fair insurance as the probability of loss increased from .001 to .25 while the expected loss was held constant. To explain these and related findings, Slovic et al. proposed (1) that the utility function is convex rather than concave and (2) that below certain probability thresholds, people refuse to worry about losses. In summary, Slovic et al. suggested that preferences for insurance relate monotonically (positively) to the probability of loss (p) in the low probability range ($.001 \leq p \leq .25$).

In view of the evidence presented in Chapter 5, however, it is reasonable to postulate a function that could explain both risk seeking for large losses and risk aversion for small ones. We will therefore specifically test whether the results are compatible with Markowitz's (1952) utility function, which is concave for small losses and convex for larger ones. This function has generally received little attention either in the literature of finance or in insurance literature.

7.2.1 A Markowitz Type of Utility Function

We will first examine insurance preferences under a Markowitz type of utility function (see Figure 7.1), for hazards of equal expected loss only. Since these analyses assume insurance to be actuarially fair, the choice will be between a sure loss of S_0 (i.e., the insurance premium) and a potential loss of L_i that has a probability p_i of occurring, with $p_i = S_0/L_i$.[1]

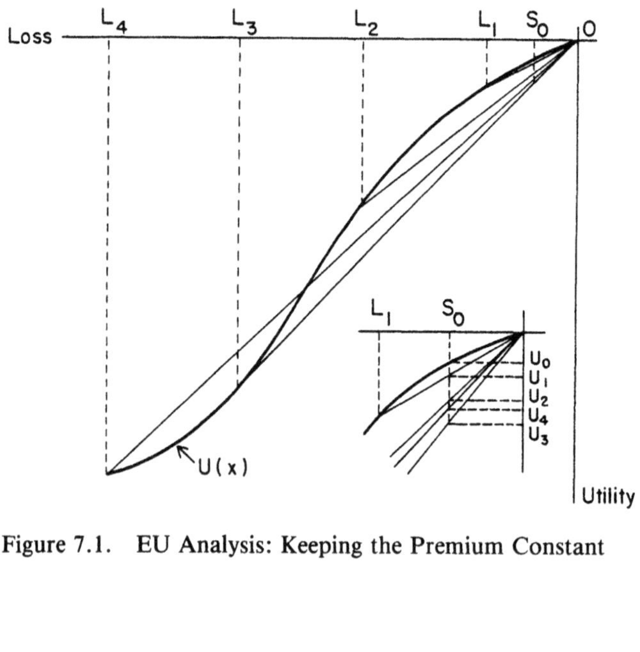

Figure 7.1. EU Analysis: Keeping the Premium Constant

Figure 7.1 shows four hazards with increasing loss levels of L_1 through L_4 and associated probabilities of p_1 through p_4, with $p_i = S_0/L_i$. In considering (p_1, L_1), the choice will be between $U(S_0)$ and $p_1 U(L_1) + (1 - p_1)U(0)$. Setting $U(0) = 0$, this leaves $U(S_0)$ versus $p_1 U(L_1)$. Graphically, $U(S_0)$ corresponds to the utility level u_0 (Figure 7.1); similarly, $p_1 U(L_1)$ corresponds to the utility level u_1 since p_1 is a fraction (equal to S_0/L_1) that is applied to $U(L_1)$. By a similar reasoning process, $p_2 U(L_2)$ corresponds to utility level u_2, $p_3 U(L_3)$ to u_3, and $p_4 U(L_4)$ to u_4.[2]

Whether actuarially fair insurance will be attractive depends on whether u_0 is larger than u_1, u_2, u_3, or u_4. As can be seen from Figure 7.1, insurance should be attractive for all four hazards. However, this need not be so for all (p_i, L_i) as there will exist very large losses for which the line connecting $U(L_i)$ with the origin intersects the vertical line through S_0 above $U(x)$ so that $u_i > u_0$.

Figure 7.1 also provides insight into the strength of preference for insurance as $|L_i|$ increases, which can be measured from the difference between u_0 and u_1, u_2, u_3, or u_4.[3] The difference between u_0 and u_i grows continually larger as $|L|$ increases (starting with small values). This divergence continues to the point where the line connecting $U(L_i)$ and the origin is tangent to $U(L)$—that is, where $U'(L) = [U(L)]/L$. Increases of $|L|$ beyond this point will reduce the preference for insurance; for very large $|L|$, insurance may no longer be preferred. Hence, the Markowitz type of utility function implies a single-peaked preference function (Coombs and Avrunin, 1977) for insurance along an iso-expected loss curve.

At the aggregate level, strength of preference may be measured from the percentage of subjects who prefer insurance. Single-peaked preference functions will occur at the aggregate level (1) if many individuals have Markowitz type of utility functions with different locations for inflection points and (2) if an increase in the difference between u_0 and u_i increases the probability that subjects will prefer insurance (i.e., stochastic preference). Hence, one way of testing the hypothesis that subjects have Markowitz type of utility functions is to determine if aggregate preferences across equal expected loss hazards exhibit single peakedness and perhaps reversal of preference as well.

Note that the inflection point in the utility function in Figure 7.1 does not lead to a preference reversal in the range from L_1 to L_4 (assuming the sure loss is at S_0). Thus, a preference reversal does not necessarily follow from an inflection point. However, the existence of a preference reversal does imply an inflection point within the EU model.

To test explicitly for the existence of an inflection point in $U(x)$, an analysis of the type shown in Figure 7.2 would be more efficient. In this figure, the probabilistic loss L_0 is held constant, while the premium or sure loss is increased from $|S_1|$ to $|S_4|$. By necessity (to keep $S_i = pL_0$) the implied probability p_i increases and will equal S_i/L_0.

In Figure 7.2, the expected utility for the first lottery, $p_1\ U(L_0)$, corresponds to the utility level u_1. In this case, the individual should prefer fair insurance since it has a utility level of u_0, with $u_0 > u_1$. However, as $|S|$ grows larger, a point will be reached where $pU(L_0) = U(S)$. Beyond this point, the individual should prefer the risky alternative over fair insurance. In Figure 7.2, this intersection lies between S_2 and S_3.

Again, although a preference reversal is a sufficient condition for at least one inflection point, it is not a necessary condition. A utility function can be constructed that is concave and then convex between 0 and L_0, but that never falls below $pU(L_0)$.

Finally, consider the case in which p is held constant. Figure 7.3 illustrates two such choice situations in which p is fixed at some value, p_0. For the first choice, $S_1 = p_0L_1$; for the second choice, $S_2 = p_0L_2$. The expected utility for the first lottery, $p_0U(L_1)$, equals u_1. The expected utility for the second lottery corresponds to u_3. In both cases, insurance should be preferred because $u_0 > u_1$ and $u_2 > u_3$. Once again, preference reversals need not occur even though an inflection point between zero and L_2 does exist. However, if a reversal occurs, it would imply the existence of at least one inflection point.

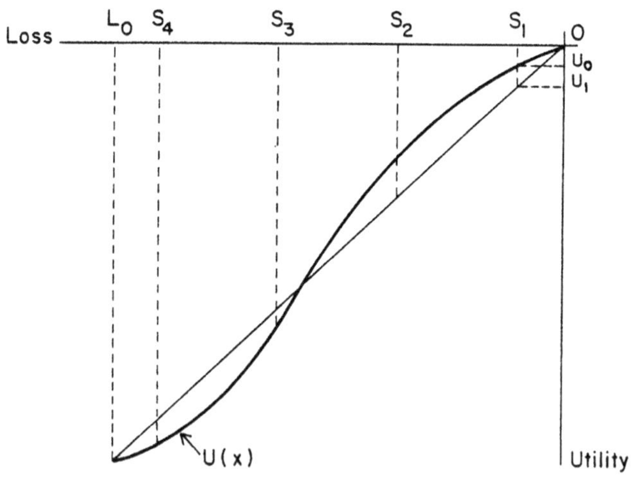

Figure 7.2. EU Analysis: Keeping the Loss Constant

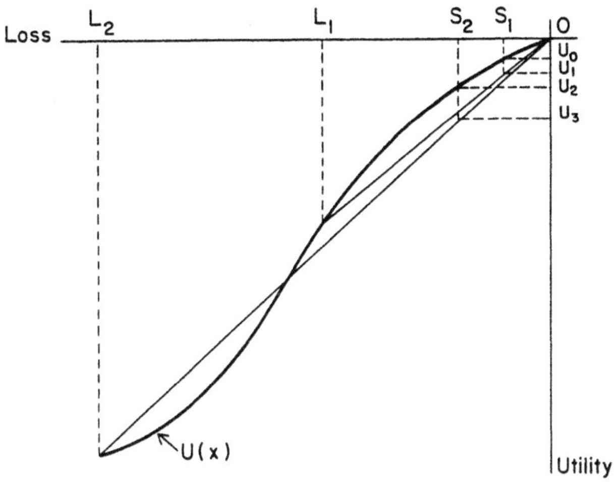

Figure 7.3. EU Analysis: Keeping the Probability Constant

7.2.2 The Influence of Problem Context

The second major hypothesis of this chapter is that the context in which a problem is presented significantly affects the extent of observed risk taking. As an example, consider the following two choice situations:

1. You stand a p chance of losing $|L|$ dollars.
   You will lose $|S|$ dollars with certainty.
2. You stand a p chance of losing $|L|$ dollars.
   You can buy insurance for $|S|$ dollars to protect you from this loss.

Ignoring taxes and assuming that $S = pL$, these situations are statistically identical, both offering actuarially fair alternatives. From a utility viewpoint, each situation involves a comparison of $U(w_0 + S)$ with $[pU(w_0 + L) + (1 - p)U(w_0)]$, with w_0 representing the customary financial position. Psychologically, however, these two situations may be quite different. In the first, the certainty of being in a losing situation is highlighted, whereas in the second, it might appear that something is to be gained (i.e., protection). Such a shift in reference point would be predicted from prospect theory.

Additionally, the problem context may evoke a different psychological set or internal problem representation in each situation. For example, social norms about prudent behavior are more likely to operate in the second situation, whereas the first expresses an implicit acceptance of the gambling nature of the choice. Hence, the second hypothesis is that problem formulation and context significantly affect risk taking for losses. More specifically, it is predicted that an insurance context will evoke more risk-averse behavior because of a shift in reference point and/or favorable societal norms toward insurance.

The third hypothesis is that the strength of the context effect varies across levels of probability and loss. An interaction is predicted because certain levels of p and L are more likely than other levels to be associated with regular insurance buying. To the extent that social norms play a role, the effect should be largest in situations that most resemble real-world insurance purchases. These are typically situations in which the hazards involve relatively high losses and relatively low probabilities, although they may not be known exactly.

7.3 THE EXPERIMENT

To assess the extent of risk taking, a series of eighteen questions was used. Each question required a choice between two unfavorable alternatives. The "risky" alternative involved a loss of $|L|$ dollars with probability p. The "safe" alternative involved the loss of $|S|$ dollars with certainty, with S always equaling the expected loss pL of the risky alternative. The eighteen questions consisted of three sets corresponding to Figures 7.1, 7.2, and 7.3. The first set kept S constant at $-\$10$ while varying p and L. The second set kept L constant at $-\$10{,}000$ while varying p and S. The third set kept p constant at .01 while varying L and S. In each question, subjects were asked to indicate which alternative they would prefer if they had to choose. However, subjects were also allowed to indicate indifference between the two alternatives. Table 7.1 lists the p, L, and S values for these eighteen questions (see also Appendix VII).

To examine the influence of the problem's formulation, the three sets of questions were presented either in an insurance context or in the context of a "pure gamble" as illustrated earlier. Hence, the experimental design involved two levels of a context-treatment factor to which subjects were randomly assigned. In addition to subjects' risk preferences, information was obtained on age, sex, wealth, and knowledge of statistical concepts.

Subjects. The subjects of the experiment were eighty-two M.B.A. students who were taking an introductory quantitative methods course at the Wharton School. The questionnaire was administered at the beginning of the course, before any discussion of probability and risk took place. The course is a required one for M.B.A. students who do not have a strong background in quantitative thinking. It is waived for about 35 percent of each entering class. Thus, in comparison to other Wharton M.B.A. students, the respondents were below average in quantitative background. The median age of the subjects was twenty-five. About half were female. Their mean wealth was about $15,000 (with a median of $6,000). Less than 7 percent indicated that they were familiar with the concept of expected utility. There were no statistical differences in age, sex, wealth, or knowledge of expected utility theory between the two subject groups (i.e., between those receiving the insurance version and those receiving the gamble version).

Method. The two versions of the questionnaire were randomly distributed during a regular class hour. Subjects were informed that there were no right or wrong answers and that each question should be answered without regard to previous questions or to those yet to come. It was emphasized that even though the questions were hypothetical, subjects should try to answer each question as if it were real. It was stressed that the subjects' responses, which would be anonymous, had no relation to the course they were taking. The experiment lasted about twenty minutes. There was no time pressure.

7.4 RESULTS

Table 7.1 shows the percentage of respondents who chose the safe alternative for each of the eighteen questions. Separate percentages are shown for the subjects given the insurance format and those given the gamble format. Of those given the insurance format, the percentage choosing the safe alternative never went beyond 80.5 percent. Of those given the gamble format, the percentage choosing the safe alternative never surpassed 63.4 percent. In many cases, fewer than 50 percent of the subjects chose the safe alternative. These results confirm the findings of Slovic et al. (1977), as well as those reported in Chapter 4, regarding significant risk taking in the domain of losses.

In these questionnaires, three questions (1, 3, and 8) were repeated at a later point, thus providing a test of within-subject consistency of preference. The results showed that 13.4 percent reversed preference between Questions 1 and 7 (even though these questions were identical); 17 percent reversed between Questions 3 and 15; and 17 percent reversed between Questions 8 and 16. Interestingly, these three types of reversals did not usually involve the same individuals. About 42 percent of the subjects changed preference at least once with respect to the repeated questions. These results confirm those of other empirical studies (Lee, 1971; Mosteller and Nogee, 1951) that have suggested that preferences can change from one moment to the next and must therefore be interpreted stochastically. As long as the stochastic noise consists of reasonably random, symmetric error terms, large samples should wash out the random disturbances, uncovering any stochastic preference that might exist across different *p-L* combinations.

In the remainder of our discussion of results, we will focus first on the extent of risk taking in the domain of losses. We will then turn our attention to the influence of problem context and the hypothesized interaction between the context effect and the levels of *p* and *L*.

7.4.1 Insurance Preferences

The results examined here concern the forty-one subjects who received the insurance version of the questionnaire. Figure 7.4(*a*) shows the findings from the first six questions.[4] This set corresponds to some of the questions of Slovic et al. (1977) if an "exchange rate" of 1 point to $10 is assumed.[5] This design was used to obtain more realistic loss magnitudes than could be obtained with an exchange rate of 1 point to $1.

Figure 7.4(*a*) reveals single peakedness. It shows a curve opposite to that reported by Slovic et al. (see Figure 7.5). In the present experiment, more people preferred insurance for low-probability, high-loss events than for high-probability, low-loss events. When individual preference patterns were analyzed, it was found that 66 percent of the subjects chose fair insurance for all six questions or for some subset of the least likely losses (e.g., Question 1; Questions 1 and 2; Questions 1, 2, and 3, etc.). This finding is in marked contrast to the results of Slovic et al., which showed only 19 percent of the subjects exhibiting such preference patterns.

How can these results be reconciled with those of Slovic et al.? One explanation is differences in subjects. To test this possibility, a small additional experiment was run (lasting about ten minutes). Its forty-five subjects were students in another section of the same course taken by the subjects of the larger experiment.[6] These subjects received exactly the same questionnaire used by Slovic et al.[7] Figure 7.5 shows the results of this replication, together with the original curve of Slovic et al. Remarkably, there were no significant (prob. > .05) differences between these two curves for any of the questions.[8] This striking similarity suggests that differences in the ques-

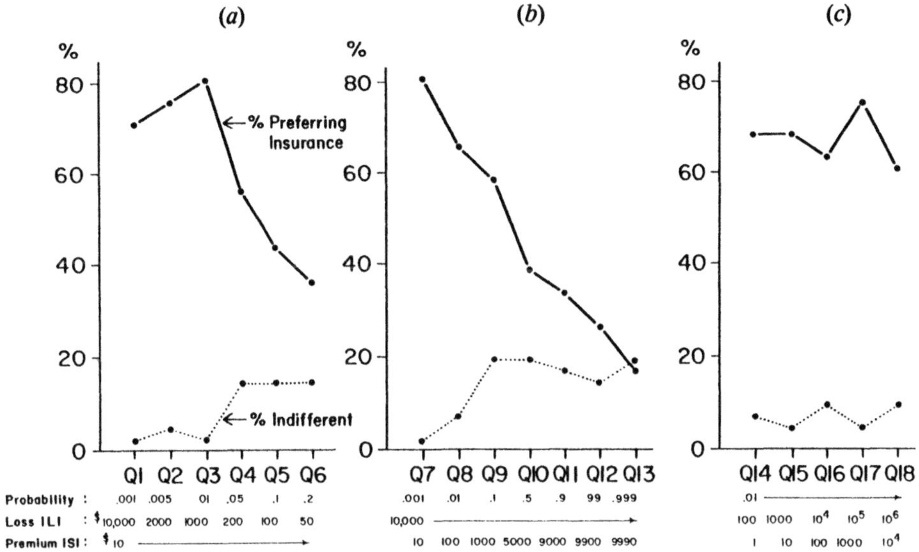

Figure 7.4. Preferences for Insurance: (*a*) when *S* is held constant; (*b*) when *L* is held constant; (*c*) when *p* is held constant. For all three figures, the solid curves denote the percentages preferring insurance; the dotted curves the percentages being indifferent.

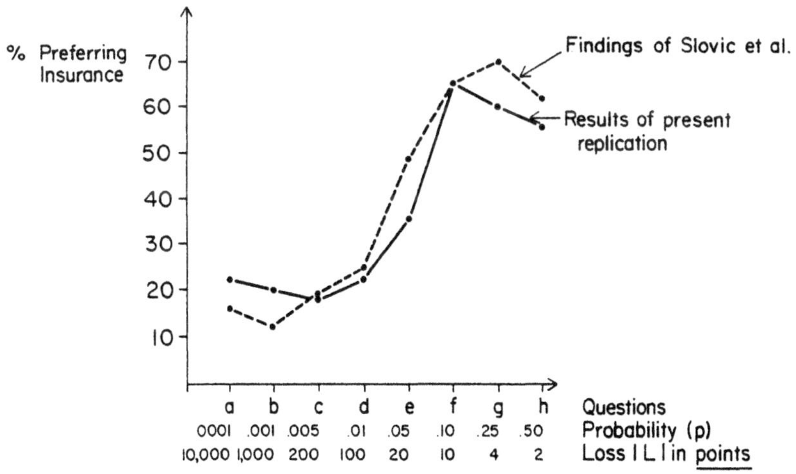

Figure 7.5. Partial Replication of the Study of Slovic et al. (1977)

tionnaires, rather than subject differences, underlie the discrepancies between Figure 7.4(*a*) and the results of Slovic et al.

Thus, one explanation might be that the internal problem representations of the subjects in the present experiment differed from those of the subjects of Slovic et al. because of differences in the contexts of the questions. For example, the subjects of Slovic et al. were asked to protect themselves from losses of abstract points. Furthermore, their instruction "to lose as little as possible" may have evoked different objectives than did the present questions, in which subjects were asked in which situation they would prefer to be if they had to choose. Finally, the exchange rate of 1 point to $10 might yield a different curve than an exchange rate of 1 point to $1. It will be shown later, however, that this last possibility is unlikely, which points to context differences as the underlying cause.[9] Since the present questions involved single events and dollar losses (as opposed to multiple urns and undefined points), the context of this experiment may more closely resemble real-world insurance decisions, leaving the upward-sloping curve of Slovic et al. open to question.

Regarding the shape of $U(x)$, Figure 7.4(*a*) shows a preference peak around Question 3, which suggests the existence of an inflection point. Nevertheless, only 10 percent of the subjects actually changed preference from gambling to insurance in going from Question 1 to Question 3. However, this latter circumstance, as noted earlier, does not imply the nonexistence of an inflection point. The hyperbolic intersection of the p-L plane examined in the first set of questions may have been at such a level that inflection points were not readily observable. Thus, to provide a better test for the possible existence of an inflection point, a second set of questions was examined. This set corresponds to Figure 7.2.

Figure 7.4(*b*) shows the results of the next set of questions (7 through 13), in which L was fixed at –$10,000 and the probability of loss p was varied from .001 to .999. The preference for fair insurance decreased monotonically from Question 7 through Question 13. Fair insurance was most attractive when it protected against a low-probability event at a low premium and was least attractive when it protected against a high-probability event (at a fair high premium).

An analysis of individual preference patterns showed that of the thirty-two subjects who preferred insurance in Question 7, thirty-one (or 97 percent) either switched preferences or became indifferent in some of the next six questions. Such changes can *only* occur (within the EU framework) if there is at least one inflection point in $U(x)$. Furthermore, only 5 percent of all the subjects exhibited behavior consistent with a convex utility function — namely, rejecting insurance for all seven questions.

Hence, the results at both the aggregate and individual levels support the first hypothesis that people are neither purely risk-averse nor purely risk-taking for losses. Instead, when analyzed from an EU perspective, their preferences imply the existence of at least one inflection point. Since simultaneous increases of p and $|S|$ lead to more risk-seeking behavior, Markowitz's function of first a concave and then a convex segment offers a good first approximation.

Figure 7.4(*c*) shows the results of the third set of questions. In this set, the probability of loss was fixed at .01, while the potential loss itself was varied from $100 to $1 million. These results are surprising in that they show a relatively constant preference for insurance when $p = .01$. Because predominantly risk-seeking behavior was observed in the second set of questions as S approached −$10,000, one would expect that most subjects would also prefer the risky alternative for Question 18, in which $S = -\$10{,}000$ and $L = -\$1$ million. To the contrary, however, fully 70.8 percent of the subjects indicated a preference for insurance or were indifferent for Question 18. This apparent inconsistency also appears when analyzing individual responses. Of the twenty-six subjects who preferred the risky alternative for Question 13, over half reversed preference to the safe alternative in Question 18.

What explanation might there be for this substantial reversal in risk attitude? One possibility is that many subjects have a second inflection point in $U(x)$ over losses, beyond which they again become risk-averse. Such a utility function, however, has not been proposed in the literature of insurance or finance and seems contrary to what introspection suggests. Instead, two other explanations of this change in risk preference are proposed. One is the influence of problem context on choices, which is discussed more fully in the next section. It will be shown that questions posed in an insurance context, when p is small and $|L|$ is large, evoke significantly greater risk aversion than do these same questions posed in the context of a pure gamble. For example, only 29.3 percent of the subjects who were given the gamble version of Question 18 chose the safe alternative. This percentage is significantly (prob. $< .01$) lower than the percentage of subjects given the insurance version who preferred insurance protection for Question 18. Furthermore, of the twenty-nine subjects with the pure gamble format who preferred the risky alternative for Question 13, only 24 percent switched preferences for Question 18. Again, this percentage is significantly (prob. $< .02$) lower than the corresponding percentage of the other subjects who switched.

As a second explanation for the observed discrepancies, consider the overweighting of low probabilities as suggested by Karmarkar (1978) and

Kahneman and Tversky (1979). The phenomenon of overweighting suggests that for low probabilities, fair insurance becomes more attractive. Such an effect would result in more risk-averse behavior for large losses and low probabilities — behavior that Figure 7.4(*c*) in fact illustrates. Thus, the large preference for insurance in Question 18 can be reconciled with the risk-taking tendencies observed in Questions 12 and 13 by assuming overweighting of low probabilities and underweighting of high ones. The latter favors risk-taking attitudes in Questions 12 and 13.

Finally, note that Figure 7.4(*c*) provides an opportunity to test one possible explanation (which we noted earlier) of the discrepancy between the results shown in Figure 7.4(*a*) and those of Slovic et al. (as duplicated in Figure 7.5). It appears that the exchange rate of 1 point to $10 does not significantly affect the results. To understand this conclusion, one must realize that Question *d* of Slovic et al. corresponds to this experiment's Questions 14 through 18 if one assumes exchange rates of $1, $10, $100, $1,000, and $10,000, respectively. While less than 20 percent of the subjects in the study of Slovic et al. (and in the replication of that study) chose insurance for their Question *d*, more than 60 percent of the subjects in this experiment chose insurance for Questions 14 through 18. Indeed, the most plausible exchange rate of 1 point to $1 yielded the same percentage as the exchange rate of 1 point to $10. Apparently, the differences in results are not due to differences in the exchange rate.

7.4.2 The Effect of Context

All the findings discussed above were based on questions posed in an insurance context. Chapter 5, however, suggested that the problem's context (particularly the context of insurance versus that of pure gamble) makes a difference. The hypothesis was that subjects will be more averse to risk when presented with insurance formulations than when presented with pure gamble formulations. In this study, both types of formulations were used with different subjects.

Figure 7.6 compares the responses of the subjects who received the insurance questions with the responses of those who received the gamble questions. The solid curves denote the preferences for fair insurance of those using the insurance formulation; the dashed curves indicate the percentage of subjects who preferred the sure loss over the risky alternative when the pure gamble formulation was employed.

As noted earlier, the two subject groups did not differ significantly (prob. > .2) with respect to age, sex, wealth, knowledge of expected utility theory, or the use of intuition in making decisions. However, there were sig-

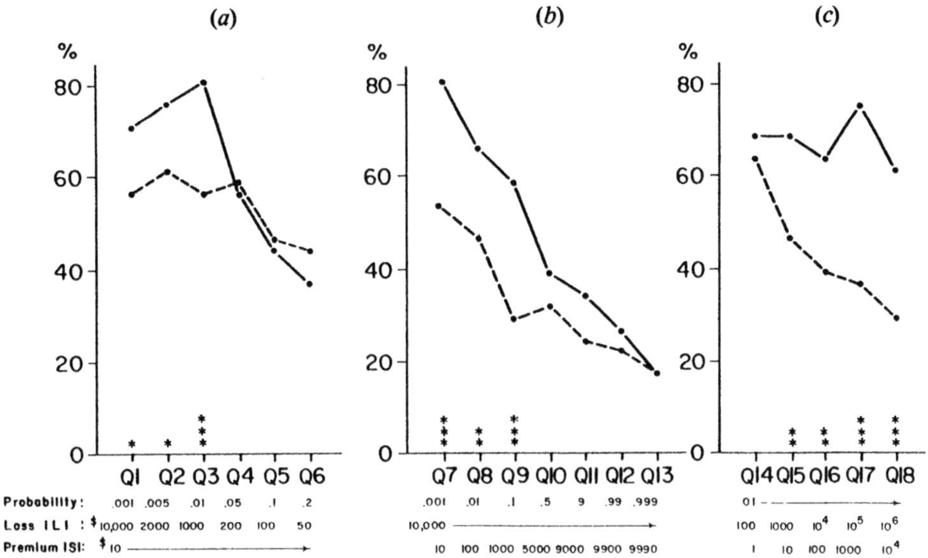

Figure 7.6. The Effect of Context: (*a*) keeping *S* constant; (*b*) keeping *L* constant; (*c*) keeping *p* constant. For all three figures, the solid curves denote the percentage of subjects using an insurance formulation who preferred insurance; the dashed curves indicate this percentage for those using a gamble formulation. The number of asterisks indicates whether the percentage difference was significant at the .1 (*), .05 (**), or .01 (***) level.

nificant differences (prob. < .05) regarding knowledge of the concepts of expected value and random variable. Because subjects randomly received either the insurance or gamble questionnaire, these differences must have been the result of sampling error. However, as statistical knowledge did not influence risk preferences within each group, we can assume that there were no between-group differences either.

The results clearly show that for many questions, problem context significantly affected risk-taking propensity. Questions for which statistically significant differences were observed are noted in Figure 7.6 by means of asterisks. In all such cases, the insurance formulation led to more risk-averse behavior, which supports this study's second hypothesis.

The differential impact of the context influence relates to the third hypothesis, which predicted the effect to be largest for realistic insurance situations. The evidence strongly indicates a significant interaction between the context effect and levels of probability and loss; furthermore, in each situation presented in Figure 7.6, this interaction is in the predicted direction. The significant differences occurred in those questions for which the potential loss was large enough to be of consequence ($L \leq -\$1{,}000$) and the probability low enough to evoke an insurance atmosphere ($p \leq .1$).

7.5 CONCLUSIONS

The present experiment examined preferences for basic loss lotteries and showed that risk taking in the domain of losses is quite prevalent.[10] However, the findings are not consistent with those of Slovic et al. (1977), who proposed a convex utility function for $.001 \leq p \leq .25$. Instead, the present findings suggest that a utility function that is concave for low losses and convex for larger ones can explain part of the results. Although this function was first suggestd by Markowitz in 1952, it has not received much attention in the literature of finance or insurance.

On the other hand, the findings are not entirely consistent with a Markowitz type of NM utility function either. An examination of low probabilities and very high loss lotteries indicates discrepancies with risk-taking attitudes revealed in earlier questions. Reconciliations would involve either the assumption of multiple inflection points or, as was suggested earlier, the overweighting of low probabilities and the underweighting of large ones. This phenomenon of probability bias has been reported in several other empirical studies, the most recent being Handa's (1977), Karmarkar's (1978) on the subjectively weighted utility model, and Kahneman and Tversky's (1979) on prospect theory.

The present investigation of risk taking adds to previous literature in that it examined several cross sections of the p-L plane rather than just hyperbolic ones for which pL is constant. Although these different cross sections present only a partial picture of the risk-taking surface across the p-L plane, they point toward the existence of at least one inflection point in $U(x)$ and, hence, at least one preference peak in the insurance-preference surface across this plane.

A second important set of findings, which is much more damaging to EU theory, concerns the pervasiveness of the context effect in which insurance formulations lead to more risk-averse behavior than do statistically equivalent gamble formulations. Although such an effect was first observed in the study described in Chapter 5, the study described in this chapter differed from the earlier study in several important ways. First, the questions did not focus on deductibles, but on premiums. Second, the choices were much simpler, in terms both of the number of alternatives and their consequences. Third, the formats were identical in each of the two contexts, whereas both the context and presentation were changed in the study in Chapter 5.

Fourth, the effect was examined over various *p-L* combinations. Finally, a between-subject design was used.

In addition to the pervasiveness of the context effect in the face of the simple choice situations examined in this study, a significant interaction was observed between the strength of the effect and the levels of p and L. It seems reasonable to conjecture that a *p-L* combination exists for which the context effect would be strongest. However, it is not clear how deviations from this "optimum" along either the p or L dimension influence the effect, which suggests the need for additional research.

In conclusion, it appears that traditional Von Neumann-Morgenstern utility theory does not offer adequate explanation of risk preference for losses, even though utility functions with one or more inflection points could explain some of the data. Instead, the recently advanced prospect theory of Kahneman and Tversky (1979) and Karmarkar's (1978) theory may offer more insight. In prospect theory, the value function over losses is convex. In both theories, there is underweighting of high probabilities and overweighting of low ones. Hence, these theories would predict either risk aversion or risk taking, depending on the *p-L* values and the exact shapes of the value and probability functions.

Finally, it should be noted that neither expected utility theory, nor Handa's (1977) CE theory, nor subjectively weighted utility theory can account for the context effects observed in this study. The effect, however, is predicted by prospect theory as a result of a shift in the reference point (Kahneman and Tversky, 1979, p. 287). As Slovic et al. remarked in their discussion of the issue, "Subtle changes in problem formulation can have marked effects upon risk taking and insurance decisions" (1977, p. 256). The normative implication of the context effect observed here is that utility functions should be constructed under various contexts. Discrepancies could be shown to the decision maker, and revision of preferences might be desired. In that case, however, whether one would still be measuring basic taste and preferences is open to question. From a descriptive viewpoint, the context effect indicates the importance of modeling for problem representation before modeling for choice. It seems that the insurance context and the gamble context evoke problem representations in which different risk-taking attitudes are deemed appropriate. To understand this influence of context on the coefficients of the utility function (or possibly its functional form) requires deeper knowledge of the psychology of problem representation in general. Finally, it is reasonable to conjecture that the context effect will be stronger yet in real-world situations in which probabilities and outcomes are not known with certainty. In those situations, probabilities and outcomes will be of less usefulness in arriving at a decision, which will thereby enhance the influence of context.

8 EPILOGUE

The research of this book has focused on the expected utility hypothesis. This hypothesis consists of two parts: (1) People's basic tastes and preferences for lotteries are compatible with the Von Neumann-Morgenstern (1947) axioms; thus, they can be represented via a well-behaved cardinal utility function. (2) People's behavior in more complex decision situations can be modeled by assuming that individuals act as if they maximize expected utility. The four research studies described in this book have bearing on both components of the EU hypothesis. They should therefore be of interest to a wide audience comprised of persons who have descriptive, as well as normative, interests in EU theory.

Whether a reader indeed finds the present results interesting would depend much on his or her prior beliefs about the two components of the EU hypothesis. As Davis (1971) has argued persuasively, the interest of research (and information in general) increases as it disconfirms prior beliefs. Wherever one has stood regarding either of the two aspects of the EU hypothesis, the results described in this book should give rise to some adjustment of belief, probably in an unfavorable direction. To assist in the revision of beliefs about the EU hypothesis, the next section highlights the major results of the four research studies. Thereafter, a conceptual framework for integrating this research is developed. In the final section, discussion centers on directions for a general theory of decision under risk, together with potentially fruitful avenues of future research.

8.1 GENERAL FINDINGS

Chapter 4 subjected the EU hypothesis to a positivistic test, evaluating the theory on the basis of its predictive power. The task involved a choice between information on true probabilities versus true outcomes. The computational complexity of this choice was high, representative of the real world about which EU theory is purported to make predictions (as an "as-if" model). It was analytically determined what information an EU maximizer should prefer. Concavity of $U(x)$ on the relevant positive payoff interval was shown to be a sufficient condition for preferring information on the true probabilities. Sixty-two subjects were tested and classified as risk-averse, risk-seeking, or mixed on the payoff intervals examined. Subjects' preferences for information were compared with those predicted from EU theory. The general finding was that EU theory did not predict better than chance. Additional violations of EU were found with respect to narrowing the probability ranges and increasing the number of urns. Hence, Chapter 4 presents strong falsifying evidence for the second component of the EU hypothesis.

Chapter 5 described an experimental insurance study whose subjects were 200 undergraduate students and 100 clients of an insurance agency; the latter had all purchased some insurance voluntarily (i.e., insurance not required by law or contract). A main finding of this study was that substantial proportions of the subjects (around 50 percent) would rather be exposed to low-probability, high-loss hazards than to high-probability, low-loss hazards when the two expected losses are equal. This finding refutes the traditional assumption of risk aversion for losses.

The extent of risk taking for losses was influenced by financial status and decision-making style. Respondents who were better off financially were generally more risk-averse. Those who were intuitive (as compared with analytical) tended to be less often indifferent between hazards with equal expected loss. Statistical knowledge increased the propensity of subjects to use analytical decision rules, even for very simple lotteries.

Various insurance questions involving deductibles also revealed considerable risk taking. At the same time, strong preferences were found for insurance policies with zero deductibles, even though such policies were much more expensive than those with small deductibles, which suggests strong risk aversion. The importance of the problem's context and presentation was highlighted when making changes that, from an EU perspective, were inconsequential. For example, insurance policies with low deductibles were perceived as more attractive when presented with an insurance context than when presented without, in spite of the mathematical equivalence of these two choice situations. Similarly, about 50 percent of the student and client groups judged comprehensive insurance to be more attractive than three separate policies that offered exactly the same coverage; about 30 percent found the comprehensive policy more attractive. According to EU theory, these alternatives should be equally attractive. Such context effects appear to be symptomatic of people's tendency to resort to simplifying strategies. These effects, however, are not recognized in the EU model.

Chapter 6 explored further the effect of statistical knowledge on decisions under risk. The research examined the extent to which such knowledge causes people to evaluate gambles multiplicatively rather than additively. Findings in favor of the former method would be compatible with EU theory. The task involved the evaluation of so-called duplex gambles. The findings of this study were that statistical knowledge reduces the mental difficulties of processing probabilities and outcomes and leads to decisions of higher quality. For example, statistically trained subjects were considerably more consistent on repeat gambles than were untrained subjects. The former tended to compute expected values much more frequently than did untrained subjects and were generally more able to focus on all four dimensions of the duplex bets. Regression analyses suggested that statistically trained subjects employ multiplicative models much more frequently than untrained subjects do. Furthermore, the former's decision rules were generally more programmable, possibly because the decision rules were more analytical.

The findings of Chapter 6 are unfavorable to the EU hypothesis in that they suggest additive information-processing strategies for untrained subjects. Since most decision tasks in the real world are more complex than duplex bets, and since most people have little statistical training, the likelihood of modeling behavior successfully from multiplicative theories seems very low.

Chapter 7 has direct bearing on the first component of the EU hypothesis. Although earlier chapters established risk taking, as well as risk aversion, for losses and a strong influence of context, it was not clear whether the effects would be present in the simple lotteries needed to construct the NM utility index. If they were, it would have direct implications for the normative status of EU theory. The task involved choosing between a simple lottery (p, L) and a sure loss (S) of equal expected value. Various p, L, and S combinations were examined.

The general finding was that people's basic tastes and preferences for losses cannot be represented with utility functions having less than two inflection points below zero, or without introducing overweighting of low probabilities and underweighting of high ones. Furthermore, utility functions constructed in an insurance context differ systematically from those derived from standard lottery questions. The formal equivalency of these two contexts implies some degree of indeterminacy in people's basic tastes and preferences for risk.

8.2 AN INTEGRATIVE FRAMEWORK

The findings summarized in the preceding section concern various types of influences on people's preferences. The present section offers a framework for classifying these different effects. It distinguishes between individual, task, and context factors.

The first group, or subsystem, consists of all influences that are specific to the decision maker (i.e., individual differences). The second subsystem contains all task-related factors that, according to normative theory, *ought* to play a role, while the third group comprises all influences that *should have no effect* and are not individual factors. These three subsystems constitute the independent variables in the framework and are discussed in more detail below. The general aim is to conceptualize variations in decision models (i.e., mathematical representations of the stimuli-response transformations) as a function of the aforementioned subsystems and to introduce concepts appropriate to such analyses.

8.2.1 The Dependent Variable

The dependent variable in the present framework is the type of selected decision model. Each possible decision model is considered to be a member of a set containing all types. This set constitutes the dependent variable, which can be a qualitative, nominal measure for the purpose of categorizing decision models or a variable scaled by the relative simplicity of the model. Decision models are defined as mathematical representations of how objectively stated inputs (e.g., probabilities and outcomes) are translated into responses (deterministically or stochastically).

The method for identifying a decision model and its parameters may be theoretical, statistical, related to protocol, or otherwise. The criterion for inferring which of several decision models best represents the decisions made could be its predictive power or its features as judged from an information-processing perspective. Clearly, trade-offs between parsimony and psychological realism are subjective. This author's preference is somewhat lexicographic: for a given task, identify the models that best predict or fit the data; next select from within that class of models the one that appears psychologically most reasonable. For example, $y_1 = x_1 + x_2$ has the same explanatory and predictive power as

$$y_2 = \sqrt{x_1^2 + x_2^2 + 2x_1^2x_2^2}, \text{ which is simply } \sqrt{y_1^2}.$$

However, the first model is probably more acceptable psychologically because of its greater computational simplicity. In any case, let it be assumed that a set of competing decision models exists. For a given task, these decision models may differ from each other in two basic ways:

1. With respect to their functional form (i.e., the manner in which different inputs are algebraically combined — linearly, multiplicatively, exponentially, or otherwise — to give an output value).
2. With respect to the weights given to the different components of the algebraic form (i.e., the coefficients or weights in the mapping function).

If a weight changes to zero, it would constitute a change in functional form, as models could otherwise never differ in functional form. Only models having identical functional forms can be meaningfully compared in terms of the relative importance of different input variables (e.g., as controlled by an experimenter). Two decision models are said to be identical if, and only if, their functional forms and weights coincide. In the present context, the term *model* is defined much more narrowly than before when speaking of the EU model or the additive model. In its broader meaning, it denotes a class of functional forms sharing some unifying characteristic (e.g., mean-risk models) or one specific functional form with unspecified coefficient values (e.g., the additive model). It will be clear from the context, however, in what connotation the term *model* is used.

8.2.2 The Independent Variables

As mentioned earlier, the factors influencing the choice of a decision model are grouped into three mutually exclusive and exhaustive categories (or subsystems). These are (1) the set of factors specific to the individual; (2) the set of factors specific to the task; and (3) the set of factors specific to the environment or context of the task.

If variations in decisions or preferences are observed across individuals for a constant task and in a constant environment, then these variations are due to individual factors. Examples of such factors are socioeconomic variables, motivational or attitudinal variables, and cognitive variables (pertaining to a person's information-processing abilities).

The task subsystem consists of all those input variables that, according to traditional normative theories of risky decision making (i.e., expected utility theory and Bayesian analysis), *should* play a role in the decision process. The notion of "playing a role" can be expressed more formally by stating that the variable must have some mathematical representation in the decision model (normatively). Examples of factors belonging to the task subsystem are probability and payoff variables, constraints on the set of alternatives, constraints on decision resources (time, computational capacity, storage capacity, etc.), and cost variables as these relate to objective and measurable costs of the decision process (opportunity costs of time and other resources, computing costs, etc.). Psychological costs (pertaining to the cognitive strain of decision making) are excluded from the task subsystem as they are included in the individual factors. Furthermore, constraints on cognitive ability are also part of the individual subsystem. However, objective constraints on time and computational resources are part of the task subsystem to the extent that they have formal recognition in normative decision models and are not specific to an individual decision maker.

The third subsystem consists of all those factors that potentially exert influence on the choice of a decision model and that are not individual or task variables. Examples of such context variables are carry-over effects, presentation formats (e.g., the sequence in which information is presented), response modes, concreteness versus abstractness of the task (as in Chapter 5), feedback mechanisms, location, experimenter, and so on. Hence, context factors are influences on choice models that do not pertain to individual differences or task variables and that should (normatively speaking) have *no effect* on decision models.

8.2.3 The Mapping Function

Having defined three mutually exclusive and exhaustive subsystems of influences on decision making under risk, we will now examine how the factors of these subsystems may influence decision models. For notational convenience, let I represent the set of individual factors, T the set of task factors, and C the set of context variables. Furthermore, let X_i represent a member of one of the sets in which X equals I, T, or C.

Next define a function (F) that maps for a given decision situation into a range (R), the elements of which represent decision models. The domain of F consists of the union of I, T, and C. R is a set containing all possible functional forms that subjects could use. For a given subject (i), define a subset (R_i) containing all functional forms that subject i could use. Similarly, F_i denotes the specific mapping function of subject i.

In a controlled experiment in which only one of the independent variables (X_i) is varied, there are three possible effects on the decision model:[1]

1. No effect on the functional form.
2. A change in the weights (or coefficients) of the functional form.
3. A change in the functional form itself.

If X_i represents (numerically) a given quantity, then denote the values of X_i for which changes in weights occur as minor critical values and the values at which changes in functional form occur as major critical values. Since the minor and major critical values of X_i may be a function of the levels at which the other independent variables are controlled, it is worthwhile to identify only those critical values that are relatively stable across control levels.

Figure 8.1 provides a graphic representation of the variables in this framework. It depicts the domain (consisting of the three subsystems), the range (consisting of model types), and the mapping function (F_i). The solid lines in Figure 8.1 denote a case in which, for given levels of individual, task, and context factors, individual i selected decision model M_1. The figure only depicts the influence of a few variables.

For example, I_1 could represent the subject's statistical knowledge; I_2 the wealth level; T_1 a probability variable; T_2 an outcome variable; C_1 the response mode (e.g., bidding versus ranking); and C_2 whether the experiment involves hypothetical or real payoffs. The dotted lines depict a case (involving the same variables) in which model M_2 was selected. This could have come about because C_1 assumed a different value or level (e.g., going from bidding to ranking).

Figure 8.2 depicts how a given independent variable can influence the weights (corresponding to minor critical values) or the functional forms (corresponding to major critical values) of a decision model. The figure illustrates such critical values for the task variable P_ℓ (the probability of losing) in the context of a duplex experiment. If all variables except P_ℓ are held constant, we find, for this example, that the subject will use model M_1 if $.5 < P_\ell < 1$. Furthermore, the figure shows that the subject will use M_2 if $.1 < P_\ell < .5$, and M_3 for P_ℓ values below .1. Since M_1 and M_2 differ only in

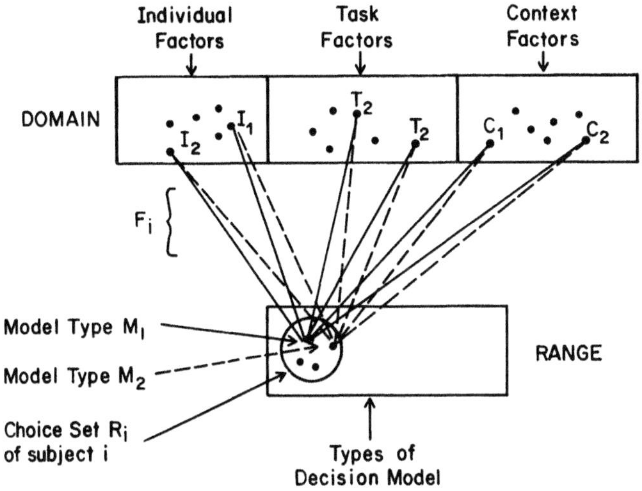

Figure 8.1. Graphic Illustration of the Conceptual Framework

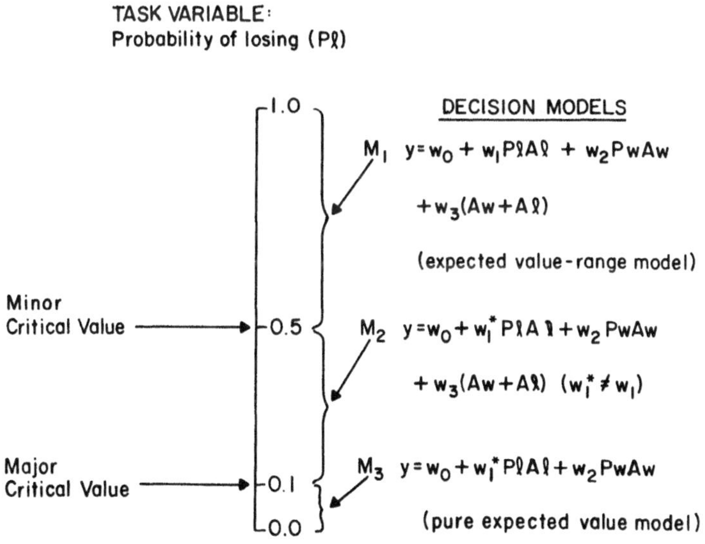

Figure 8.2. Minor and Major Critical Values

weights, $P_\ell = .5$ constitutes a minor critical value. However, because M_2 and M_3 differ in functional form, $P_\ell = .1$ represents a major critical value. To the extent that these critical values are stable across different control levels for P_w, A_w, and A_ℓ, an analysis of the type suggested in Figure 8.2 will be meaningful.

8.2.4 The Present Research

Casting the four studies of this book into the framework just outlined, Chapter 4 should be viewed as concerned with task factors only. The preferences for lotteries and types of information observed were proved to be incompatible with any functional form belonging to the class of monotonic expected utility models. Furthermore, variations in the task variable of "probability range" led to response changes counter to any deterministic monotonic EU model, as did variations in the number of urns.

The insurance study of Chapter 5 examined the influence of individual, task, and context factors. The individual factors included financial status, decision-making style, and self-assessed personality variables. The specific task variables studied were probabilities, premiums, deductibles, and loss levels. The context variables involved problem format and problem formulation.

Although both context factors affected choices, it could not be determined where, or if, critical values existed, because the variables assumed only two values (i.e., the control and the treatment level), with only one observation for each. The location of critical values and corresponding stability analyses would, of course, require more observations.

Chapter 6 examined the effect of the individual factor of "statistical training" on the decision model. It was found that this factor possesses at least one major critical value in that trained and untrained subjects used different decision models. Again, the locations of the critical values could not be determined because only two levels of the training factor were studied.

Finally, Chapter 7 focused on both task and context factors. The influence of the task variables of probability, loss, and premium was judged to be incompatible with a functional form, $y = \Sigma p_i U(x_i)$, where $U(x)$ is monotonic and has less than two inflection points below zero (assuming $U(0) = 0$). It was concluded that the results could be explained from the function $y = \Sigma f(p_i) U(x_i)$, where $f(p)$ is counter S-shaped and $U(x)$ has one inflection point for negative x.

The context factors examined involved the problem's formulations. Although the two formulation types produced different responses, it could not be ascertained whether changes in weights or functional forms were involved.

8.3 TOWARD A GENERAL THEORY

Although many previous studies on decision making under risk have sought to uncover the general nature of the function *F*, which maps probabilities and outcomes into responses, it appears that the specifics of such a function may be overshadowed by the influence that the larger problem context exerts on responses. As shown in Chapter 7, a change in context (from an insurance to a gamble formulation) may evoke a change in preference for fair insurance of the same magnitude as an increase in the probability of loss from .001 (Question 7) to somewhere between .1 (Question 9) and .5 (Question 10). For example, in Figure 7.6(*b*), each of these manipulations reduced the preference for fair insurance from about 80 percent to about 54 percent. Hence, a first component of a general descriptive theory should be to model and to explain how decisions are framed and represented psychologically.

Very much related to the component of problem representation is the role of aspiration levels. Although their importance has been noted (e.g., Siegel, 1957; Starbuck, 1963), traditional models characterize acts by probability distributions over final wealth levels without acknowledging a discontinuity in utility at the payoff level that separates losses from gains psychologically. Although this point may be the status quo, it need not be. For example, losing \$150 in a gambling casino when the budgeted loss for the evening was \$200 might be viewed as a \$50 gain and treated much differently from \$50 left after having already lost \$220. Various recent theories have attempted to incorporate some notion of aspiration levels by introducing a discontinuity in the utility function at the point of psychological neutrality. For example, in prospect theory (Kahneman and Tversky, 1979), gains are modeled as having decreasing marginal value, and losses as having increasing marginal value. Similarly, Fishburn and Kochenberger (1980) proposed two-piece Von Neumann-Morgenstern utility functions to reflect the existence of a discontinuity in $U(x)$ around the psychological zero point.

In the next phase of theory development, however, it would need to be better understood how aspiration levels vary as a function of individual, task, and context factors. A first step in this direction was offered by

Payne, Laughhun, and Crum (1979), who showed that positive translations of gambles (i.e., adding a constant amount to all outcomes) may cause strong changes in preference (e.g., reversals) as the translations move the gamble across various aspiration levels. The aspiration levels need not be fixed, however, and may themselves change as the task changes. Hence, important avenues of new research lie in the role and determinants of aspiration levels.

A second component of a more general theory concerns the psychologically relevant outcome space.[2] For example, the context effects observed in Chapters 5 and 7 could be explained by assuming different outcome spaces (i.e., different dimensionalities) for the insurance formulation than for the pure gamble formulation. In the former, such issues as the administrative inconvenience of filing a claim, lack of perfect certainty that one will collect in case the hazard occurs, or regret may be factors. Regret plays a role in that the insurance formulation implies that one will eventually know whether the hazard did occur; in case it does, one must file an insurance claim. However, in the gamble formulation, choosing the sure loss does not imply eventual knowledge of the outcome of the other option.

The role of regret might be separated into normative and non-normative components. In the former, it concerns ex-ante or anticipatory regret aimed at minimizing some expected loss or opportunity cost, and its role is thus normatively defensible. The second type, however, concerns ex-post regret and may have little normative justification. For example, the following two choice situations are normatively equivalent, but may well be judged to be different psychologically:

Situation A

	N1	*N2*
*A*1	$0	$100
*A*2	$30	$70

Situation B

	N1	*N2*
*B*1	$0	$100
*B*2	$70	$30

In this example, *N*1 and *N*2 are assumed to be equally likely future states of the world. Normatively, $E[U(A1)] = E[U(B1)] = \frac{1}{2}U(0) + \frac{1}{2}U(100)$, and $E[U(A2)] = E[U(B2)] = \frac{1}{2}U(30) + \frac{1}{2}U(70)$. Psychologically, however, *B*1 may evoke more regret (afterward) than *A*1 because an outcome of $0 will carry with it the realization that the other option would have yielded $70 in situation *B* versus only $30 in situation *A*. Of course, the other possible outcome of the first option (i.e., $100) has zero regret potential in either situation *A* or situation *B*.

It is an interesting empirical question as to whether regret considerations of the type described above enter into people's decisions. The question is important since real-world decisions may differ greatly in the extent to which the outcomes of one act reveal the outcomes that other acts would have yielded. Hence, (perceived) correlations among outcomes across acts may be important psychologically. In a recent lecture, Kahneman[3] offered a related example. Say one arrives thirty minutes late at an airport to catch a flight. Why do most people feel more regret or disutility upon learning that the plane just left (i.e., that it was late, too) than when learning that it left on time? Kahneman's explanation is that the former case suggests more ways than the latter in which one could have caught the flight; that is, regret increases as a function of the "availability of alternative worlds" that would have undone or mitigated the loss. In the present context, it would be interesting to compare these regret levels to the case of having no knowledge at all of when the plane left (other than knowing that it did leave). Hence, regret as a function of differential information about "what would have happened if" appears a fruitful area of inquiry.

A second issue regarding the outcome space concerns the way in which the EU model combines a person's risk-taking attitude and the value function under certainty into one measure. Although this is justifiable given the axioms, it leads to a psychological indeterminacy of the extent of risk aversion. As an example, consider a value function $v(x)$ that measures, via some fractionation method (see Torgerson, 1958), the value of money under certainty. Say that this interval scale is $v(x) = \sqrt{x}$ and that the person's certainty equivalent (CE) for a 50-50 chance at \$0 or \$25 is \$9. According to traditional EU theory, this person is risk-averse since \$9 is less than the gamble's expected value of \$12.50. Psychologically, however, the person is risk-taking as he or she prefers a 50-50 chance at 0 or 5 value units over 3 sure value units. Hence, a psychologically more relevant measure of risk aversion would be the difference between $v(\text{CE})$ and $\Sigma p_i v(x_i)$ or $\int f(x)v(x)dx$ in the case of a continuous random variable with density function $f(x)$. Similarly, this line of reasoning suggests definition of the NM utility function on $v(x)$ rather than x, as it would separate the risk-attitude influence from the value-function influence. The various measures of risk aversion proposed in the literature (Pratt, 1964) could then be redefined on $U[v(x)]$ and given psychologically richer interpretations. Hence, both the analytical aspects and empirical questions on the relationship between $v(x)$ and $U(x)$ merit further study, particularly since several studies suggest that they are generally not the same (Tversky, 1967a, 1967c).

Finally, there is a third component important to the development of a general descriptive theory. It concerns the notion and measurement of "basic tastes and preferences." Traditional economic theory postulates the existence of a well-behaved basic preference structure underlying people's decisions. It is often assumed that this structure is stable over time and that changes in actual decision behavior reflect changes in a person's base position (e.g., wealth level) rather than changes in basic tastes. Stigler and Becker (1977) clearly illustrated this view in their economic explanations of such seeming shifts in tastes as addiction, habitual behavior, advertising influence, and fashion. Their central proposition was that "one may usefully treat tastes as stable over time, and similar among people" (p. 76). For example, an increase in appreciation for good music as one hears more of it is interpreted as a positive relation between the marginal utility of music and the stock already consumed, as opposed to a change in taste for music. In this view, basic tastes are defined as values that cannot be influenced by obtaining new information (see Sen, 1970, p. 59).

From a psychological viewpoint, the postulate of stable tastes seems strained and artificial. It assumes away important and interesting questions — namely, how tastes are acquired, shaped, and modified. From a dynamic perspective, the traditional linear assumption of stable preferences preceding choice seems untenable (see Hogarth, 1979). Philosophically, preferences can hardly be argued to exist without some awareness of alternatives. They must be learned and constructed as the environment unfolds itself. Although basic preferences may some day be definable genotypically (i.e., independent of the environment), it seems preferable to define them in terms of environmental attributes. Understanding how preference structures are developed is a natural complement to the first component of the more general theory (that is, how decisions are framed). Both components exert considerable influence on choice behavior and do not operate independently of each other. The nature of their interaction presents a fertile ground for new research.

The above considerations may have serious implications for the EU model as a normative theory. The type of reference lotteries typically used in the construction of $U(x)$ are probably very abstract and unfamiliar to people. Instead of tapping into an existing preference structure, the procedure may prompt the construction of such a structure. This construction may, however, involve a considerable amount of decision framing as the abstract lotteries are psychologically translated into more concrete choice situations. The influence of such decision framing on the measurement of basic tastes (i.e., $U(x)$) is clearly illustrated by the context effects described in Chapters 5 and 7.

To reduce the influence of decision framing on the measurement of basic tastes will require greater realism in the elicitation of preferences. An important aspect of such elicitation is the utilization of representative designs (Brunswik, 1952). For example, a .89 chance at winning $1 million (as in the Allais paradox) is highly unrepresentative of choices encountered in the real world. It is therefore unlikely that people will have learned and developed preference structures for such choice situations. Hence, an important area of study will be the nature of preference structures — specifically, their degree of development (e.g., fuzzy vs. explicit) and their domains as a function of people's daily experiences (i.e., for what tasks they exist). A more general theory will need new conceptions, assumptions, and modeling procedures regarding basic tastes (see also March, 1978).

In sum, three components are envisioned as crucial to the development of a more general descriptive theory of decisions under risk. They concern (1) a theory of decision framing; (2) a better understanding of the psychologically relevant outcome space — its dimensionality, as well as its nature within and across dimensions; and (3) a psychologically richer theory of the determinants and role of basic tastes in choice behavior. The research of the present book should be an impetus to such a theory, as it has shown the inadequacy of expected utility theory on each of these three counts.

APPENDIX I
A GENERALIZATION OF THE FORMULAS FOR EU WITH INFORMATION

In Chapter 4, it was assumed that $f_i = f_j$ and $g_i = g_j$. In that case, the decision rule for choosing an urn after having received information on either p_i^* or x_i^* is very simple — namely, choose the urn with the higher p_i^* or x_i^* value. In this appendix, the urn problem is analyzed on the assumption that $f_i \neq f_j$ and $g_i \neq g_j$ for $i \neq j$.

In case the experimenter discloses the values of p_1^* and p_2^*, the decision rule is to choose urn 1 if, and only if, $p_1^* E[U(x_1)] \geq p_2^* E[U(x_2)]$. If this inequality does not hold, the decision maker should prefer urn 2. Assuming that this decision rule is applied correctly, the expected utility of the experiment, conditional on knowing p_1^* and p_2^*, averaged over all p_i^*, becomes

$$E[E[U(\widetilde{R}|p_1^*, p_2^*)]] = \int_0^1 p_1 g_1(p_1) \int_0^{p_1 k_1} g_2(p_2) dp_2 dp_1 E[U(x_1)] + \int_0^1 p_2 g_2(p_2) \int_0^{p_2/k_1} g_1(p_1) dp_1 dp_2 E[U(x_2)] \qquad \text{(A.1)}$$

in which

$$k_1 = \frac{E[U(x_1)]}{E[U(x_2)]} .$$

Note that terms containing $U(a)$ are omitted. $U(a)$ was arbitrarily set equal to zero since NM utility functions are unique up to positive linear transformations.

In case the experimenter discloses the values of x_1^* and x_2^*, the decision rule is to choose urn 1 if, and only if, $\bar{p}_1 U[(x_1^*)] \geq \bar{p}_2[U(x_2^*)]$. The expected utility of the experiment, conditional on knowing x_1^* and x_2^*, averaged over all x_i^*, is

$$E[E[U(\tilde{R}|x_1^*, x_2^*)]] = \bar{p}_1 \int_0^b f_1(x_1) \int_0^{U^{-1}(k_2 U(x_1))} f_2(x_2)dx_2 U(x_1)dx_1$$
$$+ \bar{p}_2 \int_a^b f_2(x_2) \int_a^{U^{-1}(U(x_2)/k_2)} f_1(x_1)dx_1 U(x_2)dx_2 \qquad \text{(A.2)}$$

in which $k_2 = \bar{p}_1/\bar{p}_2$ and $U^{-1}(x)$ is the inverse function of $U(x)$.

Note that substituting $g_1 = g_2$ and $f_1 = f_2 = 1/(b - a)$ in Equations (A.1) and (A.2) will yield

$$\frac{2}{3} E[U(x)] \text{ and } \frac{1}{2} \int_a^b \frac{2(x - a)}{(b - a)^2} U(x)dx,$$

respectively, which are the same as Equations (4.2) and (4.3).

APPENDIX II
QUESTIONNAIRE OF THE PREFERENCES FOR INFORMATION STUDY

GENERAL INFORMATION AND INSTRUCTIONS: (Please read carefully)

This questionnaire is part of a research effort at the Wharton School which investigates how people make decisions under conditions of risk. The answers you are asked to provide are statements of preference for which there are no right or wrong answers per se (i.e. it is a matter of taste). Your responses should reflect your true preferences and feelings at the time.

The questionnaire asks you to decide which of several alternatives is most preferred by you, assuming you had to make a choice. Although some questions may be difficult to answer, please give your best estimate of how you think you would decide if this were a real situation.

All the questions deal with hypothetical choices in which you stand to gain or lose money. If the amount of the loss exceeds your current wealth, please view the loss as a debt which you must pay at the earliest possible occasion. In this questionnaire we have combined several questions. However, please try to treat each question individually, without regard to previous questions or those yet to come. You may answer each question on the basis of intuition or calculations. Please answer them in the order given.

Thank you for your cooperation and willingness to treat these questions seriously and realistically.

PART I:

For each of the following choice situations, please circle the alternative you would prefer if you had to make the choice as given. When indifferent between the two alternatives, circle BOTH "a" and "b".

1. a. 50/50 chance of winning $10 or $20
   b. $15 gain for certain

2. a. 30% chance of winning $10, 70% chance at $20
   b. $17 gain for certain

3. a. 70% chance of winning $10, 30% chance at $20
   b. $13 gain for certain

4. a. 50/50 chance of winning $12 or $18
   b. $15 gain for certain

5. a. 50/50 chance of winning $500 or $1000
   b. $750 gain for certain

6. a. 30% chance of winning $500, 70% chance at $1000
   b. $850 gain for certain

7. a. 70% chance of winning $500, 30% chance at $1000
   b. $650 gain for certain

8. a. 50/50 chance of winning $600 or $900
   b. $750 gain for certain

9. a. 50/50 chance of losing $10 or $20
   b. $15 loss for certain

10. a. 30% chance of losing $10, 70% chance of losing $20
    b. $17 loss for certain

11. a. 70% chance of losing $10, 30% chance of losing $20
    b. $13 loss for certain

12. a. 50/50 chance of losing $12 or $18
    b. $15 loss for certain

13. a. 50/50 chance of losing $500 or $1000
    b. $750 loss for certain

14. a. 30% chance of losing $500, 70% chance of losing $1000
    b. $850 loss for certain

15. a. 70% chance of losing $500, 30% chance of losing $1000
    b. $650 loss for certain

16. a. 50/50 chance of losing $600 or $900
    b. $750 loss for certain

<u>PART II</u>: (Please carefully read the following description.)

Suppose you were presented with two urns and you would be asked to choose one of these urns in order to play the following game: Somebody would draw a ball randomly from the urn you picked. If it were red you would win a pre-specified amount of money (as of yet unknown to you) between $10 and $20. If the ball were white, you would win $10.

At present the following is known to you:
(1) Each urn contains a large mixture of red and white balls. The probabilities of winning (i.e. drawing a red ball) are unknown to you, and could be anywhere from 0 to 1. The probabilities of winning would in all likelihood be different between the two urns as each was determined independently by spinning a pointer on a wheel of chance such that each probability between 0 and 1 is equally likely to be the actual probability (or mixture of balls).

(2) Similarly, the payoffs to be received by you upon drawing a red ball were determined by spinning a pointer such that each amount between and including $10 and $20 was equally likely to be the actual amount. Again, the amounts to be won from Urn 1 would probably differ from that of Urn 2. Pictorially, you are faced with the following situation:

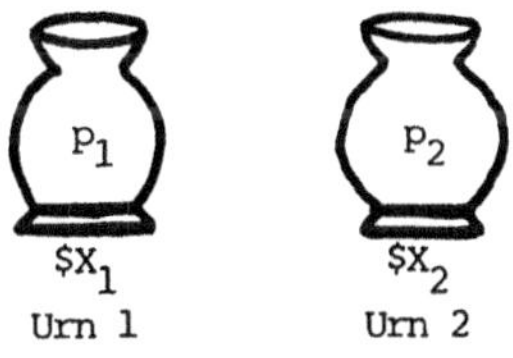

$0 \leq p_1 \leq 1$
$0 \leq p_2 \leq 1$
$\$10 \leq X_1 \leq \$20$
$\$10 \leq X_2 \leq \$20$

The actual values of p_1, p_2, X_1, and X_2 were determined <u>independently</u> of each other through four independent spinnings of a wheel of chance.

To help you choose the urn with which you want to play the game, you may know either the payoffs for each of the urns or you may know the chance of winning (drawing a red ball) with each urn. In other words, you have the option of knowing one of the following two types of information:

(a) The payoff in Urn 1 is $\$X_1$ and the payoff in Urn 2 is $\$X_2$ if a red ball is drawn (i.e. the actual dollar values of the two payoffs are given).

(b) The probability of drawing a red ball is p_1 in Urn 1 and p_2 in Urn 2 (i.e. the actual probabilities are given to you).

Each of the following questions outlines an urn game similar to the one described above. However, each of the following games will differ as to whether you win or lose money, the amounts you could win or lose, and the chances of winning or losing. For each question, please circle the type of information you would prefer to know before choosing an urn with which to play the game (circle BOTH if indifferent between the two types of information).

17. Game: Payoff on red ball ranges between \$10 and \$20. Payoff on white ball is \$10. Chance of drawing red ball is between 0 and 1.

a. Payoffs in each of the two urns (i.e. the values of X_1 and X_2
b. Chances of winning (drawing a red ball) in each urn (i.e. the values of P_1 and P_2).

18. Game: Payoff on red ball ranges between \$500 and \$1000. Payoff on white ball is \$500. Chance of drawing red ball is between 0 and 1.

a. Payoffs in each of the two urns
b. Chances of drawing a red ball in each urn

19. Game: Loss on red ball ranges between \$10 and \$20. Loss on white ball is \$10. Chance of drawing a red ball is between 0 and 1.

a. Losses in each of the two urns
b. Chances of drawing a red ball in each urn

20. Game: Loss on red ball ranges between \$500 and \$1000. Loss on white ball is \$500. Chance of drawing a red ball is between 0 and 1.

a. Losses in each of the two urns
b. Chances of drawing a red ball in each urn

21. Game: Payoff on red ball ranges between \$10 and \$20. Payoff on white ball is \$10. Chance of drawing a red ball is between 0 and 0.4.

a. Payoffs in each of the two urns
b. Chances of drawing a red ball in each urn

22. Game: Payoff on red ball ranges between \$10 and \$20. Payoff on white ball is \$10. Chance of drawing a red ball is between 0 and 0.1.

a. Payoffs in each of the two urns
b. Chances of drawing a red ball in each urn

23. Game: Payoff on red ball ranges between $500 and $1000. Payoff on white ball is $500. Chance of drawing a red ball is between 0 and 0.4.

a. Payoffs in each of the two urns
b. Chances of drawing a red ball in each urn

24. Game: Payoff on red ball ranges between $500 and $1000. Payoff on white ball is $500. Chance of drawing a red ball is between 0 and 0.1.

a. Payoffs in each of the two urns
b. Chances of drawing a red ball in each urn

25. Game: Loss on red ball ranges between $10 and $20. Loss on white ball is $10. Chance of drawing a red ball ranges between 0 and 0.4.

a. Losses in each of the two urns
b. Chances of drawing a red ball in each urn

26. Game: Loss on red ball ranges between $10 and $20. Loss on white ball is $10. Chance of drawing a red ball is between 0 and 0.1.

a. Losses in each of the two urns
b. Chance of drawing a red ball in each urn

27. Game: Loss on red ball ranges between $500 and $1000. Loss on white ball is $500. Chance of drawing a red ball is between 0 and 0.4.

a. Losses in each of the two urns
b. Chances of drawing a red ball in each urn

28. Game: Loss on red ball ranges between $500 and $1000. Loss on white ball is $500. Chance of drawing a red ball is between 0 and 0.1.

a. Losses in each of the two urns
b. Chances of drawing a red ball in each urn

29. Suppose that instead of having two urns you had ten urns, one of which you had to choose. The payoffs on drawing a red ball range between $10 and $20 and the payoff on a white ball is $10. The chance of drawing a red ball is between 0 and 1 in each urn. Before choosing one of the ten urns and drawing one random ball, would you prefer to know:

a. The probabilities of drawing red ball in all ten urns?

b. The payoffs in all ten urns?

<u>PART III:</u> (Please fill in the following information. Leave blank any items which you do not care to reveal.)

AGE:_______ SEX:_______ How many college statistics courses have you had?_____

Please estimate your current wealth (i.e. current assets minus current liabilities):_______________

Please estimate your annual budget (exclusive of tuition):___________

How many dependents do you have?______________

THANK YOU FOR YOUR COOPERATION

APPENDIX III
QUESTIONNAIRE OF THE INSURANCE STUDY

Note: The last part of this appendix contains the questions that differed in the second version of the questionnaire.

GENERAL INFORMATION AND INSTRUCTIONS (Please read carefully)

This questionnaire is part of a research effort based at the Wharton School of the University of Pennsylvania which investigates how people process information about risky decisions. The answers you are asked to provide are statements of preference for which there are no right or wrong answers per se (i.e. it is a matter of taste). Your responses should reflect your true feelings and preferences at the time.

The questionnaire asks you to decide which of several undesirable situations is most preferred by you (i.e. least undesirable) if you had to make a choice. Although some questions may be difficult to answer, please give your best estimate or guess of how you think you would decide if it were for real.

All our questions deal with hypothetical situations in which you stand to lose money. If the amount of loss exceeds your current wealth, please view the loss as a debt which you must pay at the earliest occasion. In this questionnaire we have combined several questions. However, try to treat each question individually without regard for previous questions or those yet to come. You may answer each question on the basis of intuition or calculations. Please do as you would if it were for real.

After most answers we will ask you to state to what extent your response was based on pure intuition versus explicit calculation (either mental or on paper). You can indicate this by placing an "X" mark on a scale which has "intuition" at one extreme and "calculation" at the other. By "calculation" we mean additions, subtractions, multiplications or divisions. If you did not perform any calculations you should place an "X" mark in the box nearest the "intuition" side.

Similarly, where appropriate, we shall ask you to indicate how strongly you preferred one choice over another. Again you should place an "X" mark on a scale which has "strong preference" at one extreme and "weak preference" at the other (see sample question on page 2.)

Thank you for your cooperation and willingness to treat these questions seriously and realistically. Please answer all questions in the sequence in which they appear. Please do not return to questions already answered. THANK YOU.

SAMPLE QUESTION. Imagine that you are faced with two risky situations, neither one of which you want to be in. However, suppose you have to make a choice. Which situation would you rather be in?

Situation A: you stand a 2 out of 100 chance of losing $60.
Situation B: you stand a 9 out of 10 chance of losing $40.

If, for example, you have a strong preference for situation A and you did not make any calculations, you would respond as follows:

ANSWER: (I prefer A) I prefer B I am indifferent
(please circle ONE only)

strong preference [X][ ][ ][ ][ ][ ][ ] weak preference

intuition [X][ ][ ][ ][ ][ ][ ] calculation

Question 1. Imagine that you are faced with two risky situations, neither one of which you want to be in. However, suppose you have to make a choice. Which situation would you rather be in?

Situation A: you stand a 2 out of 1,000 chance of losing $9,000.
Situation B: you stand a 9 out of 10 chance of losing $20.

ANSWER: I prefer A I prefer B I am indifferent
(please circle ONE only)

strong preference [ ][ ][ ][ ][ ][ ][ ] weak preference

intuition [ ][ ][ ][ ][ ][ ][ ] calculation

If there is any particular reason why you have this preference, please indicate this in one or two brief phrases. If you are not sure as to why you have the above preference, please write "not sure" on the "COMMENT ON WHY" line below.

COMMENT ON WHY: ______________________________

____

Question 2. Please answer the same question for the following situations:

Situation A: 6 out of 10 chance of losing $100.
Situation B: 1 out of 100 chance of losing $6,000.

ANSWER: Prefer A Prefer B Indifferent

strong preference [ ][ ][ ][ ][ ][ ][ ] weak preference

intuition [ ][ ][ ][ ][ ][ ][ ] calculation

COMMENT ON WHY: ______________________________

____

Question 3. Before evaluating the situations below, please describe briefly what a loss of $10,000 would mean to you in terms of your current possessions. If you do not have $10,000, please indicate how long you think it will take you to pay back your debt (if such a loss occured):

Which of the following situations would you rather be in, if you had to choose?

Situation A: 1 out of 2 chance of losing $400.
Situation B: 1 out of 50 chance of losing $10,000.

ANSWER: Prefer A | Prefer B | Indifferent

strong preference [| | | | | | |] weak preference

intuition [| | | | | | |] calculation

COMMENT ON WHY: ______________________________

Question 4. Suppose you are faced with a potential loss which has a 1 out of 100 chance of occurring. If it occurs you will lose somewhere between $10,000 and $30,000. Fortunately there are four different insurance policies (called 1, 2, 3 and 4) which offer you protection against this potential loss. The policies differ in their costs (called premiums) and deductibles. The deductible is the amount which you will have to pay yourself in case the loss occurs. The insurance company will pay the rest (i.e. the loss minus the deductible). The coverage is for one year, which is the time-period during which the loss could occur.
Please indicate how attractive you find EACH of the four policies (assuming you can only buy one). Place the numbers of the policies on the scale below. The relevant information is summarized as follows:

A 1 OUT OF 100 CHANCE OF LOSING SOMEWHERE BETWEEN $10,000 AND $30,000.

POLICY NUMBER	PREMIUM (cost)	AMOUNT YOU PAY IF LOSS OCCURS (i.e. deductible).
1	$ 70	$ 200
2	$ 80	$ 100
3	$ 90	$ 0
4	$ 20	$ 500

ANSWER: [| | | | | | | | | | |]
Very Attractive | Neutral | Very Unattractive
(put the numbers 1,2,3 and 4 in the above boxes)

intuition [| | | | | | |] calculation

COMMENT ON WHY: ______________________________

Question 5. Please answer the same question as above, but now assume that there is:

A 1 OUT OF 1000 CHANCE OF LOSING SOMEWHERE BETWEEN $10,000 AND $30,000.

ANSWER: [| | | | | | | | | | |]
Very Attractive | Neutral | Very Unattractive

COMMENT ON WHY: ______________________________

Question 6. Imagine that you are faced with three potential losses, any combination of which may occur. What would be the maximum amount that you would be willing to pay to avoid each, assuming that the losses are independent of each other. If you cannot give an exact figure for the maximum amount, try to give your best estimate or a range. If you cannot specify a range which you feel comfortable with, just write "don't know" (for that loss).

LOSS	CHANCE	MAXIMUM AMOUNT (you would pay to avoid i
$ 5000	1 out of 50	________
$ 3000	1 out of 100	________
$ 500	3 out of 50	________

intuition ☐☐☐☐☐☐☐ calculation

Question 7. Imagine that you just incurred a loss of $40, and now you are faced with the following two situations. Assuming you have to make a choice, which one would you prefer?

Situation A: a certain loss of $8.
Situation B: a 1 out of 1000 chance of losing $10,000.

ANSWER: Prefer A Prefer B Indifferent

strong preference ☐☐☐☐☐☐☐ weak preference

intuition ☐☐☐☐☐☐☐ calculation

COMMENT ON WHY: ____

____

Question 8. Assuming that you had to make a choice, which of the following two situations would you rather be in ?

Situation A: a certain loss of $90.
Situation B: a certain loss of $20 AND a 1 out of 100 chance of losing $500.

ANSWER: Prefer A Prefer B Indifferent

strong preference ☐☐☐☐☐☐☐ weak preference

intuition ☐☐☐☐☐☐☐ calculation

COMMENT ON WHY: ____

____

Question 9. Suppose that you are faced with two potential losses, neither of which depends on the other. There are two insurance policies which give you complete protection against these losses but at different premiums. Suppose that you <u>had to</u> buy one of these policies, which one would you choose?

Policy A: $1 premium to protect against a 1 out of 4 chance of losing $5.
Policy B: $100 premium to protect against a 1 out of 4 chance of losing $500.

ANSWER: Prefer A Prefer B Indifferent

strong preference ☐☐☐☐☐☐☐ weak preference

Suppose now that you are free to do as you choose. Would you buy both policies, one policy or neither policy ?

Question 10. Suppose that you are faced with three potential losses which are independent of each other. An insurance company is willing to offer you comprehensive insurance against all three losses. This means that you pay one premium only, which completely covers you against any and all of these losses. That is, you may collect on one, two or all three losses depending on how many occur. Please indicate the maximum amount you would be willing to pay for this comprehensive insurance plan. If you cannot specify an exact number, please give your best guess or a range. If you cannot specify a range, please write "don't know".

LOSS	CHANCE
$ 5000	2 out of 100
$ 3000	1 out of 100
$ 500	6 out of 100

MAXIMUM AMOUNT: [ ]

intuition [| | | | | |] calculation

Question 11. Imagine that you are faced with two potential losses which are independent of each other. An insurance company is willing to offer complete protection against each of them, as follows:

Policy A: $8 premium to protect against a 1 out of 1000 chance of losing $10,000.
Policy B: $40 premium to protect against a 1 out of 100 chance of losing $ 5,000.

Suppose that you must decide for each potential loss whether to buy the above insurance or not. In effect you will have four alternatives:

1. Do not purchase policy A nor policy B.
2. Purchase policy A and not policy B.
3. Purchase policy B and not policy A.
4. Purchase both policy A and policy B.

Please rank the above four alternatives (1, 2, 3, and 4) according to preference on the scale below. Put the numbers 1, 2, 3, and 4 in the boxes of this scale.

ANSWER: [| | | | | | | | | |]

Very Attractive Neutral Very Unattractive

intuition [| | | | | | |] calculation

COMMENT ON WHY: ______________________________

____

Question 12. Supposing you had to make a choice, which of the following two situations would you rather be in?

Situation A: a certain loss of $70 and a 1 out of 100 chance of losing $200.
Situation B: a certain loss of $80 and a 1 out of 100 chance of losing $100.

ANSWER: Prefer A Prefer B Indifferent

strong preference [| | | | | | |] weak preference

intuition [| | | | | | |] calculation

COMMENT ON WHY: ______________________________

PERSONAL DATA The data requested below will be kept in the strictest confidence and will only be analyzed by the researchers themselves. However, if you prefer not to give certain types of information, please leave the corresponding answer space blank. Note that your name is NOT requested. Hence all information is and remains ANONYMOUS.

PROFESSION (if student, list year of study): ______________________________

AGE:________ SEX: Male - Female (circle one) EDUCATION: High-School College Graduate School (circle highest education)

NATIONALITY: USA - Other______ RELIGION:______________ MARITAL STATUS:______________

KNOWLEDGE OF STATISTICS: Expected Value - Random Variable - Expected Utility Theory (cirlce concepts you are familiar with)

WEALTH AND INCOME Please use the scales below to indicate your current annual income and wealth (according to your best estimates). Income is defined in the sense of the IRS's gross income. By wealth we mean the total of all your possessions minus your debts. If you are married, please indicate your joint annual income and wealth. If you are a dependent, please indicate your own wealth (not your family's) and your yearly allowance plus earnings.

INCOME: negative | $0 | $5,000 | $10,000 | $15,000 | $20,000 | $30,000 | $40,000 | $60,000

WEALTH: -$30,000 | -$10,000 | $0 | $5,000 | $10,000 | $30,000 | $50,000 | $100,000 | $150,000

PERSONALITY Please indicate for each of the following descriptions to what extent you think they typify you. Each scale consists of two extremes. Please compare yourself to the average American and indicate how you think you differ from him or her. Place an "X" mark near the side that you think describes you more correctly. If you feel that you are not different from the average American, please place an "X" mark in the middle of the scale.

Prudent	☐	☐	☐	☐	☐	☐	☐	Adventuresome
Leader	☐	☐	☐	☐	☐	☐	☐	Follower
I control life	☐	☐	☐	☐	☐	☐	☐	Life controls me
Very private person	☐	☐	☐	☐	☐	☐	☐	Very outgoing person
Religious	☐	☐	☐	☐	☐	☐	☐	Not religious
Tight with money	☐	☐	☐	☐	☐	☐	☐	Generous with money
Find making decisions easy	☐	☐	☐	☐	☐	☐	☐	Find making decisions difficult
Like to decide on my own	☐	☐	☐	☐	☐	☐	☐	Like others to help me decide
Optimistic	☐	☐	☐	☐	☐	☐	☐	Pessimistic

THANK YOU VERY MUCH FOR YOUR COOPERATION. PLEASE USE FRONT PAGE FOR ANY COMMENTS YOU MAY HAVE.

Note: The following four questions were different in the second version of the questionnaire.

Question 3. Which of the following situations would you rather be in, if you had to choose?

Situation A: 1 out of 2 chance of losing $400.
Situation B: 1 out of 50 chance of losing $10,000.

ANSWER: Prefer A Prefer B Indifferent

strong preference ☐☐☐☐☐☐☐ weak preference

intuition ☐☐☐☐☐☐☐ calculation

COMMENT ON WHY: ______________________________

____

Question 4. Suppose you are faced with a potential loss which has a 1 out of 100 chance of occurring. If it occurs you will lose somewhere between $10,000 and $30,000. Fortunately there are four different insurance policies (called 1, 2, 3 and 4) which offer you protection against this potential loss. The policies differ in their costs (called premiums) and deductibles. The deductible is the amount which you will have to pay yourself in case the loss occurs. The insurance company will pay the rest (i.e. the loss minus the deductible). The coverage is for one year, which is the time-period during which the loss could occur.
Please indicate how attractive you find EACH of the four policies (assuming you can only buy one). Place the numbers of the policies on the scale below. The relevant information is summarized as follows:

A 1 OUT OF 100 CHANCE OF LOSING SOMEWHERE BETWEEN $10,000 AND $30,000.

POLICY NUMBER	PREMIUM (cost)	AMOUNT YOU PAY IF LOSS OCCURS (i.e. deductible).
1	$ 20	$ 500
2	$ 70	$ 200
3	$ 80	$ 100
4	$ 90	$ 0

ANSWER: ☐☐☐☐☐☐☐☐☐☐☐

Very Attractive Neutral Very Unattractive

(put the numbers 1,2,3 and 4 in the above boxes)

intuition ☐☐☐☐☐☐☐ calculation

COMMENT ON WHY: ______________________________

____

Question 6. Imagine that you are faced with three potential losses, any combination of which may occur. What would be the maximum amount that you would be willing to pay to avoid each, assuming that the losses are independent of each other. If you cannot give an exact figure for the maximum amount, try to give your best estimate or a range. If you cannot specify a range which you feel comfortable with, just write "don't know" (for that loss).

LOSS	CHANCE	MAXIMUM AMOUNT (you would pay to avoid it)
$ 500	3 out of 50	________
$ 3000	1 out of 100	________
$ 5000	1 out of 50	________

intuition ☐☐☐☐☐☐☐ calculation

Question 9. Suppose that you are faced with two potential losses, neither of which depends on the other. There are two insurance policies which give you complete protection against these losses but at different premiums. Suppose that you <u>had to</u> buy one of these policies, which one would you choose?

Policy A: $100 premium to protect against a 1 out of 4 chance of losing $500.
Policy B: $1 premium to protect against a 1 out of 4 chance of losing $5.

ANSWER: Prefer A Prefer B Indifferent

strong preference ☐☐☐☐☐☐☐ weak preference

Suppose now that you are free to do as you choose. Would you buy both policies, one policy or neither policy ?

APPENDIX IV
ANALYSIS OF A DUPLEX GAMBLE

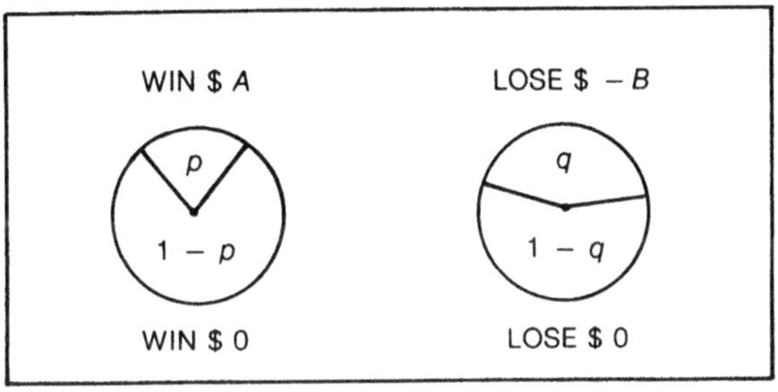

(Note that B is negative)

1. *Probability function:*

$$f(x) = \begin{cases} \textit{Outcome} & \textit{Probability} \\ A + B & pq \\ A & p(1 - q) \\ B & q(1 - p) \\ 0 & (1 - p)(1 - q) \end{cases}$$

2. $\text{EV} = pq(A + B) + p(1 - q)A + q(1 - p)B + (1 - p)(1 - q)0$
$= pA + qB.$

3. $\text{Var} = pq(A + B)^2 + p(1 - q)A^2 + q(1 - p)B^2 + (1 - p)(1 - q)0^2 - (pA + qB)^2 = pA^2(1 - p) + qB^2(1 - q).$

APPENDIX V
QUESTIONNAIRE OF THE STATISTICAL KNOWLEDGE STUDY

None of the information given by you will be published or otherwise made public, other than in the form of statistics and/or aggregate findings. Personal data will only be used for research purposes and will not be given to anyone other than the researchers.

PERSONAL DATA:

NAME (if you prefer not to give your name for further contact and/or feedback, please leave this blank)

____

PROFESSION (if student, please list current or intended major)

____

AGE (if you prefer not to give this information, please leave this blank ________________

SEX (Please, circle one): MALE FEMALE

EDUCATION (if student, please list year of study. Otherwise, please list highest education received)

____

ADDRESS (where we may reach you for feedback or questions--if you want to)

Street: ______________________________

City & State: ____________________________________

Phone: _______________________

PLEASE, TURN TO THE NEXT PAGE WHEN REQUESTED TO DO SO.

****

TRY TO ANSWER THE FOLLOWING QUESTIONS AS HONESTLY AS YOU CAN, ACCORDING TO THE WAY YOU FEEL AND THINK RIGHT AT THIS MOMENT.

****

Suppose someone offered you to flip a coin for ten dollars ($10). You are certain the coin is fair (i.e., the chances of getting heads or tails are equal), and that the person will pay you if you win. If heads comes up you have to pay him ten dollars, but if tails comes up he will pay you ten dollars. You will play this gamble only once. Would you go along with his offer?

1. Definitely Yes
2. Probably Yes
3. Indifferent
4. Probably Not
5. Definitely Not

Please, answer this question by putting down 1, 2, 3, 4, or 5 (but ONE NUMBER ONLY).

Answer: ____________________

Please, answer the same question if you were to flip this coin for five dollars ($5).

Answer: ____________________

Please, answer the same question if you were to flip this coin for two dollars ($2).

Answer: ____________________

PLEASE, TURN TO THE NEXT PAGE WHEN REQUESTED TO DO SO.

I. A large urn contains one hundred (100) balls in total which are either white or black. Someone will draw one ball from this urn without looking. Each ball has equal chances of being drawn. If the ball drawn is white you will win nothing. However, if the ball is black you will win a certain amount of money. Unfortunately, you do not know how large this amount is. You only know that it is at least zero dollars ($0) and no more than ten dollars ($10). Furthermore, you do not know how many of the 100 balls are black. There could be anywhere from zero to one hundred black balls.

Naturally you would like to play this gamble because you can never lose. However, you cannot play it for free. To make it easier for you to decide how much this gamble is worth to you at most, you may either know what the amount is you will win if a black ball is drawn, or you may know how many of the 100 balls are black. However, you can only get ONE PIECE of information.

Which piece of information would you prefer to have before having to decide how much the gamble is worth to you?

Please, circle the answer that best describes your preference:

1. I would much rather know the amount I could win than the number of black balls.
2. I would rather know the amount I could win than the number of black balls.
3. I am indifferent between the two pieces of information.
4. I would rather know the number of black balls than the amount I may win.
5. I would much rather know the number of black balls than the amount.
6. Although I am not indifferent, I really do not know which to prefer.

If you would not get any of this information, which part of the gamble would seem more uncertain to you? (circle the appropriate one)

a. Not knowing how much you can win.
b. Not knowing the number of balls that are black.
c. Both seem equally uncertain.

II. Imagine that we have the same urn as before but this time, a black ball means that you will lose anywhere between zero and ten dollars, and a white ball means that you do not lose anything. Of course, this gamble is not very attractive anymore and you would have to be paid some money before you would be willing to play it. Before deciding on how much you would have to be paid, you may again choose between two pieces of information. You may either know what the amount is that you will lose if a black ball is drawn, or you may know how many of the 100 balls are black. Again, you will only get ONE piece of information.

Please, indicate which of the above answers best describes your preference (i.e., 1, 2, 3, 4, 5, or 6?):

Answer: ________________

If you would not get any of this information, which part of the gamble seems more risky to you? Please, answer a, b, or c of the above answers.

Answer: ________________

Instructions (read carefully)

You will be asked to judge the degree of attractiveness of certain gambles (bets). In order to do this you will have to rank these gambles on a scale from -10 to +10. The ranking procedure is as follows:

Attractive gambles are given a rank from +1 to +10. The higher the rank, the more attractive the gamble. Unattractive gambles are given a rank from -1 to -10; the lower the rank, the more unattractive the gamble. The degree of attractiveness (i.e., whether it is +4, +5 or something else) should be determined by viewing the rank as the dollar amount which you would be willing to pay at most for that gamble. For example, if you rank an attractive gamble as +3, that means that you would be willing to pay up to $3 to have the right to play that gamble. Similarly, "+6" means that you would pay up to $6 to play that gamble.

Conversely, an unattractive gamble will receive a rank of -1 through -10 depending on how much you have to be paid, at minimum, before you would be willing to play this unattractive gamble. Hence a rank of "-4" means that you have to be paid at least $4 before you would be willing to play the gamble. Similarly, "-7" means that you must be paid at least $7 in order to play the gamble. When you are indifferent between playing a particular gamble and not playing it, you should give that gamble a rank of zero.

The gambles (bets) will be presented in the following form:

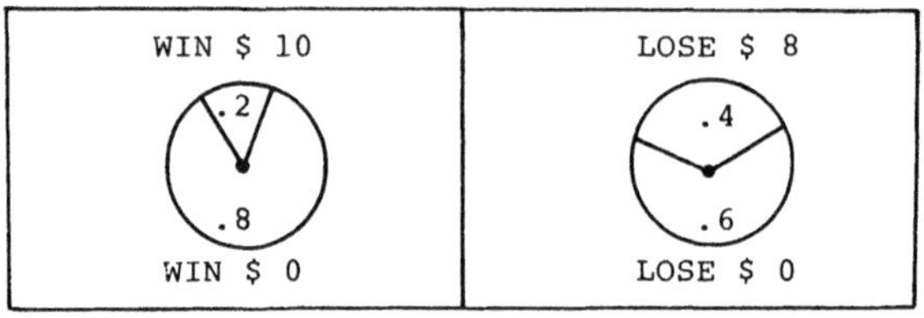

Imagine each disc having a pointer on it. The first disc's pointer will be spun to determine if you win $10 or $0. Next, the second disc's pointer will be spun to determine if you lose $8 or $0. The chance of winning $10 is 20% (.2), and the chance of winning nothing is 80% (.8) for the first disc. Note that the upper segment of the disc represents 20% of its total area. If the pointer stops in that area, after spinning around for a while, you will have won $10 from the first disc. The bet consists of playing both discs, and the difference between your winnings and losses is the actual "win" of this bet.

In judging this bet (gamble), first determine if you find it attractive. If so, give it a rank from +1 to +10 according to how much you are willing to pay for it at most. If you find it unattractive, give it a rank from -1 to -10 reflecting how much you want to be paid at minimum before you would play this gamble. If you are indifferent, give it a rank of zero.

Please, evaluate the above gamble as follows: circle whether you find it attractive, unattractive or indifferent, and give it a rank accordingly.

Bet (gamble) 0: Attractive - Unattractive - Indifferent - Rank____

For all of the following bets, to be projected on the screen, repeat the above procedure.

GAMBLE

1. Attractive - Unattractive - Indifferent - Rank________
2. Attractive - Unattractive - Indifferent - Rank________
3. Attractive - Unattractive - Indifferent - Rank________
4. Attractive - Unattractive - Indifferent - Rank________
5. Attractive - Unattractive - Indifferent - Rank________

---

6. Attractive - Unattractive - Indifferent - Rank________
7. Attractive - Unattractive - Indifferent - Rank________
8. Attractive - Unattractive - Indifferent - Rank________
9. Attractive - Unattractive - Indifferent - Rank________
10. Attractive - Unattractive - Indifferent - Rank________

---

11. Attractive - Unattractive - Indifferent - Rank________
12. Attractive - Unattractive - Indifferent - Rank________
13. Attractive - Unattractive - Indifferent - Rank________
14. Attractive - Unattractive - Indifferent - Rank________
15. Attractive - Unattractive - Indifferent - Rank________

---

16. Attractive - Unattractive - Indifferent - Rank________
17. Attractive - Unattractive - Indifferent - Rank________
18. Attractive - Unattractive - Indifferent - Rank________
19. Attractive - Unattractive - Indifferent - Rank________
20. Attractive - Unattractive - Indifferent - Rank________

---

21. Attractive - Unattractive - Indifferent - Rank________
22. Attractive - Unattractive - Indifferent - Rank________
23. Attractive - Unattractive - Indifferent - Rank________
24. Attractive - Unattractive - Indifferent - Rank________
25. Attractive - Unattractive - Indifferent - Rank________

---

26. Attractive - Unattractive - Indifferent - Rank________
27. Attractive - Unattractive - Indifferent - Rank________
28. Attractive - Unattractive - Indifferent - Rank________
29. Attractive - Unattractive - Indifferent - Rank________
30. Attractive - Unattractive - Indifferent - Rank________

We are interested to learn <u>how</u> you made your decisions regarding the previous gambles. Please, be so kind as to answer the following questions with reference to how you actually made your evaluations as opposed to how you think you should have done it.

(a) Was there any part of the bets that you focused more on than other parts (such as for example, the chance of winning versus the amount of winning, or versus the chance of losing)? Please, explain:

____

____

(b) Did you use the same method to judge attractive bets as unattractive bets? If you judged them differently, please try to explain in which way(s) your evaluation methods were different? ________________

____

____

(c) In making your evaluations of the bets, did you make any calculations (mentally) or did you judge the gambles intuitively by thinking about them?

Please, <u>circle</u> one: Made some calculations - Made no calculations

(d) If you made calculations of any type, please, try to explain what you calculated?

____

____

(e) Was it difficult for you to develop some method or system by which you could judge these gambles? Please, explain:

____

____

(f) How many gambles, would you say, passed by before you had some method or methods developed to judge them?

____

____

(g) If you used more than one method to judge the bets, please, attempt to describe how many methods you used and in which sequence. Try to estimate for how many bets each method was used.

____

____

(h) Did you find it interesting to judge all these bets or boring? Please, circle ONE:

Very Interesting - Interesting - Neutral - Boring - Very Boring

(i) If you found it boring, after how many gambles did you lose interest?

Answer:__________

(j) Were you familiar with gambles of this general form (i.e., bets in which you are given the chances of winning and losing and the amounts you can lose or gain)? Please, explain:

____

____

(k) Suppose we were to repeat some of the previous gambles. Do you think you would judge them similarly to the first time? How much do you think your second ranking would be off <u>at most</u>? Please circle one:

one rank - two ranks - three ranks - four ranks - five or more ranks.

(l) If you indicated above that your second ranking of an identical gamble would possibly be off by more than three ranks, please try to think of some reasons why this could be? (because you really did not care that much, because it was a difficult task, because you really did not understand the gambles, because you did not have a good system developed, or any other reason). Please, explain:

____

____

(m) Which bets were easier to rank: attractive or unattractive ones? Why?

____

____

(n) Did you have sufficient time to think about the bets to give them a reliable ranking, or were you hurried? Please explain:

____

____

(o) Are you familiar with the statistical concept of expected value? If yes, please define it or give an example:

____

____

____

THANK YOU VERY MUCH FOR YOUR COOPERATION

APPENDIX VI
EU ANALYSIS OF DIMENSION PREFERENCES

Dimension preference (i.e., whether a subject focuses more on probabilities or on payoffs) was directly assessed in the statistical knowledge study (Appendix V) by asking whether the subject, in determining the worth of an urn, prefers knowing the chance of winning or the amount to be won.

To analyze this question in an expected utility framework, we shall assume that the subject attends an auction where an urn gamble is for sale at the cost (price) of c dollars for one play. If the subject buys the urn gamble, the auctioneer will randomly draw one ball from the urn. If the ball is white, nothing will have been won; however, if it is black, the subject will have won a prespecified amount of money somewhere between \$0 and \$$A$. Before the subject has to decide whether or not to buy this urn game, the auctioneer will, at no charge, reveal *either* the chance of drawing a black ball *or* the amount to be won in case a black ball is drawn. The issue to be examined here is which type of information a subject should prefer before deciding whether or not to buy the game, for a given Von Neumann-Morgenstern utility function $U(x)$.

In the ensuing analysis, the following symbols will be used:

c = cost of the urn (i.e., sales price).
x = change in the current financial level of the decision maker.
$U(x)$ = Von Neumann-Morgenstern utility function defined on all relevant x values.
p^* = true probability of drawing a black ball (i.e., winning).
x^* = actual amount to be won if a black ball is drawn.
A = upper limit on x^*.
$f(\cdot)$ = prior density function on $\tilde{p}^*$.
$g(\cdot)$ = prior density function on $\tilde{x}^*$.
$\tilde{O}$ = outcome of the experiment (trip to the auction).
$E[\cdot]$ = mathematical expectation operator.

For purposes of this analysis, all random variables are assumed to be continuous.

(i) Without any information on p^* or x^*, the decision maker should only purchase the urn if

$$\bar{p}E[U(x - c)] + (1 - \bar{p})U(-c) > U(0)$$

in which

$$E[U(x - c)] = \int_0^A g(x)U(x - c)dx$$

with

$$\bar{p} = \int_0^1 pf(p)dp.$$

(ii) If p^* is known, the decision rule is to purchase the urn if, and only if,

$$p^*E[U(x - c)] + (1 - p^*)U(-c) > U(0)$$

or

$$p^* > \frac{U(0) - U(-c)}{E[U(x - c)] - U(-c)} = k_1.$$

The expected utility of the experiment conditional on knowing p^*, averaged over all p^*, is

$$E[E[U(\tilde{O}|p^*)]] = \int_{k_1}^1 f(p)dp[PE[U(x - c)] + (1 - P)U(-c)]$$
$$+ \int_0^{k_1} f(p)dpU(0)$$

in which

$$P = \int_{k_1}^{1} pf(p) \left\{ \frac{1}{\int_{k_1}^{1} f(p)dp} \right\} dp.$$

(iii) If x^* is known, the decision rule is to purchase the urn if, and only if,

$$\bar{p}U(x^* - c) + (1 - \bar{p})U(-c) > U(0)$$

or

$$x^* > U^{-1} \left\{ \frac{U(0) - (1 - p)U(-c)}{\bar{p}} \right\} + c = k_2.$$

The expected utility of the experiment conditional on knowing x^*, averaged over all x^*, is

$$E[E[U(\tilde{O}|x^*)]] = \int_{k_2}^{A} g(x)dx \left\{ \bar{p} \int_{k_2}^{A} G(x)U(x - c)dx + (1 - \bar{p})U(-c) \right\} + \int_{0}^{k_2} g(x)dxU(0)$$

in which

$$G(x) = \frac{g(x)}{\int_{k_2}^{A} g(x)dx}.$$

If the expected utility under (ii) is greater than under (iii), then the decision maker should prefer knowing p^* over x^*.

The second part of the question on dimension preference changes the "win" urn into a "loss" urn. Of course, a similar analysis is needed to see which type of information (p^* or x^*) should be preferred. The above expressions for the expected utility of the urn with knowing p^* or x^*, respectively, do not allow for any general statement as to which information should be preferred. Depending on $U(x)$, the expression in (ii) may be smaller, equal, or greater than that of (iii).

APPENDIX VII
QUESTIONNAIRE OF THE RISK TAKING AND CONTEXT EFFECT STUDY

Note: The last part of this appendix shows the sample question and the first question using an insurance formulation. The remaining questions are not shown as they followed the same format as the corresponding questions in the gamble version and contained identi cal sure losses, probabilities, and stochastic losses.

QUESTIONNAIRE

GENERAL INFORMATION AND INSTRUCTIONS

This questionnaire asks you to decide which of several undesirable situations is most preferred by you (i.e. least undesirable) if you had to make a choice. Although some questions may be difficult to answer, please give your best estimate or guess of how you think you would decide if it were for real.

The answers you are asked to provide are statements of preference for which there are no right or wrong answers per se (i.e. it is a matter of taste). Your responses should reflect your true preferences at the time.

All of these questions deal with hypothetical situations in which you stand to lose money. Try to treat each question individually without regard for previous questions or those yet to come. You may answer each question on the basis of intuition or calculations. Please do as you would if it were for real.

After each answer, we shall ask you to indicate how strongly you preferred one choice over another. You should place an "X" mark on a scale which has "strong preference" at one extreme and "weak preference" at the other.

Thank you for your cooperation and willingness to treat these questions seriously and realistically. Please answer all questions in the sequence in which they appear. Please do not return to questions already answered.

THANK YOU.

SAMPLE QUESTION

Imagine that you are faced with two unfavorable situations, neither one of which you want to be in. However, suppose you have to make a choice. Which situation would you rather be in?

Situation A: you stand a 1 out of 10 chance of losing $100.

Situation B: you will lose $1 with certainty.

If, for example, you have a strong preference for situation B, you would respond as follows:

ANSWER: I prefer A (I prefer B) Indifferent
(please circle ONE only)

strong preference [X][ ][ ][ ][ ][ ][ ] weak preference

1. Imagine that you are faced with two unfavorable situations, neither of which you want to be in. However, suppose you have to make a choice. Which situation would you rather be in?

Situation A: you stand a 1 out of 1000 chance of losing $10,000.

Situation B: you will lose $10 with certainty.

ANSWER: I prefer A I prefer B Indifferent

strong preference [ ][ ][ ][ ][ ][ ][ ] weak preference

2. Situation A: 1 out of 200 chance of losing $2000.

Situation B: you will lose $10 with certainly.

ANSWER: I prefer A I prefer B Indifferent

strong preference [ ][ ][ ][ ][ ][ ][ ] weak preference

3. Situation A: 1 out of 100 chance of losing $1000.

Situation B: you will lose $10 with certainty.

ANSWER: I prefer A I prefer B Indifferent

strong preference [ ][ ][ ][ ][ ][ ][ ] weak preference

4. Situation A: 1 out of 20 chance of losing $200.

Situation B: you will lose $10 with certainty.

ANSWER: I prefer A I prefer B Indifferent

strong preference [| | | | | | |] weak preference

5. Situation A: 1 out of 10 chance of losing $100.

Situation B: you will lose $10 with certainty.

ANSWER: I prefer A I prefer B Indifferent

strong preference [| | | | | | |] weak preference

6. Situation A: 1 out of 5 chance of losing $50.

Situation B: you will lose $10 with certainty.

ANSWER: I prefer A I prefer B Indifferent

strong preference [| | | | | | |] weak preference

7. Situation A: 1 out of 1000 chance of losing $10,000.

Situation B: you will lose $10 with certainty.

ANSWER: I prefer A I prefer B Indifferent

strong preference [| | | | | | |] weak preference

8. Situation A: 1 out of 100 chance of losing $10,000.

Situation B: you will lose $100 with certainty.

ANSWER: I prefer A I prefer B Indifferent

strong preference [| | | | | | |] weak preference

9. Situation A: 1 out of 10 chance of losing $10,000.

Situation B: you will lose $1000 with certainty.

ANSWER: I prefer A I prefer B Indifferent

strong preference [| | | | | | |] weak preference

10. Situation A: 1 out of 2 chance of losing $10,000.

Situation B: you will lose $5000 with certainty.

ANSWER: I prefer A I prefer B Indifferent

strong preference [| | | | | | |] weak preference

11. Situation A: 9 out 10 chance of losing $10,000.

Situation B: you will lose $9,000 with certainty.

ANSWER: I prefer A I prefer B Indifferent

strong preference [| | | | | | |] weak preference

12. Situation A: 99 out of 100 chance of losing $10,000.

Situation B: you will lose $9900 with certainty.

ANSWER: I prefer A I prefer B Indifferent

strong preference [| | | | | |] weak preference

13. Situation A: 999 out of 1000 chance of losing $10,000.

Situation B: you will lose $9990 with certainty.

ANSWER: I prefer A I prefer B Indifferent

strong preference [| | | | | |] weak preference

14. Situation A: 1 out of 100 chance of losing $100.

Situation B: you will lose $1 with certainty.

ANSWER: I prefer A I prefer B Indifferent

strong preference [| | | | | |] weak preference

15. Situation A: 1 out of 100 chance of losing $1000.

Situation B: you will lose $10 with certainty.

ANSWER: I prefer A I prefer B Indifferent

strong preference [| | | | | |] weak preference

16. Situation A: 1 out of 100 chance of losing $10,000.

Situation B: you will lose $100 with certainty.

ANSWER: I prefer A I prefer B Indifferent

strong preference [| | | | | |] weak preference

17. Situation A: 1 out of 100 chance of losing $100,000.

Situation B: you will lose $1000 with certainty.

ANSWER: I prefer A I prefer B Indifferent

strong preference [| | | | | |] weak preference

18. Situation A: 1 out of 100 chance of losing $1,000,000.

Situation B: you will lose $10,000 with certainty.

ANSWER: I prefer A I prefer B Indifferent

strong preference [| | | | | |] weak preference

PERSONAL DATA

The information requested below will remain anonymous. Note that your name is NOT requested. However, if you prefer not to give certain types of information, please leave the corresponding answer space blank.

AGE:________ SEX: Male or Female (circle one) Nationality: USA - other (circle one)

KNOWLEDGE OF STATISTICS: Expected Value - Random Variable - Expected Utility Theory (circle concepts you are familiar with)

Please use the scale below to indicate your current wealth (according to your best estimate). By wealth we mean the total of all your possessions minus your debts. If you are married, please indicate your joint wealth. If you are a dependent, please indicate your own wealth, not your family's.

WEALTH

-$30,000 -$10,000 $0 $5000 $10,000 $30,000 $100,000 $150,000

Note: The following are the sample question and the first actual question given to subjects who received the insurance version of the questionnaire. The remaining questions are not shown as they are identical to the gamble format ones, except for wording.

SAMPLE QUESTION

Imagine that you are faced with two unfavorable situations, neither one of which you want to be in. However, suppose you have to make a choice. Which situation would you rather be in?

Situation A: you stand a 1 out of 10 chance of losing $100.

Situation B: you can buy insurance for $1 to protect you from this loss.

If, for example, you have a strong preference for situation B, you would respond as follows:

ANSWER: I prefer A (I prefer B) Indifferent
(please circle ONE only)

strong preference [X][ ][ ][ ][ ][ ][ ] weak preference

1. Imagine that you are faced with two unfavorable situations, neither of which you want to be in. However, suppose you have to make a choice. Which situation would you rather be in?

Situation A: you stand a 1 out of 1000 chance of losing $10,000.

Situation B: you can buy insurance for $10 to protect you from this loss.

ANSWER: I prefer A I prefer B Indifferent

strong preference [ ][ ][ ][ ][ ][ ][ ] weak preference

APPENDIX VIII
INSURANCE AND EU THEORY

This appendix offers an elementary analysis of insurance within the EU framework. Its aim is to present some of the insights necessary for the interpretations of the experimental results of Chapters 5 and 7. A similar, more detailed analysis is provided in Friedman and Savage (1948). As an illustration of how insurance is analyzed within the expected utility framework, consider a situation in which a decision maker is faced with a potential loss of L dollars that has a probability p of occurring. An insurance company offers complete coverage against this potential loss at a cost of c dollars. Let W_0 represent the current wealth of the decision maker and $U(w)$ represent his Von Neumann-Morgenstern (1947) utility function. If we assume that the decision maker has only two options (i.e., full coverage or no coverage), expected utility theory dictates that full coverage should only be purchased if the following inequality holds:

$$U(W_0 - c) > pU(W_0 - L) + (1 - p)U(W_0);$$

that is, the utility associated with buying insurance is greater than the expected utility associated with not buying insurance. It can easily be shown graphically that if the utility function is concave (i.e., $U(w)$ increases monotonically at a decreasing rate) and if $c < pL$ (meaning that the insurance is subsidized), full coverage should always be purchased regardless of the values of c, p, and L. (In general, concavity of $U(x)$ implies risk aversion, in that a sure amount \$$x$ will always be preferred to any gamble with an EV of \$$x$.) Figure VIII.1 depicts a situation in which $U(w)$ is concave. Points A, B, and C correspond to the utilities of $(W_0 - L)$, $(W_0 - c)$, and W_0, respectively.

The point $X(p)$ represents the value of $pU(W_0 - L) + (1 - p)U(W_0)$ and will be located somewhere on line segment AC, the exact location depending on the value of p. As long as $X(p)$, which represents the expected utility associated with not buying insurance, is to the left of point E (i.e., below point B), the decision maker should prefer insurance to no insurance because point B represents the utility associated with buying insurance.

If $c = pL$ (i.e., the premium is actuarially fair), then $p = c/L = DC/AC = X(p)/AC$; hence, $X(p)$ will be located at point D. If $U(w)$ is concave, point D will always lie below B, and actuarially fair insurance should thus always be attractive to risk averters. When $c < pL$, then $X(p)$ will be to the left of D, and if $c > pL$, it will be to the right of D (on line segment AC). It is obvious that even if $c > pL$, the decision maker may still want to buy insurance, provided $X(p)$ has not moved to the right of point E. The distance between $X(p)$ and E is a measure of how much "premium loading" the decision maker will tolerate. Of course, if $U(w)$ is convex, the decision maker would never buy insurance unless it were sufficiently subsidized.

To explain insurance-purchasing behavior at premiums above actuarial rates, economists (e.g., Arrow, 1973; Ehrlich and Becker, 1972; Marshall, 1974) have traditionally assumed that $U(w)$ is concave on the loss side. Friedman and Savage (1948) postulated a utility function with a concave and a convex portion to account for people's desire to buy insurance, on the one hand, and their willingness to gamble (e.g., buying lotteries), on the other (see Figure VIII.2.)

Markowitz (1952) suggested another shape of the utility function; it assumes concavity near the customary wealth level (W_0) and convexity when further away from this level (for losses). Markowitz argued that beyond some point, people would become numbed to further losses and would thus be willing to take risks. However, the Markowitz utility function did not receive widespread acceptance in the economic community because the customary wealth level and the inflection points were not well defined. Figure VIII.2 depicts Markowitz's utility function, as well as that proposed by Friedman and Savage. When inflection points are present in $U(x)$ for $x < 0$, the graphical insurance analysis becomes more complex, as described in Chapter 7.

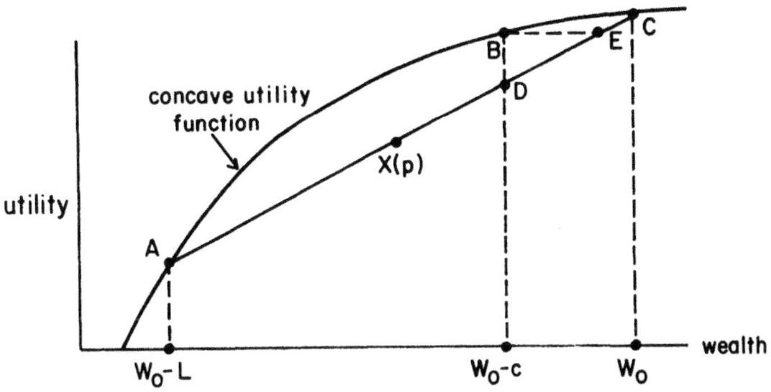

Figure VIII.1. A Graphic Analysis of the Insurance Decision Assuming a Concave Utility Function for Losses

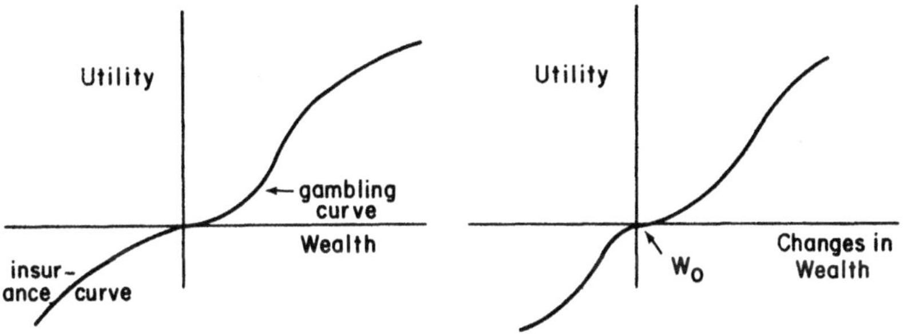

Figure VIII.2. Two General Shapes of the Utility Function as Proposed by Friedman and Savage (*left*) and Markowitz (*right*)

NOTES

1. INTRODUCTION

1. The notion of rationality is a multifaceted one. As Lee (1971) has pointed out, it can mean (1) knowledge through reason only (as opposed to experience, or empiricism); (2) the opposite of knowledge through revelation (i.e., religion); (3) the essence of ethics (i.e., the road to right action); or (4) principles of logic. In this book, rationality will only mean abidance by the axioms of expected utility theory. These axioms are stated in Chapter 2.
2. Of course, much criticism within economics exists as well. Particularly penetrating in this regard is Georgescu-Roegen (1971), who criticized economics for being a science about man from which man has been mostly excluded, reduced to a subscript in a mathematical equation.
3. When Lichtenstein and Slovic (1973) repeated their laboratory experiments in Las Vegas with professional gamblers who played with their own money for much higher stakes, they found the same biases and inconsistencies as they had among college students who provided hypothetical judgments (Lichtenstein and Slovic, 1971). Similar successful replications (with real money) were performed by Grether and Plott (1979).
4. General reviews of decision theory can be found in Edwards (1954b, 1961); Simon (1959); Becker and McClintock (1967); Milburn and Billings (1976); Lee (1971); Rapoport and Wallsten (1972); Janis and Mann (1977); and Slovic, Fischhoff, and Lichtenstein (1977). Reviews and discussions of utility theory are offered in Stigler (1950); Marschak (1950); Arrow (1951); Edwards and Tversky (1967); Borch (1968); Fishburn (1968); and Coombs, Dawes, and Tversky (1970).

2. EXPECTED UTILITY THEORY

1. It is interesting to note here that Bernoulli postulated a function that Fechner (1860) suggested a century later for subjective magnitudes in general. Fechner's law states that sensation intensity is proportional to the logarithm of the stimulus intensity. Cramer (1728) had initially suggested a power function, which Stevens (1957) later used extensively in his psychophysical scaling research.
2. In case $U(x)$ is unbounded (i.e., $\lim_{x \to \infty} U(x) = \infty$), the paradox will still exist if one makes the payoff for the n-th coin toss x_n where $U(x_n) = 2^n$. This possibility was first pointed out by Menger (1934) in his criticism of Bernoulli's explanation.
3. Karmarkar (1978) and Van Dam (1973) found that utility functions constructed with 50-50 lotteries differ systematically from those constructed with, say, 75-25 lotteries. Which is the more faithful one is open to debate.
4. As a normative theory, expected utility maximization is at the heart of statistical decision theory. Classics in this area are Savage (1954); Raiffa and Schlaifer (1968); Raiffa (1968); and DeGroot (1970). Recent expositions on normative decision theory are contained in White (1975, 1976) and Holloway (1979).
5. This general issue of safety first was analyzed in more detail by Kunreuther and Wright (1979).
6. Contingent claims are contracts for which the payoffs depend on the prevailing state of nature. For example, insurance policies may yield a payoff or no payoff depending on whether legitimate losses were incurred.

3. ALTERNATIVE DESCRIPTIVE MODELS

1. For other classification schemes, see MacCrimmon (1973); Libby and Fishburn (1977); Anderson (1979).
2. The vector notation $\bar{x}$ emphasizes the multidimensionality of an alternative; the notation $\tilde{x}$ emphasizes its probabilistic nature.
3. For more formal definitions of the various non-holistic judgment models, see Green and Wind (1973, chap. 2).
4. DeFinetti's theory contains several important axioms about coherency of beliefs that Savage (1954) later synthesized, together with the NM axioms, into a rational theory of choice based on subjective or personalistic probabilities. Hence, SEU is an important normative model as well.
5. There also exist expectation models in which the expected utility does not consist of separable functions of probability and outcomes. An example is Krelle's (1968) g-function theory in which $E[U(x)] = E[g[u(x),p]]$, with $u(x)$ being a value function and g a risk-preference function of the utilities and the amount of information available on the probabilities. A similar model was developed by Bernard (1974). These more complicated models are not discussed further because of their minor place in the general literature.

6. A recent study by Hershey and Schoemaker (1980a) questions the generality of this reflection effect. The data offered by Kahneman and Tversky (1979) concern only across-subject reflectivity, which need not imply significant individual reversals. Hershey and Schoemaker's (1980a) data suggest weak reflectivity to none at all at both aggregate and individual levels.
7. The general theory underlying single-peaked preference functions is discussed in Coombs and Avrunin (1977).
8. Additional discussions of Coombs's portfolio theory are provided in Coombs, Bezembinder, and Goode (1967); Coombs and Bowen (1971); Coombs and Huang (1970a, 1970b); and Coombs and Pruitt (1960).
9. Norman and Rumelhart (1975) and Schank and Colby (1973) provide various formal models of thought and language. Philosophical discussions of computer models and intelligence are contained in Feigenbaum and Feldman (1963). A nontechnical discussion is offered by Weizenbaum (1976) in his lucid and somewhat controversial book on computers and human thought. Also see Neisser (1963, 1967) and Newell and Simon (1961, 1972).
10. Interesting debates on administrative man and his desire and ability to be rational are contained in Argyris (1973a, 1973b) and Simon (1973).
11. Mathematically, a disjunctive rejection rule is isomorphic with a conjunctive acceptance rule. Psychologically, however, they represent different search and evaluation strategies.

4. A POSITIVISTIC TEST OF EU THEORY: PREFERENCES FOR INFORMATION

1. The proof presented here is a generalization of one first suggested to me by Dr. Dorit Hochbaum, currently with Carnegie-Mellon University in Pittsburgh. The presentation has been much improved through suggestions from Dr. Homan, St. Joseph's College in Philadelphia; Dr. Joop van Nunen, Graduate School of Management, Delft, The Netherlands; and Dr. Robert Verrecchia, Graduate School of Business, University of Chicago.
2. Acknowledgment is made to Garret Davies for his assistance with this experiment.
3. The randomness of this assignment was ascertained from the socioeconomic data. Sex, age, statistical knowledge, and the number of dependents did not differ significantly ($p < .05$) among the four subject groups (using chi-square tests). The financial status variables were excluded from this analysis because of an excessive amount of missing data.
4. The test statistic used here is

$$z = \frac{|\bar{p} - .5|}{1/2\sqrt{1/N}},$$

where $\bar{p}$ is the percentage of correct predictions and N the sample size. It is identical to Massy's (1965) discriminatory power test for confusion matrices, where the relevant test statistic is

$$Q = \frac{(N - nK)^2}{N(K - 1)},$$

with K equal to the dimensionality of the table and n the number of correct predictions; Q is approximately chi-square with one degree of freedom. Note that for $K = 2$,

$$\sqrt{Q} = \frac{|N - 2n|}{\sqrt{N}} = \frac{|1/2 - n/N|}{1/2\sqrt{1/N}} = z,$$

as stated above. This correspondence also holds for $K > 2$, provided the z-test is against H_0: $p = 1/K$.

5. This generalization was pointed out to me by Dr. Joop van Nunen, Graduate School of Management, Delft, The Netherlands. His proof is omitted because of its tangential relationship to the experiment.

5. AN EXPERIMENTAL STUDY OF INSURANCE DECISIONS

1. Appendix VIII offers a graphic analysis of the expected utility of actuarially fair insurance. The insights developed there are prerequisite to understanding the issues and analyses of this chapter, as well as those of Chapter 7.
2. Since the survey was anonymous, only limited tests of response biases could be conducted. For further detail on this, see Schoemaker (1977).
3. As a hypothetical example of Simpson's paradox, consider two independent studies on racial integration in schools. Say the first study reports 50 percent ($N = 2{,}000$) whites in private schools and 33 percent ($N = 300{,}000$) whites in public schools. Assume that a second study (conducted in another state) shows 20 percent ($N = 500{,}000$) whites in private schools and 16 percent ($N = 6{,}000$) whites in public schools. Hence, both studies show more whites in private schools than in public ones. However, aggregation of the two studies shows 20 percent ($N = 502{,}000$) whites in private schools and 33 percent ($N = 306{,}000$) whites in public schools, which is a paradoxical reversal of the earlier finding. This extreme example illustrates the care that must be taken when aggregating studies that differ in sample sizes and in percentage values of the dichotomous variable under study.
4. Subjects were told that losses exceeding their current assets were to be viewed as debts to be paid off as soon as possible; this was intended to eliminate budget constraints as a factor in the decision.
5. These figures denote 1976 dollars.

6. Question 1 was singled out for this analysis (as opposed to Question 2 or other questions) because it was closest to the instruction concerning the meaning of the calculation-intuition scales. The intuition score of Question 1 correlated highly with the other eight intuition scores for both the student and client groups. In each of the sixteen cases, the correlation was positive and significant at at least the .004 level (using a two-tailed test for Pearson product-moment correlation).
7. The reason for not comparing with those who circled none of the statistical concepts was that we were not sure whether those respondents skipped the question or indeed knew none of the concepts.
8. The sequence in which the policies of Question 4 were presented was controlled for in the client group. On a random basis, some received a \$20, \$70, \$80, \$90 sequence (with respect to premiums), and others a \$70, \$80, \$90, \$20 sequence. None of the mean ranks of any policy differed significantly at the .1 level between the two groups receiving the different sequences (for both Questions 4 and 5). Hence, there is no evidence of a sequence bias. (Note that the labels for the policies — *P*1, *P*2, *P*3, and *P*4 — of Table 5.6 were chosen for ease of readability and analysis and do not correspond to the questionnaire labels; see Appendix III, Questions 4 and 5.)
9. This concept was defined in Chapter 2 as the ratio of the "expected" cost of insurance should no disaster occur to the "expected" net gain in assets from insurance after a disaster has occurred. This ratio is .102 for *P*1 (assuming an average loss magnitude of \$20,000), and .35, .398, and .446 for *P*2, *P*3, and *P*4, respectively.
10. A similar analysis of *P*2 and *P*3 (see Question 12) also revealed that the low deductible policy (*P*3) was more attractive within an insurance context (relative to *P*2) than without. This context effect was again strongest for the student group ($p < .002$).
11. Since Questions 11 and 7 were different in the questionnaire given to the student group, this analysis pertains to the client group only.
12. The order in which the hazards of Question 6 were listed was controlled for; no sequence bias was observed.
13. To ascertain the extent to which these findings apply to real-world situations requires further investigation since neither study included systematic observations on such influences as vividness, social pressures, aspiration levels, and regret considerations.
14. The order of alternatives was controlled for (see the two versions of Question 9 in Appendix III); no significant order effect was observed.

6. STATISTICAL KNOWLEDGE AND GAMBLING DECISIONS: MOMENTS VS. RISK DIMENSIONS

1. An interesting discussion of the implications of differences in cognitive style (intuitive versus systematic) for decision making and the use of analytical techniques is provided by Keen and McKenney (1974).

2. Payne (1975) and Slovic (1967) also found that perceptions as to the riskiness of gambles are more related to risk dimensions than to moments.
3. Wright (1975) provides some empirical marketing data and a discussion of the type of compromise that consumers must make between "optimizing eventual consumption benefits and reducing the strains of decision making" (p. 62). He notes that surprisingly little attention has been paid to the effect of cognitive strain on decision processes. Indeed, to my knowledge, no studies involving gambles have explicitly examined that effect.
4. Decision quality here refers to decision making that maximizes expected utility. As noted in Chapter 2, looking just at means and variances is, strictly speaking, only justifiable if $U(x)$ is quadratic. However, the general compatibility of the moment approach with EU maximization becomes readily apparent when $U(x)$ is expanded into a Taylor's series around the mean — that is,

$$U(x) = U(\mu) + \frac{U'(\mu)}{1!}(x - \mu) + \frac{U''(\mu)}{2!}(x - \mu)^2 + R,$$

$$\text{with } R = \sum_{n=3}^{\infty} \frac{U^n(\mu)}{n!}(x - \mu)^n.$$

Taking the expected value of $U(x)$ for some random variable $\tilde{x}$ then yields

$$E[U(\tilde{x})] = U(\mu) + \frac{U''(\mu)}{2!}\sigma^2 + \frac{U''(\mu)}{3!}E(\tilde{x} - \mu)^3$$

$$+ \sum_{n=4}^{\infty} \frac{U^n(\mu)}{n!}E(\tilde{x} - \mu)^n.$$

If the remainder (i.e., sum of the higher-order terms) is small, $E[U(\tilde{x})]$ can well be approximated through the first two or three moments of $\tilde{x}$ (e.g., see Hirshleifer, 1970, pp. 278–84).
5. Dimension preference is not independent of a person's risk-taking attitude, as is shown in the expected utility analysis of Appendix VI.
6. Although differences generally exist between volunteer and nonvolunteer subjects (Rosenthal and Rosnow, 1974), the implications are minimal for the present experiment.
7. Slovic, Lichtenstein, and Edwards's (1965) finding that boredom leads to simpler strategies, and hence to less cognitive strain, supports the assumption of an inverse relationship. It may appear that this assumption is inconsistent with the hypothesis that trained subjects (who supposedly are more bored) use more complex decision rules. The paradox is resolved, however, when distinguishing between cognitive complexity and mathematical complexity. Although multiplicative models are mathematically more complex than additive ones, they may be cognitively easier for trained subjects than additive models are for untrained subjects. Indeed, Table 6.3 suggests that this is the case.

8. Readers concerned about the use of z-tests when expected cell frequencies are less than five are referred to Roscoe and Byars (1971) or Camilli and Hopkins (1978).
9. It should be noted that the additive model will generally provide a much better fit (i.e., higher R^2) than the multiplicative model when both are misspecified. To give an example, when the additive model was misfitted to a data set in which the bids were exactly equal to each duplex bet's EV, the resulting R^2 equalled .78. The thirty-one bets used were those shown in Table 6.1. However, when the EV-variance model was misfitted to an artificial data set computed from an additive model with equal weights, the R^2 was as low as .23. Hence, the additive model appears significantly less sensitive to model misspecification than does the multiplicative one (see also Dawes and Corrigan, 1974).

7. RISK TAKING AND PROBLEM CONTEXT IN THE DOMAIN OF LOSSES

1. Throughout this chapter, S and L denote negative amounts of money.
2. Appendix VIII contains a more detailed graphic EU analysis, the insights of which are prerequisite to this discussion.
3. It is generally not advisable to measure strength of preferences by differences in expected utilities, as this is usually meaningless. However, Figure 7.1 has a common reference point (S_0), which makes inversion of the expected utilities into certainty equivalents unnecessary for comparison of the degrees of insurance preferences across different hazards.
4. The analyses in this chapter do not utilize the information that subjects provided on the strengths of preference (see Appendix VII), as these cannot be meaningfully compared across questions. The general findings, however, would have been the same if mean strengths of preference had been plotted in Figures 7.4, 7.5, and 7.6.
5. The similarity between the present questions and those of Slovic et al. does not hold for Question 6 in which $p = .2$ and $L = -\$50$, as opposed to $p = .25$ and $L = -4$ points in Slovic et al. (their Question g; see Figure 7.5).
6. The students used in this replication did not differ from the present subjects in terms of age, sex, wealth, or statistical knowledge.
7. Acknowledgement is made to Paul Slovic and Baruch Fischhoff for making available a copy of their questionnaire.
8. To avoid confusion between p as a probability level in a lottery and p as a significance level in a statistical test, we will use "prob. > . . ." to indicate the latter.
9. Discussions with subjects after this replication suggested that the portfolio context, the instruction to "lose as little as possible," and the aggregation of abstract loss points across urns induced a gambling atmosphere and a desire to

win the "game." Most subjects felt that losing abstract points meant little to them, other than not winning or doing well in the game.

10. Note that in this chapter the question is not whether people maximize expected utility, but whether their basic tastes and preferences can be represented through a utility function. This latter condition is necessary to guarantee EU theory's operationality as a normative model, as well as its validity as a descriptive model for more complex decision situations.

8. EPILOGUE

1. It is implicitly assumed that the decision model does not already capture these influences by, for example, being discontinuous for certain values of one or more of the independent variables. For illustration purposes, it is useful to think of F as a continuous function of the X_i; however, the distinctions made here may apply as well to discontinuous models (e.g., algorithmic or flow-chart representations) after modifying some of the terminology (e.g., see Einhorn, Kleinmuntz, and Kleinmuntz, 1979).
2. Vlek and Stallen (1979) offer an important step in this direction by providing a psychological categorization of various aspects of risk.
3. Kahneman's lecture (October 8, 1979) was part of the Cognitive Science Lecture Series and the Decision Research Workshop of the University of Chicago. Its title was "The Psychology of Possible Worlds."

REFERENCES

Allais, M. 1953. Le comportement de l'homme rationel devant le risque: critique des postulats et axiomes de l'école Américaine. *Econometrica* 21:503–46.

Anderson, D. R. 1974. The national flood insurance program — problems and potentials. *Journal of Risk and Insurance* 41:579–99.

Anderson, J. R. 1979. Perspective on models of uncertain decisions. In *Risk, uncertainty and agricultural development*, chap. 3. J. A. Roumasset, J. M. Boussard, and I. Singh, eds. New York: Agricultural Development Council.

Anderson, N. H. 1970. Functional measurement and psychological judgment. *Psychological Review* 77:153–70.

Anderson, N. H., and J. C. Shanteau. 1970. Information integration in risky decision making. *Journal of Experimental Psychology* 84:441–51.

Andriessen, J. H. 1971. Comments on a new risk taking model. *Acta Psychologica* 35:173–87.

Argyris, C. 1973a. Some limits of rational man organizational theory. *Public Administration Review* 33, no. 3 (May/June).

_______. 1973b. Organization man: rational and self-actualizing. *Public Administration Review* 33, no. 4 (July/August).

Armstrong, J. S. 1978. *Long-range forecasting: from crystal ball to computer,* chap. 10. New York: Wiley.

Arrow, K. J. 1951. Alternative approaches to the theory of choices in risk taking situations. *Econometrica* 19:405–37.

———. 1971. *Essays in the theory of risk-bearing*. Chicago: Markham.

———. 1973. Optimal insurance and generalized deductibles. Rand Report R-1108-E. Santa Monica, Calif.

Bar-Hillel, M. 1973. On the subjective probability of compounded events. *Organizational Behavior and Human Performance* 9:396–406.

———. 1980 (in press). The base-rate fallacy in probability judgments. *Acta Psychologica*.

Baron, D. P. 1977. On the utility theoretic foundations of mean-variance analysis. *Journal of Finance* 32, no. 5 (December).

Baumol, W. J. 1958. The cardinal utility which is ordinal. *Economic Journal* 68 (December): 1–6.

———. 1972. *Economic theory and operations analysis*. Englewood Cliffs, N.J.: Prentice-Hall.

Becker, G. M., M. H. DeGroot, and J. Marschak. 1963. An experimental study of some stochastic models for wagers. *Behavioral Science* 8:199–202.

Becker, S. W., and F. O. Brownson. 1964. What price ambiguity? Or the role of ambiguity in decision-making. *Journal of Political Economy* 72:62–73.

Becker, S. W., and C. G. McClintock. 1967. Value: behavioral decision theory. *Annual Review of Psychology* 18:239–86.

Bernard, G. 1974. On utility functions. *Theory and Decision* 5:205–42.

Bernoulli, D. 1738. Specimen theoriae novae de mensura sortis. *Commentarri Academiae Scientiarum Imperialis Petropolitanae* 5:175–92. Translated by L. Sommer as Expositions of a new theory on the measurement of risk. *Econometrica* 22 (1954):23–26.

Bernoulli, J. 1713. *Ars conjectandi*. Translated into German by R. Haussner as Wahrscheinlichkeitsrechnung. *Ostwald's Klassiker der Exakten Wissenschaften*, nos. 107 and 108. Leipzig: W. Englemann, 1899.

Bickel, P. J., E. A. Hammel, and J. W. O'Connell. 1975. Sex bias in graduate admissions: data from Berkeley. *Science* 187 (February):398–404.

Birnbaum, M. H. 1973. The devil rides again: correlation as an index of fit. *Psychological Bulletin* 4:239–42.

Blyth, C. R. 1972. On Simpson's paradox and the sure thing principle. *Journal of the American Statistical Association* 67 (338):364–81.

Borch, H. K. 1968. *The economics of uncertainty*. Princeton, N.J.: Princeton University Press.

Bower, G. H. 1975. Cognitive psychology: an interpretation. In *Handbook of learning and cognitive processes*, vol. 1. W. K. Estes, ed. Hillside, N.J.: Erlbaum Associates.

Bowman, E. H. 1963. Consistency and optimality in managerial decision making. *Management Science* 9 (2):310–21.

Břicháček, V. 1970. Use of subjective probability in decision making. *Acta Psychologica* 34:241–53.

Bruner, J. S., J. L. Goodnow, and G. A. Austin. 1956. *A study of thinking*. New York: Wiley.

Brunswik, E. 1952. *Conceptual framework of psychology*. Chicago: University of Chicago Press.

Burks, A. W. 1977. *Chance, cause, reason: an inquiry into the nature of scientific evidence*. Chicago: University of Chicago Press.

Camilli, G., and K. D. Hopkins. 1978. Applicability of chi-square to 2 × 2 contingency tables with small expected frequencies. *Psychological Bulletin* 85 (1):163–67.

Campbell, D. T., and J. C. Stanley. 1963. *Experimental and quasi-experimental designs for research*. Chicago: Rand McNally.

Carnap, R. 1971. A basic system of inductive logic. In *Studies in inductive logic and probability*, vol. 1. R. Carnap and R. C. Jeffrey, eds. Berkeley: University of California Press.

Churchman, C. W. 1961. *Prediction and Optimal Decision*. Englewood Cliffs, N.J.: Prentice-Hall.

Cook, T. D., and D. T. Campbell. 1976. The design and conduct of quasi-experiments and true experiments in field settings. In *Handbook of industrial and organizational psychology*, pp. 224–46. M. D. Dunnette, ed. Chicago: Rand McNally.

Coombs, C. H. 1964. *A theory of data*. New York: Wiley.

_______. 1975. Portfolio theory and the measurement of risk. In *Human judgment and decision processes*. M. F. Kaplan and S. Schwartz, eds. New York: Academic Press.

Coombs, C. H., and G. S. Avrunin. 1977. Single-peaked functions and the theory of preference. *Psychological Review* 84:216–30.

Coombs, C. H., T. C. Bezembinder, and F. M. Goode. 1967. Testing expectation theories of decision making without measuring utility or subjective probability. *Journal of Mathematical Psychology* 4:72–103.

Coombs, C. H., and J. N. Bowen. 1971. A test of VE-theories of risk and the effect of the central limit theorem. *Acta Psychologica* 35:15–28.

Coombs, C. H., R. M. Dawes, and A. Tversky. 1970. *Mathematical psychology: an elementary introduction*. Englewood Cliffs, N.J.: Prentice-Hall.

Coombs, C. H., and L. C. Huang. 1970a. Polynomial psychophysics of risk. *Journal of Mathematical Psychology* 7:317–38.

_______. 1970b. Tests of a portfolio theory of risk preference. *Journal of Experimental Psychology* 85:23–29.

Coombs, C. H., and R. C. Kao. 1955. Nonmetric factor analysis. Research Bulletin no. 38, Engineering Research Institute, University of Michigan.

Coombs, C. H., and D. G. Pruitt. 1960. Components of risk in decision making: probability and variance preference. *Journal of Experimental Psychology* 60:256–77.

Cramer, G. 1728. Letter to Bernoulli's cousin. (See Bernoulli, 1738.)

Cyert, R. M., and J. G. March. 1963. *A behavioral theory of the firm*. Englewood Cliffs, N.J.: Prentice-Hall.

Davidson, D., P. Suppes, and S. Siegel. 1957. *Decision making: an experimental approach*. Stanford, California: Stanford University Press.

Davis, M. S. 1971. That's interesting! *Philosophy of Social Science* 1:309–44.

Dawes, M. D., and B. Corrigan. 1974. Linear models in decision making. *Psychological Bulletin* 81 (2):95–106.
Deegan, J. 1976. The consequences of model misspecification in regression analysis. *Multivariate Behavioral Research* 11, no. 2 (April).
DeFinetti, B. 1937. La prévision: ses lois logiques, ses sources subjectives. *Annales de l'Institut Henri Poincaré* 7:1–68.
———. 1974. *Theory of probability: a critical introduction*, vol. 1. London: Wiley.
DeGroot, M. H. 1970. *Optimal statistical decisions*. New York: McGraw-Hill.
De La Place, P. S. 1951. *A philosophical essay on probabilities*. Translated by F. W. Truscott and F. L. Emory. New York: Dover.
Edgeworth, F. Y. 1881. *Mathematical psychics*. London: Kegan Paul.
Edwards, W. 1953. Probability-preferences in gambling. *American Journal of Psychology* 66:349–64.
———. 1954a. Probability preferences among bets with differing expected values. *American Journal of Psychology* 67:56–67.
———. 1954b. The theory of decision making. *Psychological Bulletin* 51:380–97.
———. 1954c. Variance preferences in gambling. *American Journal of Psychology* 67:441–52.
———. 1955. The prediction of decisions among bets. *Journal of Experimental Psychology* 50:201–14.
———. 1959. Subjective probability in decision theories. Working Paper, Willow Run Laboratories, University of Michigan.
———. 1961. Behavorial decision theory. *Annual Review of Psychology* 12:473–98.
———. 1968. Conservatism in human information processing. In *Formal representation of human judgment*. B. Kleinmuntz, ed. New York: Wiley.
Edwards, W., and A. Tversky. 1967. *Decision making*. New York: Penguin Books.
Ehrlich, I., and G. S. Becker. 1972. Market insurance, self-insurance, and self-protection. *Journal of Political Economy* 80 (July/August).
Einhorn, H. J. 1970. The use of nonlinear, noncompensatory models in decision making. *Psychological Bulletin* 73:221–30.
———. 1971. Use of nonlinear, noncompensatory models as a function of task and amount of information. *Organizational Behavior and Human Performance* 6:1–27.
Einhorn, H. J., D. N. Kleinmuntz, and B. Kleinmuntz. 1979. Linear regression and process-tracing models of judgment. *Psychological Review* 86:465–85.
Eisner, R., and R. Strotz. 1961. Flight insurance and the theory of choice. *Journal of Political Economy* 69:355–68.
Ellsberg, D. 1961. Risk, ambiguity and the Savage axioms. *Quarterly Journal of Economics* 75:643–69.
Etzioni, A. 1967. Mixed scanning: a third approach to decision making. *Public Administration Review* 27:385–92.
Fechner, G. T. 1966. *Elemente der psychopsysik*, 1860. English translation of vol. 1 by H. E. Adler, D. H. Howes, and E. G. Boring, eds. New York: Holt, Rinehart and Winston.

Federal Insurance Administration. 1974. Full insurance availability. Washington, D.C.: U.S. Department of Housing and Urban Development.

Feigenbaum, E. A., and J. Feldman. 1963. *Computers and thought*. New York: McGraw-Hill.

Fellner, W. 1961. Distortion of subjective probabilities as a reaction to uncertainty. *Quarterly Journal of Economics* 75:670–89.

Fischhoff, B. 1975. Hindsight = foresight: the effect of outcome knowledge on judgment under uncertainty. *Journal of Experimental Psychology: Human Perception and Performance* 1 (August):288–99.

_______. 1976. The effect of temporal setting on likelihood estimates. *Organizational Behavior and Human Performance* 15:180–94.

_______. 1977. Perceived informativeness of facts. *Journal of Experimental Psychology: Human Perception and Performance* 3 (May):349–58.

Fischhoff, B., and R. Beyth. 1975. 'I knew it would happen.' Remembered probabilities of once-future things. *Organizational Behavior and Human Performance* 13:1–16.

Fishburn, P. C. 1968. Utility theory. *Management Science* 14:335–78.

_______. 1970. *Utility theory for decision making*. New York: Wiley.

_______. 1974. Lexicographic orders, utilities and decision rules: a survey. *Management Science* (July):1442–71.

_______. 1977. Mean-risk analysis with risk associated with below-target returns. *American Economic Review* 67, 2 (March):116–26.

_______. 1978. On Handa's "new theory of cardinal utility" and the maximization of expected return (comments). *Journal of Political Economy* 86 (2, 1):321–24.

Fishburn, P. C., and G. A. Kochenberger. 1980 (in press). Two-piece Von Neumann-Morgenstern utility functions. *Decision Sciences*.

Friedman, M. 1935. *Essays in positive economics*. Chicago: University of Chicago Press.

Friedman, M., and L. J. Savage. 1948. The utility analysis of choices involving risk. *Journal of Political Economy* 56:279–304.

Fryback, D. G., B. C. Goodman, and W. Edwards. 1973. Choices among bets by Las Vegas gamblers: absolute and contextual effects. *Journal of Experimental Psychology* 98 (2):271–78.

Georgescu-Roegen, N. 1971. *The entropy law and the economic process*. Cambridge, Mass.: Harvard University Press.

Goldberg, L. R. 1968. Simple models or simple processes? Some research on clinical judgments. *American Psychologist* 23, no. 7 (July).

_______. 1970. Man versus model of man: a rationale, plus some evidence, for a method of improving on clinical inferences. *Psychological Bulletin* 73 (6):422–32.

_______. 1971. Five models of clinical judgment: an empirical comparison between linear and nonlinear representations of the human inference process. *Organizational Behavior and Human Performance* 6:458–79.

Gould, J. P. 1969. The expected utility hypothesis and the selection of optimal deductible for a given insurance policy. *Journal of Business* 42 (2):143–51.

Green, P. E., and Y. Wind. 1973. *Multiattribute decision making in marketing*. Hinsdale, Ill.: Dryden Press.

Greene, M. R. 1963. Attitudes toward risk and a theory of insurance consumption. *Journal of Insurance* 30:165–82.

———. 1964. Insurance mindedness — implications for insurance theory. *Journal of Insurance* 31.

Grether, D. M., and C. R. Plott. 1979. Economic theory of choice and the preference reversal phenomenon. *American Economic Review* 69:623–38.

Hadar, J., and W. R. Russell. 1969. Rules for ordering uncertain prospects. *American Economic Review* 59:25–34.

Halter, A. N. 1956. Measuring utility of wealth among farm managers. Ph.D. dissertation, Michigan State University.

Handa, J. 1977. Risk, probabilities and a new theory of cardinal utility. *Journal of Political Economy* 85:97–122.

Henderson, J. M., and R. E. Quandt. 1971. *Microeconomic theory: a mathematical approach.* New York: McGraw-Hill.

Hershey, J. C., and P. J. H. Schoemaker. 1980a (in press). Prospect theory's reflection hypothesis: a critical examination. *Organizational Behavior and Human Performance.*

———. 1980b. Risk taking and problem context in the domain of losses: an expected utility analysis. *Journal of Risk and Insurance* 47 (March).

Hershman, R. L., and J. R. Levine. 1970. Deviations from optimum information-purchase strategies in human decision-making. *Organizational Behavior and Human Performance* 5:313–29.

Hicks, J. R. 1939. *Value and capital.* London: Oxford University Press.

Hirshleifer, J. 1970. *Investment, interest and capital.* Englewood Cliffs, N.J.: Prentice-Hall.

Hoffman, P. J. 1960. The paramorphic representation of clinical judgment. *Psychological Bulletin* 57 (2).

Hogarth, R. M. 1979. Functional and dysfunctional aspects of judgmental heuristics: a dynamic perspective. Working Paper, Center for Decision Research, University of Chicago.

Holloway, C. A. 1979. *Decision making under uncertainty: models and choices.* Englewood Cliffs, N.J.: Prentice-Hall.

Irwin, F. W. 1953. Stated expectations as functions of probability and desirability of outcomes. *Journal of Personality* 21:329–35.

Isaac, R. M., and C. R. Plott. 1979. Price controls and the behavior of auction markets: an experimental examination. Social Science Working Paper no. 253, California Institute of Technology.

Janis, I. L., and L. Mann. 1977. *Decision making: a psychological analysis of conflict, choice and commitment.* New York: Free Press.

Johnson, G. L., et al. 1961. *Managerial processes of midwestern farmers.* Ames: Iowa State University Press.

Kahneman, D., and A. Tversky. 1972. Subjective probability: a judgment of representativeness. *Cognitive Psychology* 3:430–54.

———. 1973. On the psychology of prediction. *Psychological Review* 80 (4).

———. 1979. Prospect theory: an analysis of decision under risk. *Econometrica* 47:263–91.

Kanuk, L., and C. Berenson. 1975. Mail surveys and response rates: a literature review. *Journal of Marketing Research* 12 (November): 440–53.

Karmarkar, U. S. 1978. Subjectively weighted utility: a descriptive extension of the expected utility model. *Organizational Behavior and Human Performance* 21:61–72.

_______. 1979. Subjectively weighted utility and the Allais paradox. *Organizational Behavior and Human Performance* 24:67–72.

Katona, G. 1965. *Private pensions and individual saving*. Monograph no. 40, Survey Research Center Institute for Social Research, University of Michigan.

_______. 1975. *Psychological economics*. New York: Elsevier.

Keen, P. G. W., and J. L. McKenney. 1974. The implications of cognitive style for implementation of analytic models. Sloan Working Paper 694, M.I.T.

Keeney, R. L., and H. Raiffa. 1976. *Decisions with multiple objectives: preferences and value tradeoffs*. New York: Wiley.

Keynes, J. M. 1921. *A treatise on probability*. London: Macmillan.

Klatzky, R. L. 1975. *Human memory: structures and processes*. San Francisco: W. H. Freeman.

Kogan, N., and M. A. Wallach. 1967. Risk taking as a function of the situation, the person, and the group. In *New directions in psychology*, pp. 111–278. T. M. Newcomb, ed. New York: Holt, Rinehart and Winston.

_______. 1974. *Risk taking: a study in cognition and personality*. New York: Holt, Rinehart and Winston.

Krantz, D. H., et al. 1971. *Foundations of measurement*, vol. 1. New York: Academic Press.

Krantz, D. H., and A. Tversky. 1971. Conjoint-measurement analysis of composition rules in psychology. *Psychological Review* 78:151–69.

Krelle, W. 1968. *Präferenz- und Entscheidungstheorie*. Tübingen: Mohr.

Kuhn, H. W., and A. W. Tucker. 1951. Nonlinear programming. In *Proceedings of the second Berkeley symposium on mathematical statistics and probability*. Berkeley: University of California Press.

Kunreuther, H. 1969. Extensions of Bowman's theory on managerial decision-making. *Management Science* 15, no. 8 (April).

_______. 1976. Limited knowledge and insurance protection. *Public Policy* 24, no. 2 (Spring).

Kunreuther, H., et al. 1978. *Disaster insurance protection: public policy lessons*. New York: Wiley.

Kunreuther, H., and G. Wright. 1979. Safety-first, gambling, and the subsistence farmer. In *Risk, uncertainty and agricultural development*, chap. 12. J. A. Roumasset, J. M. Boussard, and I. Singh, eds. New York: Agricultural Development Council.

Kyburg, H. E. 1974. *The logical foundations of statistical inference*. Dordrecht, The Netherlands: Reidel.

Kyburg, H. E., and H. E. Smokler. 1964. *Studies in subjective probability*. New York: Wiley.

Lawler, E. E. 1973. *Motivation in work organizations*. Monterey, Calif.: Brooks/Cole.

Lazarsfeld, P. F. 1949. The American soldier: an expository review. *Public Opinion Quarterly* 13:380.

Lee, W. 1971. *Decision theory and human behavior*. New York: Wiley.

Levy, H., and H. M. Markowitz. 1979. Approximating expected utility by a function of mean and variance. *American Economic Review* 69, no. 3 (June):308–17.

Libby, R. 1976. Man versus model of man: some conflicting evidence. *Organizational Behavior and Human Performance* 16:1–26.

Libby, R., and P. C. Fishburn. 1977. Behavioral models of risk-taking in business decisions: a survey and evaluation. *Journal of Accounting Research* (Autumn).

Lichtenstein, S. 1965. Bases for preferences among three-outcome bets. *Journal of Experimental Psychology* 69:162–69.

Lichtenstein, S., and P. Slovic. 1971. Reversals of preference between bids and choices in gambling decisions. *Journal of Experimental Psychology* 89:46–55.

———. 1973. Response-induced reversals of preferences in gambling: an extended replication in Las Vegas. *Journal of Experimental Psychology* 101:16–20.

Lichtenstein, S., P. Slovic, and D. Zink. 1969. Effect of instruction in expected value on optimality of gambling decisions. *Journal of Experimental Psychology* 79:236–40.

Lindblom, C. E. 1964. The science of muddling through. In *The making of decisions*. W. T. Gore and J. W. Dyson, eds. New York: Free Press.

Lindman, H. R. 1971. Inconsistent preferences among gambles. *Journal of Experimental Psychology* 89:390–97.

Lindsay, R. B. 1968. Physics — to what extent it is it deterministic? *American Scientist* 56:93–111.

Luce, R. D., and H. Raiffa. 1957. *Games and decisions*. New York: Wiley.

Luce, R. D., and P. Suppes. 1965. Preference, utility, and subjective probabilities. In *Handbook of mathematical psychology*, pp. 42–49. R. D. Luce, R. R. Bush, and E. Galanter, eds. New York: Wiley.

Luce, R. D., and J. W. Tukey. 1964. Simultaneous conjoint measurement — a new type of fundamental measurement. *Journal of Mathematical Psychology* 1:1–27.

MacCrimmon, K. R. 1968. Descriptive and normative implications of decisions theory postulates. In *Risk and uncertainty*, pp. 3–23. K. Borch and J. Mossin, eds. New York: Macmillan.

———. 1973. An overview of multiple objective decision making. In *Multiple criteria decision making*, pp. 18–44. J. L. Cochrane and M. Zeleny, eds. Columbia: University of South Carolina Press.

MacCrimmon, K. R., and S. Larsson. 1975. Utility theory: axioms versus "paradoxes." In *Rational decisions under uncertainty*. M. Allais and O. Hagen, eds.

McGrath, J. E. 1964. Toward a "theory of method" for research on organizations. In *New perspectives in organizational research*, pp. 533–37. W. W. Cooper, H. L. Leavitt, and M. W. Shelby, eds. New York: Wiley.

Machlup, F. 1967. Theories of the firm: marginalist, behavioral, managerial. *American Economic Review* 57, no. 1 (March).

March, J. G. 1978. Bounded rationality, ambiguity, and the engineering of choice. *Bell Journal of Economics* 9:587–608.

March, J. G., and H. A. Simon. 1958. *Organizations*. New York: Wiley.

Markowitz, H. 1952. The utility of wealth. *Journal of Political Economy* 60, no. 2 (April):151–58.

_______. 1959. *Portfolio selection: efficient diversification of investments*. New York: Wiley.

Marks, R. W. 1951. The effect of probability, desirability, and "privilege" on the stated expectations of children. *Journal of Personality* 19:332–51.

Marrow, A. J. 1969. *The practical theorist: the life and work of Kurt Lewin*. New York: Basic Books.

Marschak, J. 1950. Rational behavior, uncertain prospects, and measurable utility. *Econometrica* 18:111–41.

Marshall, A. 1890. *Principles of economics*. London: Macmillian.

Marshall, J. 1974. Insurance as a market in contingent claims: structure and performance. *Bell Journal of Economics and Management Science* 5.

Massy, W. F. 1965. On methods: discriminant analysis of audience characteristics. *Journal of Advertising Research* 5:39–48.

Menger, K. 1934. Das Unsicherheitsmoment in der Wertlehre. *Zeitschrift für Nationalokönomie* 51:459–85.

Meyer, R. F., and J. W. Pratt. 1968. The consistent assessment and fairing of preference functions. *CEEE Systems Science and Cybernetics* (SSC-4):270–78.

Milburn, T. W., and R. S. Billings. 1976. Decision-making perspectives from psychology: dealing with risk and uncertainty. *American Scientist* 20, no. 1 (September/October).

Miller, G. A. 1956. The magical number seven, plus or minus two. *Psychological Review* 63 (2).

Mosteller, F., and P. Nogee. 1951. An experimental measurement of utility. *Journal of Political Economy* 59:371–404.

Murray, M. L. 1971. A deductible selection model — development and application. *Journal of Risk and Insurance* 38.

_______. 1972. Empirical utility functions and insurance consumption decisions. *Journal of Risk and Insurance* 39.

Neisser, U. 1963. The imitation of man by machine. *Science* 139:193–97.

_______. 1967. *Cognitive psychology*. Des Moines: Meredith.

Neter, J., and C. A. Williams, 1971. Acceptability of three normative methods in insurance decision making. *Journal of Risk and Insurance* 38.

Newell, A., J. C. Shaw, and H. A. Simon. 1958. Elements of a theory of human problem solving. *Psychological Review* 65 (3).

Newell, A., and H. A. Simon. 1961. Computer simulation of human thinking. *Science* 134:2011–17.

_______. 1972. *Human problem solving*. Englewood Cliffs, N.J.: Prentice-Hall.

Nisbett, R. E., and T. D. Wilson. 1977. Telling more than we know: verbal reports on mental process. *Psychological Review* 84:231–59.

Norman, D. A., and D. E. Rumelhart. 1975. *Explorations in cognition*. San Francisco: W. H. Freeman.

Officer, R. R. 1967. Decision making under risk: a brief examination of the Bayesian approach and an empirical study of utility analysis in agriculture. Master's thesis, University of New England, Armidale, Australia.

Officer, R. R., and A. N. Halter. 1968. Utility analysis in a practical setting. *American Journal of Agricultural Economics* 50, no. 2 (May).

Pareto, V. 1909. *Manuel d' economic politique*. Paris: Girard.

Pashigian, B. P., L. Schkade, and G. H. Menefee. 1966. The selection of an optimal deductible for a given insurance policy. *Journal of Business* 39:35–44.

Payne, J. W. 1973. Alternative approaches to decision making under risk: moments versus risk dimensions. *Psychological Bulletin* 80 (6):439–53.

———. 1975. Relation of perceived risk to preferences among gambles. *Journal of Experimental Psychology* 104 (1):86–94.

———. 1976. Task complexity and contingent processing in decision making: an information search and protocol analysis. *Organizational Behavior and Human Performance* 16:366–87.

Payne, J. W., and M. L. Braunstein. 1971. Preferences among gambles with equal underlying distributions. *Journal of Experimental Psychology* 87:13–18.

Payne, J. W., D. J. Laughhun, and R. Crum. 1979. Levels of aspiration and preference reversals in risky choice. Working Paper, Graduate School of Business Administration, Duke University.

Pollatsek, A. 1971. The inconsistency of expected utility theory with certain classes of single-peaked preference functions. *Journal of Mathematical Psychology* 8:225–34.

Pratt, J. W. 1964. Risk aversion in the small and in the large. *Econometrica* 32:122–36.

Pratt, J. W., H. Raiffa, and R. Schlaifer. 1965. *Introduction to statistical decision theory*. London: McGraw-Hill.

Press, J. S. 1972. *Applied multivariate analysis*. New York: Holt, Rinehart and Winston.

Preston, M. G., and P. Baratta. 1948. An experimental study of the auction value of an uncertain outcome. *American Journal of Psychology* 61:183–93.

Pruitt, D. G. 1962. Pattern and level of risk in gambling decisions. *Psychological Review* 69:187–201.

Quirk, J., and R. Saposnik. 1968. *Introduction to general equilibrium theory and welfare economics*. New York: McGraw-Hill.

Raiffa, H. 1961. Risk, ambiguity and the Savage axioms: comment. *Quarterly Journal of Economics* 75:690–94.

———. 1968. *Decision analysis: introductory lectures on choices under uncertainty*. Reading, Mass.: Addison-Wesley.

Raiffa, H., and H. Schlaifer. 1968. *Applied statistical decision theory*. Cambridge, Mass.: M.I.T. Press.

Ramsey, F. P. 1931. *The foundations of mathematics*. New York: Harcourt Brace.

Ranyard, R. H. 1976. Elimination by aspects as a decision rule for risky choice. *Acta Psychologica* 40:299–310.

Rapoport, A., and T. S. Wallsten. 1972. Individual decision behavior. *Annual Review of Psychology* 23:131–75.

Reder, M. W. 1947. A reconsideration of the marginal productivity theory. *Journal of Political Economy* (October):450–58.

Reichenbach, H. 1949. *The theory of probability*. Translated by E. H. Hutton and M. Reichenbach. Berkeley: University of California Press.

Robertson, L. 1974. Urban area safety belt use in automobiles with starter interlock belt systems: a preliminary report. Washington, D.C.: Insurance Institute for Highway Safety.

Ronen, J. 1973. Effects of some probability displays on choices. *Organizational Behavior and Human Performance* 9:1–15.

Roscoe, J. T. 1975. *Fundamental research statistics for the behavioral sciences*. New York: Holt, Rinehart and Winston.

Roscoe, J. T., and J. A. Byars. 1971. An investigation of the restraints with respect to sample size commonly imposed on the use of the chi-square statistic. *Journal of the American Statistical Association* 66:755–59.

Rosenthal, R., and R. Rosnow. 1974. *The volunteer subject*. New York: Wiley.

Rosett, R. N. 1971. Weak experimental verification of the expected utility hypothesis. *Review of Economic Studies* (October):481–92.

Russo, J. E., and B. A. Dosher. 1976. An information processing analysis of binary choice. Working Paper, Carnegie-Mellon University.

Savage, L. J. 1954. *The foundations of statistics*. New York: Wiley.

Schank, R. C., and K. M. Colby, eds. 1973. *Computer models of thought and language*. San Francisco: W. H. Freeman.

Schmitt, N., and R. L. Levine. 1977. Statistical and subjective weights: some problems and proposals. *Organizational Behavior and Human Performance* 20:15–30.

Schneeweiss, H. 1974. Probability and utility — dual concepts in decision theory. In *Information, inference and decision*, pp. 113–44. G. Menges, ed. Dordrecht, The Netherlands: Reidel.

Schoemaker, P. J. H. 1977. Experimental studies on individual decision making under risk: an information processing approach. Ph.D. dissertation, Wharton School, University of Pennsylvania.

_______. 1978. Context credibility and format bias in retrospective judgment. *Proceedings of the American Institute for Decision Sciences* (October). St. Louis: American Institute for Decision Sciences.

_______. 1979. The role of statistical knowledge in gambling decisions: moment vs. risk dimension approaches. *Organizational Behavior and Human Performance* 24:1–17.

Schoemaker, P. J. H., and H. Kunreuther. 1979. An experimental study of insurance decisions. *Journal of Risk and Insurance* 46 (December):603–18.

Sen, A. K. 1970. *Collective choice and social welfare*. San Francisco: Holden-Day.

Shepard, R. N. 1964. On subjectively optimum selections among multi-attribute alternatives. In *Human Judgment and Optimality*. M. W. Shelly and G. L. Bryan, eds. New York: Wiley.

Siegel, S. 1957. Level of aspiration and decision making. *Psychological Review* 64:253–62.

Simon, H. A. 1955. A behavioral model of rational choice. *Quarterly Journal of Economics* 69:99–118.

———. 1956. Rational choice and the structure of the environment. *Psychological Review* 63:129–38.

———. 1957. *Models of man: social and rational*. New York: Wiley.

———. 1959. Theories of decision making in economics and behavioral science. *American Economic Review* 49 (3):253–80.

———. 1964. On the concept of an organizational goal. *Administrative Science Quarterly* 9 (1):1–22.

———. 1969. *The sciences of the artificial*. Cambridge, Mass.: M.I.T. Press.

———. 1973. Organization man: rational or self-actualizing? *Public Administration Review* 33, no. 4 (July/August).

Simon, H. A., and M. Barenfeld. 1967. Information processing analysis of perceptual processes in problem-solving. *Psychological Review* 76:473–83.

Simon, H. A., and A. Newell. 1971. Human problem solving: the state of the theory in 1970. *American Psychologist*, pp. 145–59.

Sjöberg, L. 1968. Studies of the rated favorableness of offers to gamble. *Scandinavian Journal of Psychology* 9:257–73.

Slovic, P. 1966a. Risk-taking in children: age and sex differences. *Child Development* 37, no. 1 (March).

———. 1966b. Value as a determiner of subjective probability. *Transactions of the Institute of Electronic Engineers: Human Factors Issue* HFE-7, no. 1 (March):22–28.

———. 1967. The relative influence of probabilities and payoffs upon perceived risk of gamble. *Psychonomic Science* 9:223–24.

———. 1969a. Differential effects of real versus hypothetical payoffs on choices among gambles. *Journal of Experimental Psychology* 80:434–37.

———. 1969b. Manipulating the attractiveness of a gamble without changing its expected value. *Journal of Experimental Psychology* 79:139–45.

———. 1972a. Information processing, situation specificity, and the generality of risk-taking behavior. *Journal of Personality and Social Psychology* 22, no. 1 (April).

———. 1972b. From Shakespeare to Simon: speculations — and some evidence — about man's ability to process information. *Research Bulletin* 12, no. 2 (April). Oregon Research Institute.

———. 1972c. Psychological study of human judgment: implications for investment decision making. *Journal of Finance* 27, no. 4 (September).

———. 1975. Choices between equally valued alternatives. *Journal of Experimental Psychology: Human Perception and Performance* 1:280–87.

Slovic, P., et al. 1977. Preferences for insurance against probable small losses: insurance implications. *Journal of Risk and Insurance* 44.

Slovic, P., B. Fischhoff, and S. Lichtenstein. 1977. Behavioral decision theory. *Annual Review of Psychology* 28:1-39.

Slovic, P., D. Fleissner, and W. S. Bauman. 1972. Analyzing the use of information in investment decision making: a methodological proposal. *Journal of Business* 45:283-301.

Slovic, P., and S. Lichtenstein. 1968a. The relative importance of probabilities and payoffs in risk taking. *Journal of Experimental Psychology* 78.

_______. 1968b. Importance of variance preferences in gambling decisions. *Journal of Experimental Psychology* 78:646-54.

_______. 1971. Comparison of Bayesian and regression approaches to the study of information processing in judgment. *Organizational Behavior and Human Performance* 6:649-744.

Slovic, P., S. Lichtenstein, and W. Edwards. 1965. Boredom-induced changes in preferences among bets. *American Journal of Psychology* 78 (June):208-17.

Slovic, P., and D. Lyon. 1976. Dominance of accuracy information and neglect of base rates in probability estimation. *Acta Psychologica* 40:287-98.

Slovic, P., and A. Tversky. 1974. Who accepts Savage's axiom? *Behavioral Science* 19:368-73.

Slovic, P., M. S. Weinstein, and S. Lichtenstein. 1967. Sex differences in the risks a person selects for himself and the risks he selects for someone else. *Research Bulletin* 7, no. 10 (October). Oregon Research Institute.

Smith, A. 1776. *An inquiry into the nature and causes of the wealth of nations.* Edinburgh.

Smith, V. L. 1976. Experimental economics: induced value theory. *American Economic Review* 66 (May):274-79.

Starbuck, W. H. 1963. Level of aspiration. *Psychological Review* 70:51-60.

Stevens, S. S. 1957. On the psychophysical law. *Psychological Review* 64 (3):153-81.

Stigler, G. J. 1950. The development of utility theory. Pts. 1 and 2. *Journal of Political Economy* 58 (5):307-26, 373-96.

Stigler, G. J., and G. S. Becker. 1977. De gustibus non est disputandum. *American Economic Review* 67 (2):76-90.

Torgerson, W. S. 1958. *The theory and measurement of scaling*. New York: Wiley.

Tversky, A. 1967a. Additivity, utility and subjective probability. *Journal of Mathematical Psychology* 4:175-201.

_______. 1967b. A general theory of polynomial conjoint measurement. *Journal of Mathematical Psychology* 41:1-20.

_______. 1967c. Utility theory and additivity analysis of risky choices. *Journal of Experimental Psychology* 75:27-36.

_______. 1969. Intransitivity of preferences. *Psychological Review* 76:31-48.

_______. 1972a. Choice by elimination. *Journal of Mathematical Psychology* 9, no. 4 (November).

_______. 1972b. Elimination by aspects: a theory of choice. *Psychological Review* 79:281-99.

———. 1975. On the elicitation of preferences: descriptive and normative considerations. Paper presented at Workshop on Decision Making with Multiple Conflicting Objectives, October 1975, at International Institute for Applied Systems Analysis, Schloss Laxenburg, Austria.
Tversky, A., and D. Kahneman. 1973. Availability: a heuristic for judging frequency probability. *Cognitive Psychology* 5:207–32.
———. 1974. Judgments under uncertainty: heuristics and biases. *Science* 185 (September):1124–31.
———. 1977. Causal schemata in judgments under uncertainty. In *Progress in social psychology*. M. Fishbein, ed. Hillsdale, N.J.: Erlbaum Associates.
Van Dam, C. 1973. Beslissen in onzekerheid. Leiden, The Netherlands: Stenfert Kroese.
Van Raaij, W. F. 1977. Consumer choice behavior: an information processing approach. Ph.D. dissertation, Tilburg University, The Netherlands.
Venn, J. 1866. *The logic of chance*, London: Macmillan.
Vlek, C., and P. J. Stallen. 1979. Rational and personal aspects of risk. Working Paper, Institute for Experimental Psychology, University of Groningen, The Netherlands.
Von Mises, R. 1957. *Probability, statistics and truth*. Translated by Hilda Geiringer. New York: Macmillan.
———. 1964. *Mathematical theory of probability and statistics*. New York: Academic Press.
Von Neumann, J., and O. Morgernstern. 1947. *Theory of games and economic behavior*, 2nd ed. Princeton, N.J.: Princeton University Press.
Vroom, V. H. 1964. *Work and motivation*. New York: Wiley.
Wallsten, T. S. 1968. Failure of predictions from subjectively expected utility theory in a Bayesian decision task. *Organizational Behavior and Human Performance* 3:239–52.
Walsh, V. C. 1970. *Introduction to contemporary microeconomics*. New York: McGraw-Hill.
Weick, K. E. 1967. Organizations in the laboratory. In *Methods of organizational research*. V. H. Vroom, ed. Pittsburgh: University of Pittsburgh Press.
Weinstein, M. S. 1969. Achievement motivation and risk preference. *Journal of Personality and Social Psychology* 13 (2):153–72.
Weizenbaum, J. 1976. *Computer power and human reason*. San Francisco: W. H. Freeman.
White, D. J. 1975. *Decision methodology*. New York: Wiley.
———. 1976. *Fundamentals of decision theory*. New York: Elsevier.
Williams, C. A., 1966. Attitudes toward speculative risks as an indicator of attitudes toward pure risk. *Journal of Risk and Insurance* 33:577–86.
Winkler, R. L. 1972. *Introduction to Bayesian inference and decision*. New York: Holt, Rinehart and Winston.
Wood, G. 1978. The knew-it-all-along effect. *Journal of Experimental Psychology: Human Perception and Performance* 4 (2):345–53.

Wright, P. 1975. Consumer choice strategies: simplifying vs. optimizing. *Journal of Marketing Research* 12 (February):60–67.

Yaari, M. E. 1965. Convexity in the theory of choice under risk. *Quarterly Journal of Economics*, pp. 278–90.

Zeleny, M. 1976. On the inadequacy of the regression paradigm used in the study of human judgment. *Theory and Decision* 7:57–65.

NAME INDEX

Allais, M., 18, 19, 20, 32
Anderson, D. R., 26, 67
Anderson, J. R., 182
Anderson, N. H., 31, 32, 92, 94
Andriessen, J. H., 93
Argyris, C., 183
Aristotle, 2
Armstrong, J. S., 36
Arrow, K. J., 25, 178, 181
Austin, G. A., 36
Avrunin, G. S., 113, 183

Baratta, P., 31
Barenfeld, M., 37
Bar-Hillel, M., 21, 39
Baron, D. P., 34
Bauman, W. S., 107
Baumol, W. J., 14, 16
Becker, G. M., 20
Becker, G. S., 138, 178
Becker, S. W., 20, 181
Berenson, C., 69
Bernard, G., 182
Bernoulli, D., 11, 12, 13, 16, 182
Bernoulli, J., 3
Beyth, R., 7
Bezembinder, T. C., 183
Bickel, P. J., 71
Billings, R. S., 181
Birnbaum, M. H., 107
Blyth, C. R., 71
Borch, H. K., 181
Bowen, J. N., 183
Bower, G. H., 94
Bowman, E. H., 36
Braunstein, M. L., 43, 92, 93, 110
Břicháček, V., 31
Brownson, F. O., 20

Bruner, J. S., 36
Brunswik, E., 139
Burks, A. W., 4
Byars, J. A., 187

Camilli, G., 187
Campbell, D. T., 5, 8
Carnap, R., 4
Churchman, C. W., 4
Colby, K. M., 183
Cook, T. D., 5
Coombs, C. H., 20, 21, 31, 35, 41, 92, 113, 181, 183
Corrigan, B., 36, 107, 187
Cramer, G., 11, 182
Crum, R., 136
Cyert, R. M., 39

Darwin, C., 2
Davidson, D., 17, 31
Davies, G., 183
Davis, M. S., 126
Dawes, R. M., 36, 107, 181, 187
Deegan, J., 107
DeFinetti, B., 4, 31, 182
DeGroot, M. H., 20, 182
De La Place, P. S., 3
Dosher, B. A., 42

Edgeworth, F. Y., 13
Edwards, W., 21, 31, 32, 92, 181, 186
Ehrlich, I., 178
Einhorn, H. J., 41, 42, 188
Eisner, R., 26, 67
Ellsberg, D., 19, 20
Etzioni, A., 44

Fechner, G. T., 182
Feigenbaum, E. A., 183
Feldman, J., 183
Fellner, W., 20
Fischhoff, B., 7, 181, 187
Fishburn, P. C., 14, 32, 34, 41, 43, 135, 181, 182
Fleissner, D., 107
Friedman, M., 17, 25, 45, 110, 177, 178, 179
Fryback, D. G., 21

Georgescu-Roegen, N., 181
Goldberg, L. R., 36, 107
Goode, F. M., 183
Goodman, B. C., 21
Goodnow, J. C., 36
Gould, J. P., 26, 46
Green, P. E., 182
Greene, M. R., 67, 89
Grether, D. M., 21, 44, 93, 110, 181

Hadar, J., 52
Halter, A. N., 22
Hammel, E. A., 71
Handa, J., 32, 124, 125
Heisenberg, 4
Henderson, J. M., 9
Hershey, J. C., 109, 183
Hershman, R. L., 21
Hicks, J. R., 13
Hirshleifer, J., 186
Hochbaum, D., 183
Hoffman, P. J., 36, 107
Hogarth, R. M., 138
Holloway, C. A., 182
Homan, 183
Hopkins, K. D., 187
Huang, L. C., 31, 35, 183

Irwin, F. W., 31
Isaac, R. M., 7

Janis, I. L., 44, 181
Johnson, G. L., 22

Kahneman, D., 21, 28, 32, 33, 39, 40, 87, 89, 93, 110, 111, 122, 124, 125, 135, 137, 183, 188
Kanuck, L., 69
Kao, R. C., 41

Karmarkar, U. S., 32, 121, 124, 125, 182
Katona, G., 23
Keen, P. G. W., 185
Keeney, R. L., 15
Keynes, J. M., 4
Klatzky, R. L., 36
Kleinmuntz, B., 188
Kleinmuntz, D. N., 188
Kochenberger, G. A., 135
Kogan, N., 9, 89
Krantz, D. H., 31
Krelle, W., 182
Kuhn, H. W., 24
Kunreuther, H., 23, 24, 25, 26, 36, 66, 67, 68, 87, 182
Kyburg, H. E., 4

Larsson, S., 20
Laughhun, D. J., 136
Lawler, E. E., 32
Lazarsfeld, P. F., 7
Lee, W., 2, 4, 31, 118, 181
Levine, J. R., 21
Levine, R. L., 107
Levy, H., 34
Lewin, K., 23
Libby, R., 34, 36, 41, 182
Lichtenstein, S., 21, 34, 35, 89, 92, 93, 94, 95, 100, 107, 110, 181, 186
Lindblom, C. E., 39
Lindman, H. R., 21, 44, 93, 110
Lindsay, R. B., 4
Luce, R. D., 14, 31
Lyon, D., 21

McClintock, C. G., 181
MacCrimmon, K. R., 20, 182
McGrath, J. E., 5
Machlup, F., 45
McKenney, J. L., 185
Mann, L., 44, 181
March, J. G., 39, 82, 139
Mark, R., 69
Markowitz, H. M., 34, 112, 113, 121, 124, 178, 179
Marks, R. W., 31
Marrow, A. J., 23
Marschak, J., 20
Marshall, A., 2, 181
Marshall, J., 178
Massy, W. F., 184
Menefee, G. H., 26, 46, 67
Menger, K., 182
Meyer, R. F., 15
Milburn, T. W., 181
Miller, G. A., 37
Morgenstern, 0., 13, 14, 16, 27, 33, 48, 125, 126, 135, 166, 167, 177
Mosteller, F., 17, 118
Murray, M. L., 67

Neisser, U., 183
Neter, J., 67
Newell, A. J., 37, 183
Newton, I., 2
Nisbett, R. E., 107
Nogee, P., 17, 118
Norman, D. A., 183
Nunen, J. van, 183, 184

O'Connell, J. W., 71
Officer, R. R., 22

Pareto, V., 2
Pashigian, B. P., 26, 46, 67
Payne, J. W., 43, 44, 92, 93, 107, 110, 136, 186
Plott, C. R., 7, 21, 44, 93, 110, 181
Pollatsek, A., 35
Pratt, J. W., 4, 14, 15, 137
Press, J. S., 74
Preston, M. G., 31
Pruitt, D. G., 35, 92, 183

Quandt, R. E., 9
Quirk, J., 9

Raiffa, H., 4, 14, 15, 20, 182
Ramsey, F. P., 4, 31, 32
Ranyard, R. H., 92
Rapoport, A., 181
Reder, M. W., 41
Reichenbach, H., 4
Robertson, L., 26, 67
Ronen, J., 93, 110
Roscoe, J. T., 106, 187
Rosenthal, R., 186
Rosett, R. N., 18
Rosnow, R., 186
Rumelhart, D. E., 183
Russell, W. R., 52
Russo, J. E., 42

Saposnik, R., 9
Savage, L. J., 4, 14, 17, 25, 110, 177, 178, 179, 182
Schank, R. C., 183
Schkade, L., 26, 46, 67
Schlaifer, R., 4, 14, 182
Schmitt, N., 107
Schneeweiss, H., 32
Schoemaker, P. J. H., 7, 66, 91, 97, 109, 183, 184
Sen, A. K., 138
Shakespeare, W., 2
Shanteau, J. C., 32, 92, 94
Shaw, J. C., 37
Shepard, R. N., 41
Siegel, S., 17, 31, 135
Simon, H. A., 2, 3, 28, 37, 38, 39, 41, 44, 82, 181, 183
Simpson, 71, 184
Sjöberg, L., 93
Slovic, P., 2, 9, 20, 21, 31, 35, 36, 66, 67, 68, 78, 86, 87, 89, 92, 93, 94, 95, 100, 107, 110, 111, 112, 117, 118, 120, 122, 124, 125, 181, 186, 187
Smith, A., 2
Smith, V. L., 7
Smokler, H. E., 4
Stallen, P. J., 188
Stanley, J. C., 5, 8
Starbuck, W., 135
Stevens, S. S., 182
Stigler, G. J., 138, 181
Strotz, R., 26, 67
Suppes, P., 17, 31

Torgerson, W. S., 137
Tucker, A. W., 24
Tukey, J. W., 31
Tversky, A., 19, 20, 21, 28, 30, 31, 32, 33, 39, 40, 42, 43, 69, 87, 89, 93, 110, 111, 122, 124, 125, 135, 137, 181, 183

Van Dam, C., 182
Van Raaij, W. F., 42
Venn, J., 4
Verrecchia, R., 183
Vlek, C., 188
Von Mises, R., 4
Von Neumann, J., 13, 14, 16, 27, 33, 48, 125, 126, 135, 166, 167, 177
Vroom, V. H., 32

Wallach, M. A., 9, 89
Wallsten, T. S., 21, 181
Walsh, V. C., 13
Weick, K. E., 6, 7
Weinstein, M. S., 89
Weizenbaum, J., 183
White, D. J., 182
Williams, C. A., 66, 67
Wilson, T. D., 107
Wind, Y., 182
Winkler, R. L., 4
Wood, G., 7
Wright, G., 182
Wright, P., 186

Yaari, M. E., 17, 18

Zeleny, M., 107
Zink, D., 93, 107

SUBJECT INDEX

Additive-difference model, 30, 42
Additive model, 30, 35–36, 42, 104, 135, 187
Ambiguity, 20
Anchoring, 39, 40, 61, 81
Aspiration level, 19, 23, 34, 38, 135–36
Availability, 40

Base rate ignorance, 21, 40–41
Basic tastes and preferences, 126, 138–39, 188
Betting odds, 31
Bootstrapping, 36
Bounded rationality, 37–39

Certainty effect, 19, 33, 69, 79, 137, 187
Certainty equivalent, 15, 32, 49, 65
Cognitive processes, 36–43, 82, 94, 185
Cognitive strain, 93–94, 96–101, 108, 186
Complexity, 186
Comprehensive insurance, 68, 85–86
Confusion matrices, 184
Conservatism, 9, 21
Construct validity, 6
Context effects, 82–89, 110, 125, 187–88
Critical values, 132–35
Cue utilization, 92, 107

Decision environment, 38, 39, 44
Decision framing, 135–38
Decision models
 additive-difference, 30, 42
 conjunctive, 30, 40–42, 183
 disjunctive, 30, 40–42, 183
 elimination-by-aspects, 30, 43
 lexicographic, 30, 42–43, 93
 mean-risk, 34–35
 noncompensatory, 41–43

Deductible effect, 46, 67-68, 79, 111
Differential dimension focus, 100, 103
Dimension preference, 95, 103-04, 166-68
Duplex gamble, 35, 43, 92-96, 157, 187

Elimination by aspects, 30, 43
EV model, 11, 17, 93, 102, 187
Evoking process, 82
Expected utility theory
  applications of, 46-56, 113-15
  axioms of, 13-14
  evidence against, 18-26, 57-65, 67
  historical background of, 11-13
  insurance and, 112-15, 177-79
  introduction to, 1, 13-16, 177-79
Experimental method
  challenges of, 6
  definition of, 5, 45-46
  misconceptions about, 7-8
  types of validity and, 5-6, 8
Eye-movement research, 42

Goal gradient, 23

Heuristics, 39-41
Hindsight bias, 7
Holistic models, 29-30, 44, 182
Hypothetical payoffs, 9, 181

Individual factors, 130-31
Inflection points, 111-15, 118-22, 125, 179
Information-integration model, 32
Information-processing view
  evidence for, 39-44
  statement of, 36-39
Insurance
  context effects in expected utility theory, 112-15, 177-79
  findings, 71-87, 117-24
  literature, 23-26, 67

Intuition, 21, 74-78
Irrational bids, 102
Isolation effect, 33, 90

Lexicographic models, 30, 42-43, 93

Marginal utility, 12, 17, 22, 25, 135
Mean-risk models, 34-35
Measurement, 31, 137, 182
Memory, 36, 37
Model misspecification, 107, 187
Moment approach, 34, 92-93, 186
Multiattribute choice, 36, 38, 41-44

Noncompensatory rules, 29-30, 41-43

Paradigm, 2
Paradoxes
  Allais', 18-20, 32
  Ellsberg's, 19-20
  Simpson's, 71, 184
  St. Petersburg, 11-12, 182
Paramorphic representation, 107
Portfolio
  influences, 83-85, 187
  theories, 21, 34, 183
Positivistic view, 45-46
Prediction error, 8, 15, 17, 184
Preferences
  inconsistency of, 18-20, 44, 82
  reversals of, 44, 93, 110
Probability. *See also* Subjective probability
  density function and, 15, 48, 53
  distortions of, 14, 18-21, 31, 33, 39-40, 87, 89, 121-22, 124, 182
  views of, 3-4, 93
Probability thresholds, 68, 112
Problem-solving research, 37
Prospect theory, 33-34, 89-90, 115, 125

Random utility, 43
Rationality
  bounded, 2-3, 37-39, 44

economic, 2-3, 9, 11-16
other, 39, 181, 183
Reference effect, 19
Reflection effect, 33, 183
Regression
findings, 104-08, 187
models, 42, 104-07
Regret, 136-37
Representativeness, 40
Response mode bias, 44, 93, 110
Risk taking
attitude toward, 15, 22, 25, 67, 95, 137
context effects in, 44, 81-86, 93, 110, 115-16, 135-38
factors affecting, 73-78, 89

Satisficing, 38-39, 41-42
Scale effects, 86-87
Speculative risk, 66
Statistical knowledge
cognitive strain and, 98-101, 186
decision quality and, 101-02, 186
decision strategy and, 102-04
effect of, 77-78
use of intuition and, 74-78, 186
Stochastic
dominance, 52
preference, 118
Subjective expected utility, 30-32, 35, 65, 182
Subjective probability, 17, 31, 35, 40, 182
Subjectively weighted utility, 32, 33
Substitution effect, 23

Task variables, 130-31
Taylor expansion of $U(x)$, 186
Transitivity, 13, 21, 42-43

u effect, 58-64
Uncertainty, 3
Urn problem, 46-56
Utility
cardinal type of, 13, 16, 26
measurement of, 14-15
ordinal type of, 13, 16, 26
Utility function
exponential, 15, 35
general, 26, 46, 111, 177-79, 186
quadratic, 15, 34

Value of information, 48-56, 64-65, 141-42, 166-68
Value function, 137
Vividness, 73-74

GPSR Compliance

The European Union's (EU) General Product Safety Regulation (GPSR) is a set of rules that requires consumer products to be safe and our obligations to ensure this.

If you have any concerns about our products, you can contact us on ProductSafety@springernature.com

In case Publisher is established outside the EU, the EU authorized representative is:

Springer Nature Customer Service Center GmbH
Europaplatz 3
69115 Heidelberg, Germany

Batch number: 10830937

Printed by Printforce, the Netherlands